-2020-

A Complete Guide to Beginning Your Acrylic Skills Through 30 Unique Paintings

THE ART SHERPA

This work is under copyright by Cinnamon Cooney. The International Standard Book Number (ISBN) 978-1-960894-00-7 has been assigned to "Acrylic April 2020" by Cinnamon Cooney. This book has been filed prior to publishing with the Library of Congress.

Dedication

To the inspiring and ever-supportive Art Sherpa community, my cherished Art family.

Without your constant encouragement, unyielding belief, and unwavering passion for art, the idea of teaching a 30-day painting course would have remained an elusive dream. You have provided me with the courage to take that leap and embrace the journey, each step adorned with colors and strokes of creativity.

You have taught me that art is more than just technique; it is a way of life, a language that transcends barriers, and a force that unites us all. Through the countless hours spent sharing your expertise, tips, and heartfelt stories, you have forged a bond that transcends the canvas, connecting each of us in a vibrant tapestry of inspiration.

So, it is with profound gratitude and immense admiration that I dedicate this 30-day painting course to you, my Art Sherpa family. Your influence has not only shaped my art but also my life, and for that, I am eternally grateful.

May this course serve as a testament to the transformative power of our Art family and as a beacon of light for aspiring artists who, like me, embark on their own creative journeys.

With love and admiration
The Art Sherpa

CONTENTS

Introduction to the Daily Painting Experience 6

How to succeed at Daily Painting 10

The Myths of Painting 12

Materials 14

Acrylic Paint & The Color Palette 16

Artists Brush Crash Course 22

Canvas, Board, or Paper? 25

Techniques for this Course 26

Troubleshooting and the Gridding Method 30

Glowing Sunset 32

Ladybug 38

Phoenix 44

Colorful Pig 50

Colorful Bubbles 56

Zen Stones Candle 62

Wine and Pour 68

Robins Egg Nest 74

Fluffy Baby Chick 80

Realistic Strawberries 86

Tropical Sunset 93

Lavender Field Sunset 100

A Pair of Birds 106

Boat and Red Umbrella 112

Blue Butterfly 120

Moon On Water 126

Lionfish 132

Poppies 138

Blue Rose 146

Ballet Shoes 152

Red Fox 158

Girl In Hat 164

Desert Sunset 170

Raccoon In Flowers 176

Koi Fish Pond 184

Colorful Dog 192

Storm House 198

Stone Angel 204

Jungle Bird 210

Big Ship 216

INTRODUCTION TO THE DAILY PAINTING EXPERIENCE

WHY DAILY PAINTING?

Daily painting is a creative path that helps creatives quickly grow and develop art skills and intuition. This is true for both new artists looking to learn how to paint and experienced artists that find themselves in a rut. Even simple paintings created on this regular basis nurtures a sense of confidence, design and loose expression.

OK, but why 30 paintings in 30 days?

There are learning thresholds that are typically seen with beginners. Setting a goal of 30 paintings allows you to move through several of these thresholds in quick succession. As you're gaining new painting skills your artistic brain is building on the previous day's experience. This habit of painting over the course of 30 days allows you to move past the individual project to see the totality of the artistic journey.

IS IT VERY EASY FOR NEW ARTISTS TO GET OBSESSED WITH A SINGLE PAINTING?

It's not uncommon for new artists to start a project and not complete it 2/3 of the way through. Committing to a daily painting helps you move past both of those blocks. I would love to see everyone go beyond 30 days, but within this month, if you paint daily, relax and commit to the process, you will be changed as a creative for the better. You will learn that not every painting is going to be great, and that's okay, because there will be great paintings. That's the thing to understand...every painting doesn't have to be your best painting ever. Creating your best painting ever generally comes from the experience of several previous paintings.

IS THIS DAILY PAINTING THING FOR REAL?

Daily painting is a movement. One might even say it's a whole School of Art. Daily painting was started by a group of artists trying to overcome their own creative blocks, to improve workflow, and find personal voice. These early explorers created a path for other artists, like you, to follow. They shed a light on something important about what helps us grow as artists.

IF YOU PAINT CONSISTENTLY, DAILY, FOR SHORTER SESSIONS, ON SMALL CANVASES, YOU WILL PAINT BETTER, PAINT BRAVER, AND PAINT LOOSER.

Shorter painting sessions keep you from getting overwhelmed and fatigued. A shorter time frame also means that you have to make faster, braver decisions with each brush stroke, loosening up, and relaxing into your artistic experience. This technique helps you trust and see your painting more confidently. Small canvases mean that you don't have to deal with the challenges of scale. It's a practical matter, bigger canvases require more paint, more time, and more physical work, creating another obstacle to your painting process. In combination, these are a powerful medicine to the soul of the artist. Fear of lack-of-talent and words of self-doubt transform into words of determination and commitment. You will see past the individual painting, forever evolving the goal of simply painting.

Have you seen the insurance ad that says, "we've learned a thing or two because we've seen a thing or two"? It rings true for me. I talk to new artists every day and I talk specifically with them about their challenges.

Every first painting matters. It's brave to try something new. It takes courage, and that is why I personally have so much respect for new painters. I know how brave a first time painter is. I know what it takes to share that first time painting. I encourage you to smile because you were brave enough to bare your soul and share your real art with the world. Nothing makes you more of a real artist.

With students from all over the world, from every background, you can imagine, there are a few things that I found new artists all have in common. They seem to believe deeply in "The Myths" of painting. Very often, when I first meet these amazing souls, the myths of art have become their cannon. They seem reluctant to call themselves artists because they have so much respect for art and so little belief that they can be part of something so amazing. They see every mistake in their art and miss every correct decision. They have a vision of the artist in their head and heart that they dream of being. A fantasy artist, capable of spectacular fantasy paintings. Paintings that exist in the realm of imagination, which is okay, because that's where art comes from. But the truth is that this imaginary artist in their mind has nothing to do with who they

are when they paint, what they need when they're painting, or the type of art they create.

The other thing I've learned is that criticism doesn't help a new student get better. Don't get me wrong, I think a well-executed art "critique" for an artist with enough skills to be able to receive the information AND take action on it, can be incredibly valuable. But in the beginning, the benefit of critique needs to step aside and give way to the learning of new skills. This is the time when I want to get my students to paint more and try new challenges. To worry less about every little detail and instead work consistently on their skills. As a teacher with over 500,000 students, at the time of writing this book, I've seen more than a few people begin their art journey and the one truth I know is that everyone that sticks with it becomes a better painter. Natural aptitude is fantastic but it doesn't hold a candle to dogged determination. There is a natural flow to artistic growth that is very predictable and noble.

IF YOU PAINT AND IF YOU DO IT EVERY DAY, YOU ARE GOING TO BE A BETTER PAINTER.

I'd like to help you get better at painting. Notice the use of the word better. I say this, as a teacher. because there are several metrics by which we all measure our success but many of these same metrics are poison to the creative process. Things like looking for approval from outside sources to validate your creative journey. Another one to avoid is setting arbitrary goals about what makes a painting good or not good. I'm sure you already have a preference of what you would label good art and you might have another preference of what you would call bad art. This can be attributed to all types of aspects of art. Perhaps you think realistic objective art is good art and you currently lack the skills necessary to achieve that look. Perhaps you think bright and colorful is good art and you don't know enough about color mixing to get bright colors. Maybe you think loose and expressive is the best type of painting but you don't know enough about brushstroke and value to confidently execute a loose expressive painting. I promise you that the type of painter you think you want to be will change, maybe in a big way, maybe in a small way, but it is going to evolve. So when you look at your art and you're looking for a metric to judge it by, only measure against your own personal growth.

" Are you better in some way" at painting after painting 30 then you were before?

Let's examine what I just said. "Are you better in some way?" That "way" could be that you are better at color mixing, or better at brushstrokes, or better in value. Perhaps you feel more confident when you paint. I'm sure you consider it common sense that we do get better when we practice something. Many times I see people criticize their first or second attempt at a painting when they actually have done pretty well and have managed to complete the entire project. Let's put this in another context.Let's say you were tight rope walking for the first or second time. What would you consider a successful attempt? Would you expect that you were able to balance a lot of things on your head or would you expect yourself to do a flip? I hope you'd feel amazing to successfully walk from one end of the tightrope to the other end without falling. Because that's what successfully completing your first paintings equates to. It takes time to learn new things and it takes time for your muscles and your mind to start working together as a team to start a new venture. Art is like that.

I cannot say this enough: "Artists are not born, or created magically, in faraway European art schools." That being said, all artists are born and some of them even went to good European art schools, though even these artists didn't achieve their level of success and their craft by mere luck. They all worked very hard on what they did and even if they had aptitude, they had to labor diligently to develop that aptitude into skill. Every artist is ripened over time through determination, perseverance and hard work. While pixie magic is wonderful and we all have a place in our heart for Tinkerbell, pixie dust is not a component of becoming an artist. Being an artist can help you create a world that not only yourself, but others exist in, where pixies are real and pixie dust helps little boys fly if they believe. And while we're on the subject of pixies, there is something we do have in common with pixies. We have to believe in ourselves. The first step to anything wonderful is always to believe that you can do it. To turn away from all the reasons that you have held close before this moment that fill you with fear and tell you that creativity is out of your reach. Put that negativity down and believe in the only thing that will matter here...YOU!

HOW TO SUCCEED AT DAILY PAINTING

1. **SET UP A SACRED SPACE:** Create your own sacred space that you dedicate to your daily painting. This space could be your kitchen table, or a desk off to the side, a converted bedroom, or a space in your garage. Wherever your space is, dedicate it to your journey and commit to keeping the space for painting only. Don't be afraid to ask your roommate and family members to help you keep your art space from having to do double duty and end up cluttered and unworkable. Set the space up with the tools and materials you need. Make sure that it's ready to go day 1 when you're ready to begin your painting challenge.

2. **CREATE SACRED TIME:** Set aside time every day when you know you can sit down and paint. You can plan for about an hour to an hour and a half every day, so pick a time during the day that you know can belong to you. Talk to your friends and family members and let them know that you're beginning this personal challenge and that you're not going to be available during this time. Ask them to help you keep this time for you. Spend some alone time in your sacred space and realize that you, too, have to commit to making this your time in your creative space. Whenever you're developing a lifestyle change, whether it's working out or learning a new hobby, you have to internally commit and be resolved to that change. Taking the time to be consistent can help you achieve your goals.

3. **CREATE A BUDGET:** It's important to look at your budget when beginning a long painting practice. It may not be fun but it can be a strategy that really sets you up for success. Knowing how much you have to spend each month easily, and without strain, can help you determine what types of art supplies you buy and how much of each supply you are going to need. You don't want to be in the middle of a daily painting project and run out of money and have to strain your overall economic well-being to get more art supplies. Also, I found when you know your budget ahead of time, it helps you be creative with your budgeting strategies such as using sales and coupons to make those dollars go further. I always think art is more fun when I don't feel an extreme financial strain around my creative materials. Also, a note on quality, I do think that quality art materials help the artist have a better experience with their painting. Remember, quality doesn't always mean more expensive. It's important to know that most online art companies and art stores have deep discount sales several times a year. If you have researched the materials you're looking for, you'll know a good deal when you see it. I try to make sure I don't pay full price for my art supplies. Generally, if you look, they'll have a list price. List price is the highest amount of money that particular art supply should ever be sold for. I prefer to pay 20% to 30% below the list price.

4. **USE A LIMITED PALETTE:** Another cost saver you can incorporate for daily painting is to limit the colors that you're going to be using. This not only helps you learn to mix colors, but it also prevents spending hours deciding which tube of yellow to use for the sunset. In this program we will be using 11 colors including black and white. I picked these colors because they give me a variety of mixes that allow me to paint nearly anything my eyes can see. When you look at my materials list, you'll see many recommendations for exchanges and alternatives if you can't find the exact colors listed.

5. **WORK SMALL:** It can be tempting during a daily painting to increase the size of your canvas. I don't recommend this because the larger the canvas, the more fatiguing the projects can become and the more time that they will require. Working small lets you make lots of big decisions in an easier way and you are much more likely to do a little painting then a monolithic painting.

6. **LESS BRUSHES:** It's fun to have all the newest art tools but I suggest you pick a selection of brushes that you most consistently use. This is going to allow you to become familiar with your tools and confident with your ability to use them. It is going to help free you from the idea that it's going to take a particular brush to create a singular effect. You might have a favorite brush that you make clouds with, but keep in mind that all brushes can make clouds. By using less specialty brushes you're going to become more agile and experimental. I have a nice selection of tools suggested below, but, of course, you can customize it for your particular circumstances and preferences. That being said, I softly suggest you put the giant brush bucket aside for the moment and let's go find a few workhorses and get to know them well.

7. **STUFF HAPPENS:** Breaks in the daily painting will happen. Sick days, family obligations, and deadlines for work or school need to come first sometimes. When this happens, you just jump back in on the date you were supposed to be on. That's what is fantastic about this, it's not like a video game where you have to almost begin again. You just resume. No stress. No pressure. Just your personal goals.

8. **SET TIME LIMITS:** When we paint, it's very easy to lose track of time and a daily painting is a marathon, not a sprint. Create soft limits to the amount of time you will spend each day working on a project. The projects in this book took me an hour or less to complete. There's no speed component to painting and I'm not asking you to paint faster. I am encouraging you to paint braver. Don't rework every brush stroke. Make it a goal to be bold. Limit yourself to 2 hours or less a day for your painting time. I personally prefer an hour and have friends that swear by 30 minutes. Anything between 30 minutes and 2 hours is very sustainable. Keep in mind you are an individual, a unique person, and your needs may need to adjust to fit your reality. Set realistic goals and, within reason. Put the brush down within 10 to 15 minutes of reaching the time. You can come back later for any project that you felt you had more to explore after your painting challenge is over.

9. **30 SMALL PAINTINGS INSTEAD OF 30 DAYS ON 1 PAINTING:** This challenge is about doing 30 days of different projects. Not about working on one project over 30 days. I'm not saying that wouldn't be cool. I'm not saying it couldn't create a painting habit. The value here, as I see it, is the variety of projects in this program. Beginning and finishing a painting in a single session. Face a new set of challenges every single day. A new set of techniques. Building each day on what you learned the day before.

10. **A KEY TO SUCCESS:** Be OK with Failure: During the challenge, you're possibly going to hate some of your artwork. You may even question why you began this challenge. Some projects are going to frustrate you. Try to keep in mind that it's not the make 30 most amazing paintings you'll ever paint in your life challenge. It's the painting every day challenge. Nobody's going to curate this or judge it. In fact, you shouldn't allow anyone to judge it. Consider these 30 paintings not as individual products but a collective whole. Don't judge each individual project but evaluate the progress that you've made as an artist over the course of the 30 days. It is my goal to challenge you, to stretch you. As each painting builds on the previous one, you will begin to see the worth of the project. You are the final work of art. I guarantee that when all 30 paintings are hung up on the wall, it really is something to see. You may even take pride when people ask you about it and you tell them you painted every day for 30 days.

11.

THE MYTHS OF PAINTING

It is my sincere hope that this book will be the catalyst for your art journey and that is what being creative is, a personal journey. Steps that add up together, steps that can take you to amazing places that you have not visited since you were a child.

You probably loved art when you were little, LOVED coloring, and likely only stopped because something or someone made you feel as if your creative efforts were not worthwhile. These words might have come from a family member, a teacher, a friend, and even yourself. You decided that your imagination was somehow unworthy of being expressed anymore, and so you got on with the business of serious life.

What a sad turn of events...Imagination is one of the greatest gifts we have as a species. The good news is that your imagination never really left you. Perhaps you pushed it way, way, down under all that adulting pressure, but it remains dormant, waiting for you to wake it up. I hope to share with you the greatest myths in art. Concepts that people deeply believe to be true but are, in fact, illusions. Letting go of these myths will help unburden you for the next step of your journey. Myths that have been holding you back from realizing your true creative potential.

THE MYTHS OF ART

> "IF YOU HEAR A VOICE WITHIN YOU SAY, 'YOU CANNOT PAINT', THEN BY ALL MEANS, PAINT, AND THAT VOICE WILL BE SILENCED."
>
> -VAN GOGH

1. **YOU MUST BE BORN WITH ART TALENT TO BE AN ARTIST:** Talent is misunderstood and certainly not a requirement. People are not born magically talented as winners of a genetic lottery. Amazing artists do have certain traits in common, among them...perseverance and determination. As a group, artists work at what they do, they practice their craft. We don't mind this work as it feels more like play. Remember...the path of art is a lifelong journey, not a sprint. You don't just miraculously pop into being as an artist. Artists are not made with pixie magic, they are developed through hard work over time.

2. **THE RESULT MAKES THE ARTIST:** The finished painting is NOT the goal. The process of creating the painting is, in fact, the goal. No one can look at the finished work of a painting and know what YOU got out of it. There are so many choices, and little magic moments, in every piece of art creation. Things that matter to you as an imaginative human. Personal growth is where your focus should be.

3. **YOU WILL IMPROVE FROM CRITICISM:** Let us not confuse critique with criticism. Critique is a fabulous tool that artists use. We often lean on our peers for insight into a particular and focused art goal. It is not hurtful and generally will provide understanding that allows the artist to hone in on a particular art goal.

   Criticism by contrast is how people back up the dump truck of their emotions and unload on you. It has very little value for you as a student or your growth as an artist. Snarky comments don't make artists, they just kill dreams. My advice to you is, don't ask for criticism from yourself or others.

   Self-evaluations are fine, but beating yourself up over imagined "unachieved goals in a painting" are only, at best, roadblocks to your personal art journey.

4. **TRACING OR GRIDDING IS CHEATING:** That's news to me, honestly, as proper transfer techniques are actually taught in art school. I don't grab a pricey canvas and scribble all over it until I get an idea fleshed

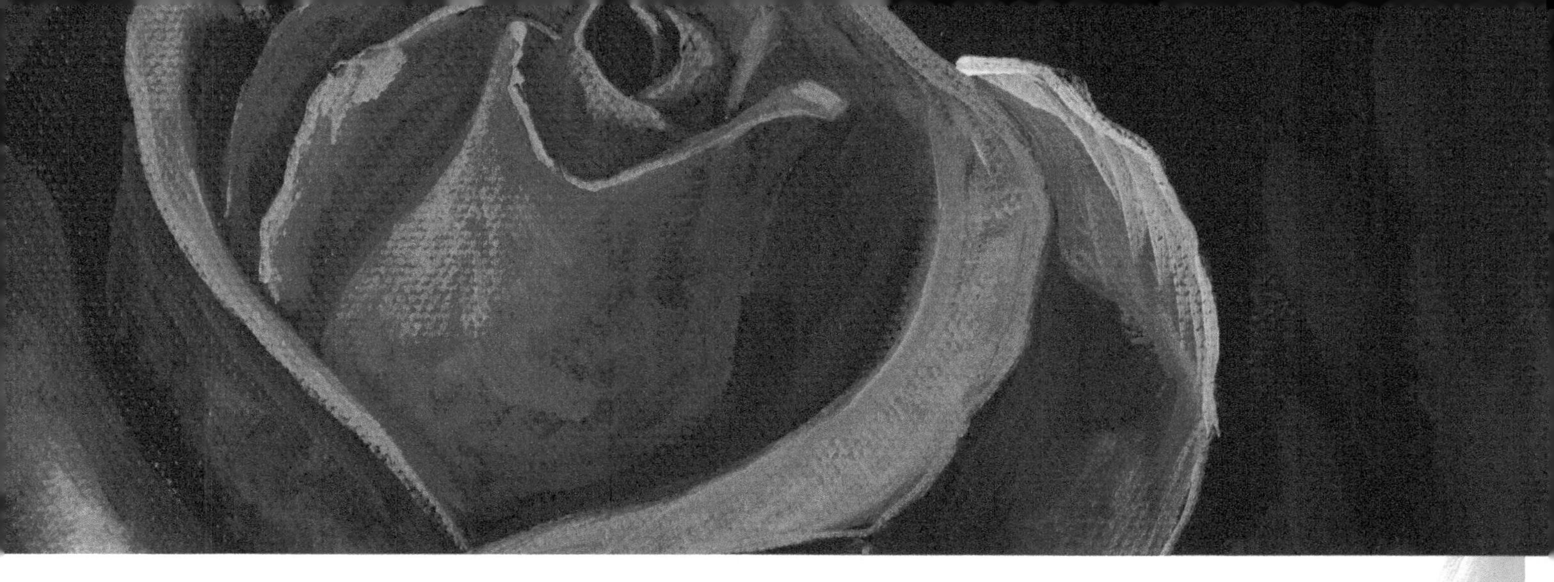

out. I grab tracing paper, sketch out my thoughts and, after several numerous iterations, transfer the image onto my canvas. Transferring images is an acceptable method of creating art. If I have a complicated design I have to work out, I will often use the gridding method to help me simplify the process, breaking down each element into smaller, more digestible parts. These are simply techniques and processes that artists use, nothing more and nothing less.

5. **I CAN'T DO THIS:** You CAN. Plain and simple. The only thing stopping you is fear and doubt. I have seen thousands of people all over the globe, at every age and skill level, with every challenge facing them, take this leap and find out they can paint. Your job here is to be a little bit brave and optimistic about your potential.

6. **ART IS EXPENSIVE:** As with anything in life, things have a range of expenses. My advice to all students is get the best art supplies you can afford within your budget. I feel confident telling you this because, between sales and coupons, this is an achievable goal. There is always a way to work it out and still not hurt your wallet. Knowing what makes a good brush or paint means that your #1 concern is not expense, but performance. You only need to know the brands to get a sense of who is committed to making quality products. There are art manufacturers out there that are amazing and still reasonable on the pocketbook.

7. **CRAFTERS ARE NOT ARTISTS:** This makes steam come out my ears when I hear it. There are so many terms in art to explain processes that have been hijacked to determine the value of an artistic practice. Crafters are artists, and many artists are also crafters. Any good quilt show or decorative painting show makes it clear that skills in the hands of imaginative people create works of art everywhere.

8. **IMAGINATION HAS NO VALUE IN THE REAL WORLD:** Thank goodness for the people who hold onto imagination so that our future can be brighter than our past. I think imagination should be taught in school as one of the most important skills we have as a species. Every great thing from sliced bread to telephones, and computers required imagination. The most difficult problems we face in life will require imagination to get through. The only way you can have hope is if you can imagine things to be different than they are. A lack of imagination traps us into situations and problems without end.

9. **ARTIST STARVE:** The legend of the starving artist is a deep part of human culture and the perception that being an artist means having no hope of making a living seems to be a universal outlook. Unless you talk to the thriving industry of working artists. Art, like everything else, has a variety of career paths and can offer as much security as any other career path. Our world is designed by artists...literally...there is very little you can see or hold that has not passed the desk or easel of a creative professional in some way.

10. **YOU NEED TO DRAW TO BE AN ARTIST:** You do not need to draw to be creative or an artist. Drawing is a wonderful skill in art, but it is not the gateway to being an artist. There is design, color theory, and medium Many art practices don't require drawing at all. I think everyone can learn to draw better than they realize, but it makes me sad to see artful people walk away from painting over drawing.

11. **IT HELPS BE A BETTER ARTIST IF YOU COMPARE YOUR ART TO OTHER PEOPLE'S ART:** Seriously, it's not. Comparison is human and we all like to see how we measure up. The first most important thing is to not compare your art to somebody else's. Comparison can take your joy balloon and deflate it quickly. I mean, think about it. How great do you feel after pouring over fashion magazines? Do you feel that the model is thin and beautiful? Yes, They are beautiful and, I think most of you will agree that looking at other other-worldly, photoshopped, pretty women does not make you personally feel prettier or amazing. We all know that fashion magazines are their own art form and that they utilise digital imagery and airbrushing to create a super human sense of femininity. Setting a personal benchmark should never leave you feeling less than. If comparing your art to someone else's art results in you feeling not as awesome as the creative powerhouse that you are, it's time to stop and just focus on your own canvas. In time, you will learn to balance being "inspired by", instead of feeling "eclipsed by'' others. It can take a lot of personal work to achieve that place, that state of creative confidence. So, DON'T compare your art or growth to anyone else's. DO take notice of your personal growth in your own paintings. That is an excellent benchmark by which to measure your growth.

MATERIALS

HEAVY BODY ACRYLIC PAINT - SENNLIER ABSTRACT ACRYLIC

PAINT COLORS:

- CADMIUM RED -PR 108
- QUINACRIDONE MAGENTA - PR 122 (AKA QUINACRIDONE FUCHSIA)
- CADMIUM YELLOW MEDIUM - PY 35
- NAPLES YELLOW LIGHT - PY53 (TITANATE YELLOW)
- PHTHALO BLUE- PB 15:3
- ULTRAMARINE BLUE - PB 29
- PHTHALO GREEN - PG 7
- DIOXAZINE PURPLE - PV 23
- BURNT SIENNA - PBR 7
- MARS BLACK - PBK 11
- TITANIUM WHITE - PW 6

BRUSHES

THE ART SHERPA® CATS TONGUE #8

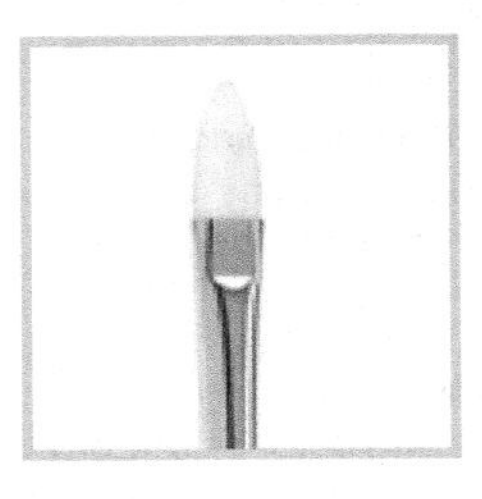

This brush is actually a pointed filbert and I really love the versatility of this brush. If you can't get access to it, a number 8 filbert brush with a firm synthetic filament will be perfectly fine.

THE ART SHERPA® ROUND #4

This brush has a very sharp tip and good spring. When selecting a brush, you want a tip that is very sharp so you can get fine lines. Also, look for a synthetic firm filament with good spring.

CAMBRIDGE™ BRIGHT #8

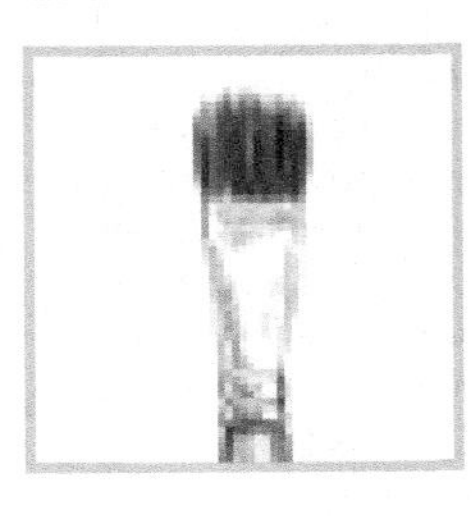

This brush is a mix of hog bristles and synthetic filaments. I do think it is nice to have a blended brush in your brush bucket. If you can't find it, a number eight bright will do.

ART SHERPA® #30 BRIGHT

A big bright for large areas of surface on a canvas. There are many economical options, but what you're looking for is a brush that is 1½ - 2" wide.

RUBY SATIN #6 BRIGHT

This particular line and bright has a very good firm filament with tons of spring and a sharp edge. There are many equivalent brushes, so just look for a brush in this size range with these qualities.

#1 MONOGRAM LINER

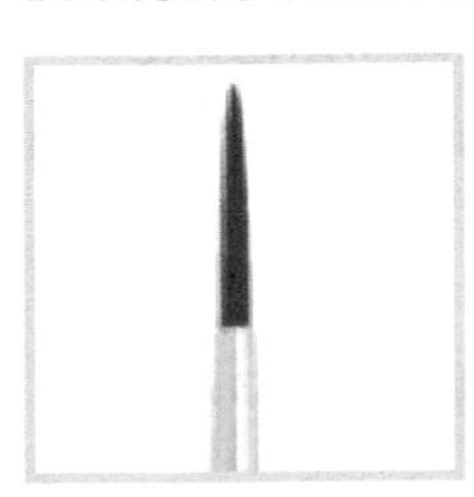

A monogram liner is a wonderful tool to have for fine line work and signatures. These brushes are in almost every type of brush brand line so make sure you purchase one that is suitable for acrylic paint. I do highly recommend the one I'm using here but you should use what you can find.

The brushes I'm using can be found at many retailers and also online. They're manufactured by Silver Brush Limited.

30 8 X 8 CANVASES OR SURFACES SUITABLE FOR ACRYLIC PAINTING

T SQUARE

ARTISTS KNIVES - PLASTIC IS OK

CHALK TOOL OR PLAIN CHALK FOR SKETCHING AND GRIDDING. DRITZ 3095 CHALK CARTRIDGE SET CAN BE FOUND ON AMAZON

LOW TACK TAPE

ACRYLIC PAINT & THE COLOR PALETTE

ACRYLIC PAINT

WHAT IS ACRYLIC PAINT

Is an acrylic polymer emulsion of water based polymers with pigment. This EMULSION is the suspension of tiny solids in a liquid and comes in several viscosities. Think of it as a spreadable plastic with coloring in it that stabilizes when dry. While it can look exactly like an oil painting, it shares none of the chemical properties of an oil painting. The stability and longevity of this paint medium is projected to far exceed any other media currently available to artists.

PROPERTIES OF ACRYLIC PAINT

It is water soluble. Dries fast and once it's dry it can not be reactivated. Acrylic can be painted in thick or thin applications and works on many surfaces. Great for multimedia. Acrylic paint can look like many other types of art mediums so I like to call it the chameleon of the art materials

TYPES OF ACRYLIC PAINT

HEAVY BODY: Thick and does not shrink when dry. You can see the texture and brush stroke.

FLUID / SOFT BODY: As much pigment as the heavy body but the polymer is more fluid and self leveling. Craft paint is like this but it may not have as much pigment as the professional brands. Also, the color may not be as reliable in mixing. Some of the craft brands make a line of bottle paints designed for artist painting needs and it will tell you on the label. It will also come in colors you see present in traditional paint brands. While I personally prefer a professional grade heavy body acrylic paint, let me be clear craft paint is real paint. There are many real artists that use brands like Deco or Plaid to create amazing works of art.

HIGH FLOW OR INK: Like water or an ink but full of color. This is great for washes, airbrush, calligraphy and fine lines You will get noticeably better results from quality paint. You will find that painting with the best quality product will make your experience significantly easier. SO MUCH EASIER. However, more than any element, more important than any particular paint product, I feel the most important thing is that you do paint. Find a paint that is easily accessible to you, whether it be in a store or online. Make sure that there's a customer support line to address any issues you have.

GOOD HEAVY BODY ACRYLIC PAINT SHOULD BE:

- **EVEN WITH A SMOOTH CONSISTENCY**
- **BLENDABLE WITH LOW BRUSH DRAG**
- **HIGH PIGMENT LOAD**
- **LOW COLOR SHIFT (PAINT DARKENS AS IT DRIES)**
- **HOLDS ITS FORM WITH MINIMAL SHRINKAGE**
- **MEET ATSM SAFETY AND QUALITY STANDARDS**
- **PIGMENT CODES AND SAFETY INFORMATION ON TUBES**
- **LIGHTFAST**
- **DRY NEITHER TOO QUICKLY OR TOO SLOWLY**
- **FLEXIBLE AND RESILIENT**

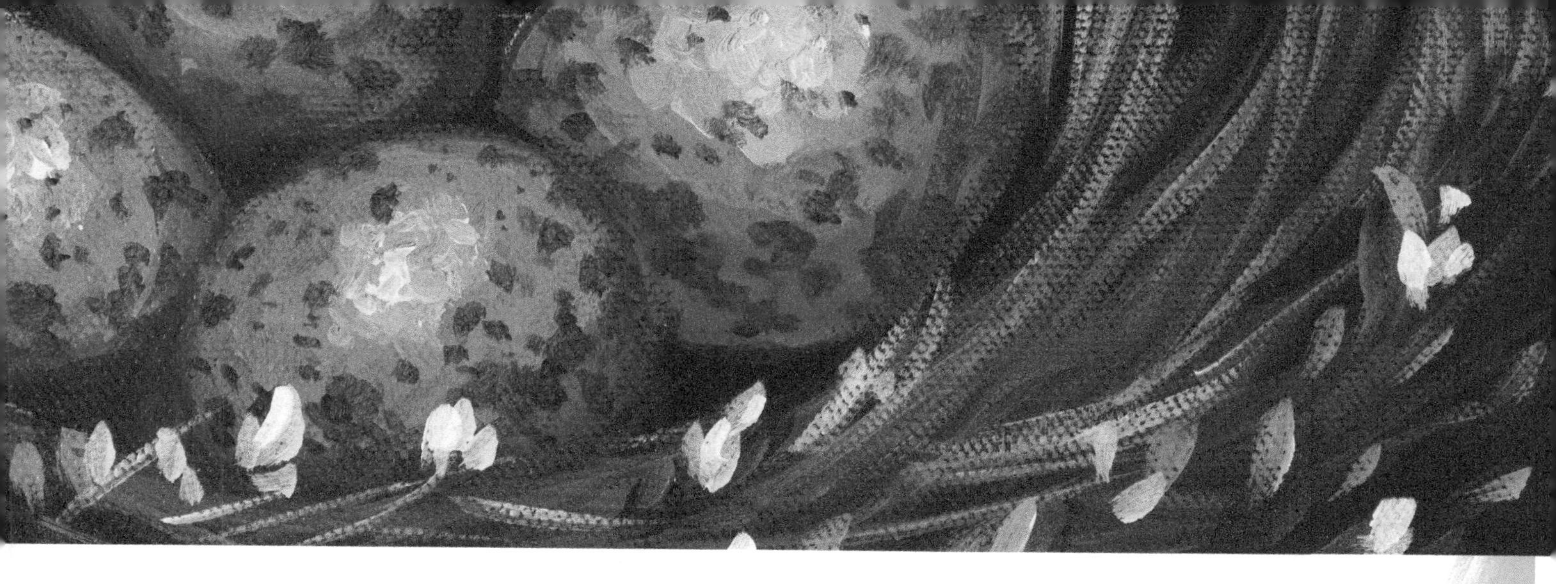

HEAVY BODY ACRYLIC PAINT SHOULD NOT BE:

- **CLUMPY LIKE COTTAGE CHEESE**
- **SEPARATED WHERE CLEAN POLYMER AND PIGMENT ARE NO LONGER INCORPORATED**
- **LABELED WITH NO INFORMATION ON TUBE**
- **HARD TO FIND THE MAKER OF THE PAINT**
- **STRANGE SMELLING OR MOLDY**

THE COLOR PALETTE

THE COLOR WHEEL

Imagine color on a wheel divided equally into Primary, Secondary and Tertiary Colors. Yellow orange and red on one side; green blue and violet on the other. The yellow, orange and red sides are referred to as warm colors. The green blue and violet are referred to as cool colors.

WARM COLOR: A warm color is bold in nature and seems to move closer to us in visual terms. They create the illusion of being closer. They are on the side of the color wheel of red, yellow and orange. Warm colors are like fire and the sun.

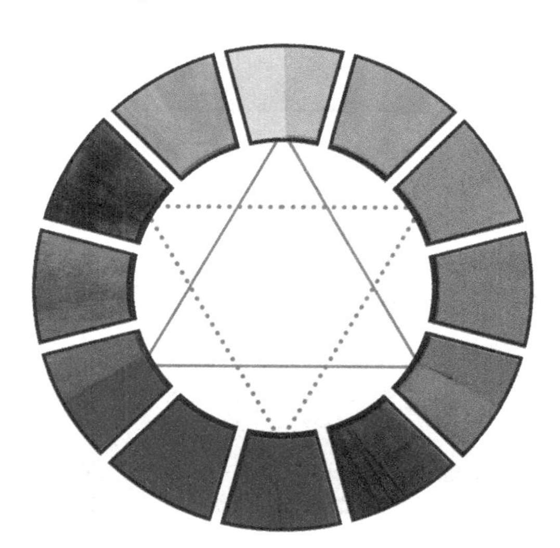

COOL COLOR: A cool color is calm or soothing in nature and tends to recede in visual terms. They create the illusion of moving into the distance, or away from the viewer. For this reason, cool colors typically make a space seem larger. They are on the side of the color wheel green, blue and violet. Sometimes greys will feel cool unless they are given a strong warm bias.

THE SECRET OF COLOR BIAS: So here is the secret of color mixing. Your color has a secret agenda. A warm color can have a cool bias and a cool color can have a warm bias. Mind blowing I know. A color may bias to one side of the color wheel or the other. A yellow may have a bias of red, making it a bit warmer to our eyes. Whereas a cool yellow might lean to the green, feeling cooler and calming.

It's always a good idea to swatch your paint and see if you can see the bias of the colors you have. I will try to describe the colors with the bias that they're leaning to. So if our yellow is cool I'll let you know it has a bias of green.

You can see how the bias of the warm and cool yellow almost seem to vibrate a bit.

On the left, we have a warm yellow outer square, with a cool yellow inner square, and flipped on the right. Can you see the effects of the color bias?

Notice how the warm bias blue and the cool bias blue play against each other.

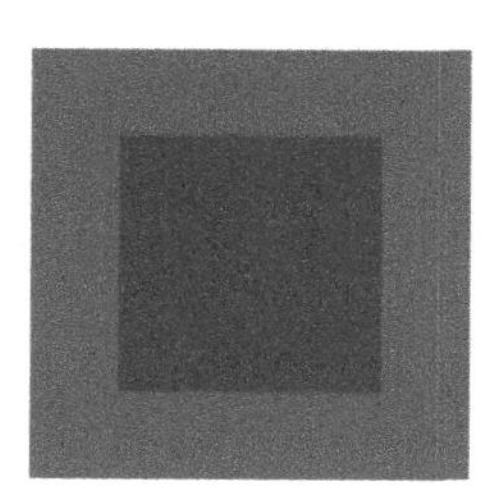

When you mix all 3 primaries they make a brownish grey. This is important to know when mixing colors because if there is a bias where all 3 primaries come into play you can not get bright vibrant color.

One of the number one questions I get asked is why someone took a red and a blue and didn't get the purple they expected. Usually the next question is, "Why did I take a blue and yellow and not end up with a good green?" This is because of the hidden bias within the color. If you take a color like ultramarine, which has a hidden bias of red, and mix it with cadmium red medium, which has a hidden bias of yellow, bright purple will never be the result. Why? Because you now have all the primaries...cadmium red with a yellow bias and ultramarine blue in the mix. The resulting color, while vaguely purple, will be very neutralized by that hidden by bias. Great when that was your goal and very frustrating when it wasn't.

We're going to take a little deeper look at the color palette for our 30 day challenge. Colors exchanges will be offered because sometimes you have different colors than what a lesson calls for and you may not have access to a certain color. I prefer you paint than not paint if you are missing a specific color. If you change the colors you will change the color palette of the painting. It will be different but it can be just as good and just as beautiful. The big thing is to get the same values. I believe that as long as your values are correct, you can use almost any colors you want. Again, different colors mean slight changes in the painting, but it's fine, it doesn't hurt anybody. Just recognize that you need to manage that expectation.

We will be using a Split Primary Palette for this challenge with some extra colors. A split pallet has 6 total primaries instead of 3.

What is super cool about this type of color scheme is that it is highly customizable and allows you to ALWAYS mix great colors once you know the trick. I am going to teach you "The Trick".

We will be using a warm bias red, cool bias red, warm bias yellow, cool bias yellow, warm bias blue, cool bias blue, a green, a brown, a purple, white and black.

You will end up with a total of eleven colors. If you use the split primary method you can do anything. Seriously, it's a powerful painting method and after this, you will buy and add paints with total confidence.

Here is what a split primary palette looks like. By understanding the bias of color and where it lives on the color wheel, we can predict the mixes that will make bright or neutral Colors. You will want to have at least 1 warm red, 1 cool red. 1 warm yellow, 1 cool yellow, 1 warm blue, 1 cool blue, phthalo green, burnt sienna, mars black and titanium white.

PRIMARIES - Red, Yellow, and Blue. A group of colors from which all other colors can be obtained by mixing. Primaries cannot be obtained by mixing other colors.

SECONDARY COLOR - A secondary color is created by mixing two primary colors together...orange, green, and purple.

TERTIARY COLOR - Tertiary color is created by mixing a primary with a secondary color. The 6 Tertiary colors are red-orange, yellow-orange, yellow-green, blue-green, blue-violet, and red-violet. The easiest simplest way to remember this is to put the primary name before the secondary color.

HUE - Refers to the underlying Color Family Yellow, Orange, Red, Violet, Blue, or Green.

COLOR - All the hue's, white, black ,tints, tones, and shades.

TINT - Simply means to add white to a color (not to be

confused with tinting strength of pigment which refers to how strongly one color can influence another color).

TONE - When you add grey to a color. This can be done

by adding pre-mixed grey or by first adding white to a color and then adding black, or vice versa.

SHADE - add black to a color. We can also sometimes

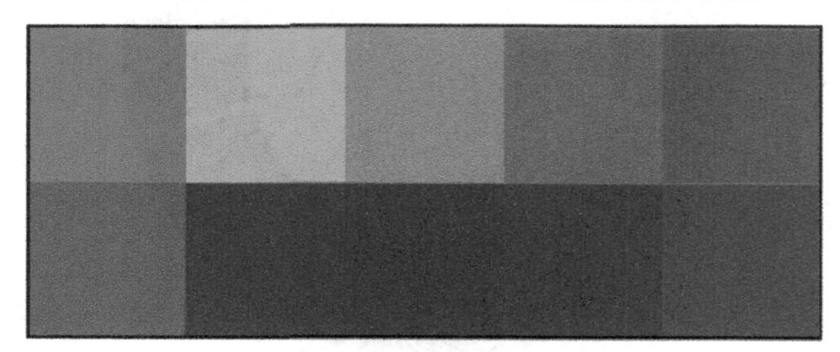

mean adding light and dark values to create shape in a painting even when we're not specifically adding black to the color.

VALUE - How light or dark something is.

COLOR PALLET - The specific colors an artist plans to use.

THE REDS

CADMIUM RED

Warm Red

This is the
basis red
warm
a yellow
You can
substitute
these
just pick

Cool Red

warm
and
means
bias.

ANY of
reds,
one:

- **NAPTHOL RED**
- **NAPTHOL RED LIGHT**
- **PYRROLE RED**
- **CADMIUM RED MEDIUM (HUE IS OK)**
- **CADMIUM RED LIGHT (HUE IS OK)**

These colors can be easier found in most paint lines and paint brands so don't be afraid of switching it out. When the red is light, it will often be a shade more to the yellow.

QUINACRIDONE MAGENTA - PR122

This is my cool red. Cool bias means a blue bias. Really, it's Quinacridone Magenta, but companies can name paint colors some unexpected things. It took me years to figure out the pigment codes on a tube of paint; lucky for you, I know them now. These pigment codes are available to you in most lines of acrylic paint. Use the pigment code for paint lines where colors are listed as Magenta Quinacridone, Quinacridone Fuchsia and Magenta Deep. Take the time to check, the pigment code you want is pr122.

You can Substitute ANY of these cool reds:

- **QUINACRIDONE MAGENTA**
- **PRIMARY MAGENTA**
- **MAGENTA DEEP**
- **QUINACRIDONE RED**
- **QUINACRIDONE ROSE.**
- **QUINACRIDONE FUCHSIA**

THE YELLOWS

CADMIUM YELLOW

This is the warm (red) bias yellow and you can substitute ANY of these warm (red) bias yellows

- **HANSA YELLOW**
- **HANSA YELLOW DEEP**
- **CADMIUM YELLOW MEDIUM HUE**
- **CADMIUM YELLOW DEEP**
- **DIARYLIDE YELLOW**
- **YELLOW AZO MEDIUM**
- **BENZIMIDAZOLONE YELLOW MEDIUM**
- **PRIMARY YELLOW**

NICKEL TITANATE YELLOW PY53
(SOMETIMES CALLED NAPLES YELLOW LIGHT)

This is the green bias yellow and, by far, my absolute favorite cool yellow. There are other cool yellows that you can substitute if you can't find it, if for some reason, you can't find it, but it is one of my favorite colors in my personal paint box. There is a problem, however, and that is the name on this package of paint. There are two colors, very different from each other, that the art world likes to call Naples Yellow. One is a light yellow green, and is in fact Nickel Titanate Yellow. I went out and found every acrylic paint company that carries the correct green yellow, regardless of what they named it. The other companies make the orange yellow that they consider to be Naples. The one on the LEFT is correct.

The one right is not on the a cool yellow.

You can substitute ANY of these cool (green) bias yellows:

- **HANSA YELLOW LIGHT**
- **CADMIUM YELLOW LIGHT**
- **CADMIUM YELLOW PALE HUE**
- **LEMON YELLOW**
- **BISMUTH VANADATE**
- **YELLOW AZO LIGHT**
- **BENZIMIDAZOLONE YELLOW LIGHT**

Below is a list of paint companies that carry this exact color or a suitable Hue. This is the hardest color to find, so feel free to use a substitute with what you have from the colors listed below these paints:

- **ARCYLIQUE BY SENNELIER CALLED NAPLES YELLOW LIGHT**
- **ABSTRACT ACRYLIC PAINT BY SENNELIER CALLED NAPLES YELLOW LIGHT**
- **AMSTERDAM ACRYLIC PAINT MADE BY ROYAL TALENS**
- **OLD HOLLAND NEW MASTERS CLASSIC ACRYLIC**
- **MATISSE STRUCTURE ACRYLIC (ALSO CALLED NAPLES YELLOW IN THIS LINE OF PAINT)**
- **DALER ROWNEY CRYLA ACRYLIC PAINT**
- **GOLDEN HEAVY BODY ARTIST ACRYLICS CALLED TITANATE YELLOW**
- **PÉBÉO STUDIO FINE ACRYLIC NAPLES YELLOW HUE 100 ML**
- **CRANFIELD ACRYLICS CALLED PRIMROSE YELLOW IS PY53**
- **AV VALLEJO ACRYLIC CALLED TITANIUM YELLOW IS PY53**

ULTRAMARINE BLUE PB 29

This is our red bias blue and available in almost every line of acrylic paint

This color is usually very consistent across several paint lines. In some fine art paint lines, you may find several shades of ultramarine blue. Choose the regular ultramarine blue and check pigment codes to be sure.

Ultramarine Blue can be exchanged for Prussian Blue Hue and Anthraquinone Blue.

PHTHALO BLUE-- PB15 OR PB15:3

This is our green bias blue and, again, available in almost every line of acrylic paint. In professional lines, you will see phthalo blue green shade or phthalo blue red shade. You will want the green shade. Sometimes this color can be referred to as Windsor Blue so be sure and check the pigment codes. Another thing you will see is paint tubes can be listed as green shade or red shade. If your paint company has that specification, please choose green shades (PB15:3). If your paint company only has one version of this color (PB15) it is likely the green shade and you don't need to worry about it.

Phthalo blue can be exchanged for Cyan Blue, Manganese Blue Hue, and Cerulean Blue Deep.

PHTHALO GREEN PG 7

Our blue bias geen (phthalo green blue shade) is available in almost every line of acrylic paint. When you get into professional lines of paint, you will see if they have green listed as blue shade or yellow shade. You will be looking for the blue shade. In the economy lines, they only manufacturer either a neutral shade or blue shade, either of which you can use.

Phthalo Green can be exchanged for Cobalt Green and Viridian Green Hue.

BURNT SIENNA PBR 7

Available in almost every line of acrylic paint, burnt sienna can range a little bit in its color variant. This is because the pigment that comes from the earth in different mines and locations results in different siennas. The good news is whether you're burnt sienna is more orange or brown, it's still an excellent color to have and will always be reliable

Burnt Sienna can be exchanged for Raw Sienna, Burnt Umber, Red Oxide and Transparent Brown Iron.

DIOXAZINE PURPLE PV 23

Available in almost every line of acrylic paint, this purple is very deep and until white is added, can appear black to the naked eye. We have the ability to mix a lot of purple shades, but dioxazine is unique. Whenever I work in an artist palette without it, I always miss it. It is very staining and it takes very little color to have a big impact.

Dioxazine Purple can be exchanged for Ultramarine Violet.

MARS BLACK PBK 11

Available in almost every line of acrylic paint, Mars Black tends to be more matte than its counterpart, Carbon Black.

Mars Black can be exchanged for Carbon Black and Primary Black.

TITANIUM WHITE PW 6

Available in almost every line of acrylic paint. You should plant on using twice as much white as you do any other color you have in your palette.

Titanium White can be exchanged for Primary White.

PIGMENT CODES

Pigment codes can be found on most tubes of paint but can be difficult to find. Sometimes found on the front, sometimes on the back, and, wow, paint companies can use creative terms to describe a color pigment. Pigments codes give us a way to be very specific about what color we are purchasing so that the vanity names of the color don't throw us off.

- **PY = PIGMENT YELLOW**
- **PO = PIGMENT ORANGE**
- **PR = PIGMENT RED**
- **PV = PIGMENT VIOLET**
- **PB = PIGMENT BLUE**
- **PG = PIGMENT GREEN**
- **PBR = PIGMENT BROWN**
- **PBK = PIGMENT BLACK**

PROP 65 AND OTHER WARNINGS

Prop 65 is a warning required to be put on labels if it contains a chemical found by two independent committees of scientists and health professionals to have been shown to cause cancer or birth defects or other reproductive harm.

OH NO! Scary right? Well, yes and no. Often these chemicals are found to be harmful in different amounts or in very specific methods of exposure. Like Cadmium is not great in your lungs or tummy. So while it's great that they warned us that there could be chemicals in our paint that we need to be aware of. What you also need to know is chances are you're not getting exposed to these chemicals in their most dangerous states or amounts. Components like cadmium pigment are most dangerous for the people making the paint because it can be powdered in its pigment form and therefore easier to get into the lungs.

So, then, why cadmium? BECAUSE IT IS stunning as a color. Artists love it, we love it a lot.

Yet there are some valid concerns about cadmium pigments. Artist grade pure cadmium pigment is coated and not as bioavailable as industrial cadmium. That being true, it is still cadmium and you should not eat it or drink it. In fact don't eat your paint in general. The other thing to consider is you don't want to turn it into particles and then breathe it. The only two ways this would happen is if you use a true cadmium pigmented paint in an airbrush or some type of aerosol method. Paint companies don't want to hurt you and some of them have made the cautious decision to not manufacture the more dangerous pigments in the airbrush line because of the greater risk to them inhaling the paint.

Burning cadmium paint is also a no-no, in fact, I recommend you don't smoke and paint at the same time. Another way that you could breathe in cadmium is if you sand a painting that is dry where cadmium paint was used. Cadmium color used as it is intended should not be too concerning. You don't absorb it through the skin, though, in rare cases, you could have an allergy to it.

Paint labeled HUE has zero cadmium in it. So a student paint called Cadmium Yellow Hue is 100% free of cadmium pigment.

Basic paint safety, in general, is NOT to smoke while painting and wash your hands after painting and before eating. We all dip our brush into our beverage, it happens, but don't drink it.

Let's not panic. In my experience with new painters, any time I suggest that there could be any dangerous situations with art materials...panic ensues. That's one of the subjects an art school provides , an understanding of Material Science and Studio safety. It's not such a shock learning that art materials used improperly can be problematic. For example, oil painting. Oil painting done correctly is incredibly safe. Painting with oils pigments and using turpentine in a closed studio with no ventilation is not safe. It sounds simple right? It sounds like common sense. Yet in the 50's, 60's, and 70's, many people painted without proper ventilation and didn't feel well because of it. Then people started saying oil painting is toxic. Oil painting is not toxic or dangerous. Lack of proper ventilation in the use of questionable turpentine is dangerous.

How does a beginner artist avoid these problems; by reading the label.

Paint companies do not want to hurt you; they actually need their customers.If there is anything you need to be warned about, they're going to put it on the label. If they have a warning on the label, their website likely has more information.

My final thought safety is about hair dryers.Have you seen a label with the illustration of somebody being electrocuted painfully because they got into a bathtub with a hair dryer. I'm often fascinated with these pictorial illustrations so they're fresh in my mind. The label is there for safety reasons, but that doesn't mean that hair dryers are intrinsically imminently dangerous. Hair dryers are dangerous if you decide to plug them in and submerge yourself in water. When you see the warning label on the hair dryer are you so afraid you don't use it? Of course not. You're a smart person and you understand not to throw your electronics in the bathtub. Labels give information that consumers need. BE INFORMED, read and follow the labels and you'll be just fine.

ARTISTS BRUSH CRASH COURSE

PARTS OF A BRUSH

HANDLE, FERRULE, AND HEAD. ON THE HEAD, WE HAVE THE: HEEL, BELLY, AND TOE.

HANDLE - The back end or control bit of the brush. This is the part of the tool that translates all that creativity, from your brain, down through your shoulder, into your hand, flowing to your fingers where you hold the brush. Can be long or short, can be wood or plastic, and may be finished or unfinished

FERRULE - This is the metal bridge between the handle and the head of the brush. It has a crimp where the metal meets the handle. This is to help the head stay attached even if the glue fails.

(ps, the glue fails a lot) Metal ferrules may be of the following; aluminum, copper, nickel, or nickel-plated steel. Many people are allergic to nickel. Many good brush companies avoid the metal all together

HEAD - The head is the business end of your brush. It's the part that does the painting. Your head can be made of natural hair bristles or synthetic elements. Its shape and makeup determines how it loads paint and how it releases that paint onto the canvas. Matching up the correct brush head to the type of paint you are using can do a lot to improve your experience.

THE HEEL - Where the filaments, hair or bristles meet the ferrule. Too much pressure on an artist's brush can break the heel. What that means is that the filament in your brush can bend or "crimp", because you pressed down too hard, disrupting the shape of your brush.

THE BELLY - This is the area in which the bristles hold water and paint in your brush. Is generally in the middle between the heel and toe.

TOE - The toe is where your brush ideally dances across the canvas. It's the end of the filaments hairs or bristles. The shape of the brush toe greatly impacts your brush stroke.

TYPES OF BRUSHES INCLUDE:

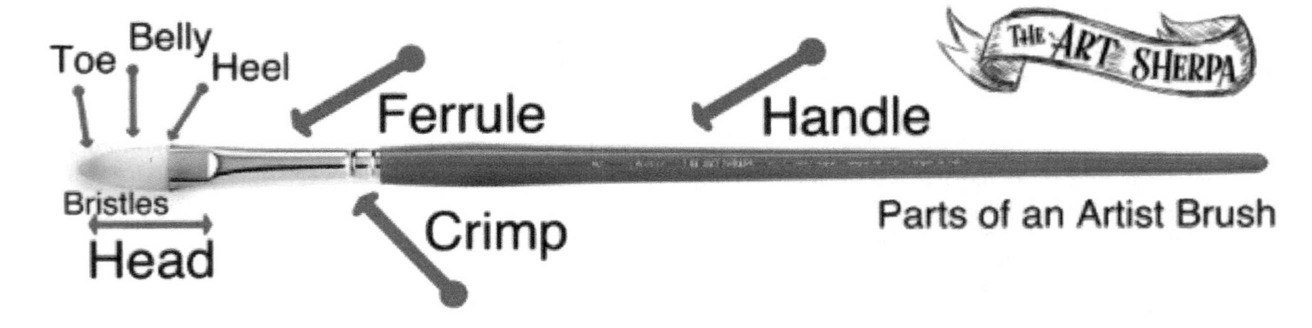

Acrylic Brushes which are almost entirely nylon or synthetic for the lion's share of the painting tasks. They can also be hog or hair when you look to techniques like Scumbling or Blending.

HEAVY BODY - Heavy body paint works best when brushes have a firm synthetic filament. The filament should also have a good spring to it. These types of brushes are expressive and easily move and control the thickness of heavy body paint.

FLUID OR SOFT BODY - Fluid acrylic paint works best when a brush has a softer smoother filament to it. I still prefer a synthetic for its resilience. I also look for filaments that are self sealing sometimes referred to as strokeless. These brushes are more ideal for smooth finishes or techniques.

HIGH FLOW OR INK - While I still prefer synthetic for acrylic brushes overall these brushes have the most in common with the watercolour brushes. They need to have sharp tips and edges with a thirsty belly. The filaments are soft and the brush head will soak up the highflow paint easily and provide you with hair fine lines.

SYNTHETIC BRISTLES - These are made of multi-diameter extruded nylon filament, Taklon or polyester. This is ideal for acrylic paint. Acrylic paint, while fun and versatile, can be hard on the lifespa of your brushes. With good brush care, you can extend the life of your brushes. In my experience, even when washing regularly, hog bristles wear out quickly compared to synthetic elements. Another thing that I really enjoy about synthetic is that it holds a more optimal amount of water for the acrylic medium, and is more resilient in holding its shape for continued enjoyable use.

FOR PAINTING STANDING AT THE EASEL - Long handle is best. This lets you back away from your artwork while you're creating it. Holding the brush handle far back, and then painting back from the artwork creates a loose expressive method of painting. Have you heard that old saying "They can't see the forest for the trees" ? This means that you're too close to the subject to be able to take it all in. Moving back from the easel changes that view. In fact, this is the view that lets you take in the whole forest and adjust where those trees need to go based on your artistic sensibility.

FOR PAINTING FROM THE TABLE WHILE SEATED

Most typically, people paint with short handle brushes at a table. This prevents a great deal of injury, mostly via eye-poking. No I'm just kidding, but the length of the handle can become problematic for the painter. It just isn't comfortable or practical for the short distances that sitting while painting creates. You're close in. So if you're sitting at a table, you may prefer a short handle. ***Pro tip: Artists that sit at a table should regularly stand up and walk away from the work to view it. If you can't do that because of mobility issues, another trick is to take a picture with your phone. This is the other way that you can see the forest for the trees.***

WATERCOLOR BRUSHES are soft, can pull in a large amount of water, and are usually made of sable or synthetic nylon. For the most part, watercolor brushes are short handled. You can invest as much as you want in a watercolor brush as with good care they will last a very long time, through many uses. Natural hair, squirrel, badger or sable are all used by watercolorists. The most prefered brushes are made by hand.

OIL PAINTING BRUSHES are usually made of natural hair, sable or hog bristle. They are firmer than Watercolor and are made for the blended effects that oils excel in. The hog Bristles will wear down over time, shaping to the artist preferences, much like breaking in a good pair of shoes. In general oil artists use long handle brushes since most of the work is done at an easel

MULTIMEDIA AND DECOR PAINTING BRUSHES - These brushes are often short handled and can come in a variety of filaments or hair. Brushes in this category have very specific jobs. They can have unique heads and shapes. And often a brush will be shaped and developed for a single brush stroke. They work with any media. While we won't be using these brushes in this course, they can be a fun thing to do research on and add to your own art kit

BRUSH SHAPES

There are a multitude of brush shapes. We're just going to discuss the basic ones that you'll be adding to your artist kit.

BRIGHT - A bright is a square brush with the sharp edge. The filaments are shorter from the feral to the toe allowing for more control and a firmer feel.

FLAT - A flat is also a square shape brush but the filament is longer from the ferulel to the toe.

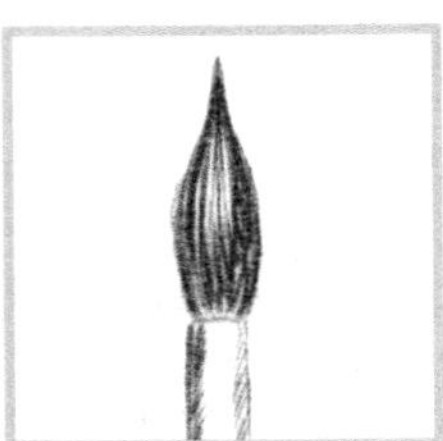

ROUND - Round with pointed tip.

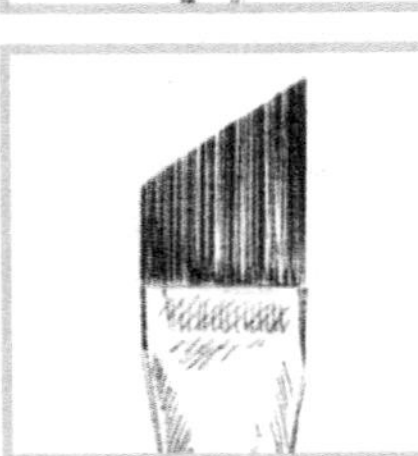

ANGLE - The brush head is shaped at an angle. These brushes are fantastic for doing a variety of jobs including hair fine lines and difficult compound curves.

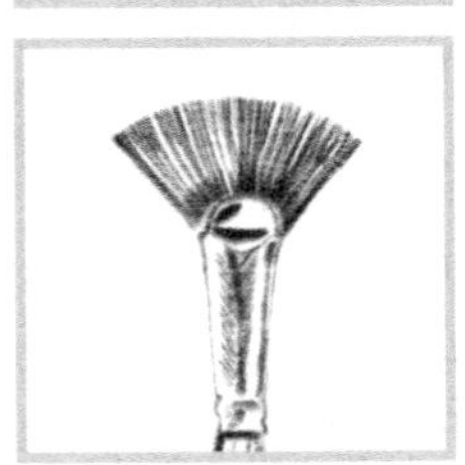

FAN - These brushes are shaped like a fan. Originally a decorative brush this has become part of the fine art brush kit for its variety of textural brush strokes. It can be difficult to find one suitable for heavy body paint.

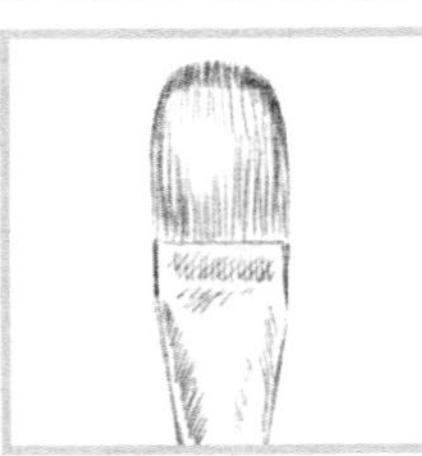

FILBERT - A filbert has a rounded head.The soft curve of the head allows for soft brush effects, some delicate blending and some nice curved edge strokes .

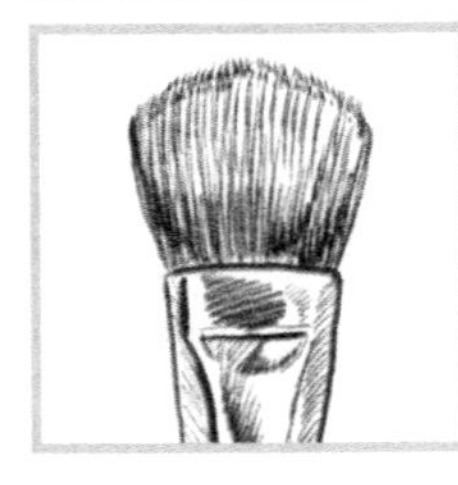

MOP - These brushes tend to be Fuller and softer with a rounded head. They're used to apply varnish. They can be used to apply glazes. they can also be used for soft diffused blending

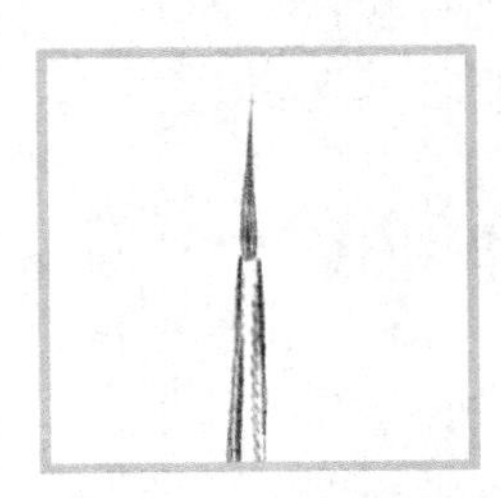

LINER OR RIGGER - These brushes have long fine detail points with great snap and spring. They do great refined lines and delicate work.

CLEANING YOUR BRUSH

Your paint brushes are an expensive investment that you will want to know how to protect and keep for years. This might surprise you to know that the future of each brush is sealed at the sink after each painting session. That leftover paint in the brush MUST ALL come out.The acrylic polymer emulsion and pigments get pushed into your bristles and the ferrules. When you get dried paint hiding in the ferrule, it can build up until it "blows out" the shape of your brush, causing splitting and stray hairs. This will give you a great cloud or scumble brush, but will ruin the shape and edge of your favorite brush.

Turpentine or thinners can destroy some types of synthetic brushes, and are not really necessary in acrylic painting. Warm water, soap, your fingers and a towel for drying are you best tools in caring for your acrylic brush

ART SHERPA SPA BRUSH CLEANING INSTRUCTIONS

MATERIALS- Art Sherpa Brush Spa Soap, paper towels, container of swishing water, cup of hot water (not hot enough to burn your fingers)

1. Place cleaning supplies by the sink and lay your drying towels out next to the sink.
2. Remove excess thick paint that is on your brush (if you have any) on a disposable towel.
3. Vigorously Swish the brush in a container of water.
4. Wet Brush in warm running water and rub across the soap. Build up the suds as you use the directional stroke method. Do this Firmly, but gently. Don't scrub or bend the filaments of the brush.
5. Take fingers and work the soap gently through the brush.
6. Rinse and Repeat step 4.
7. Now take your clean brush and stroke firmly but gently dragging across a dry white paper towel. If you see any color, go to step 8, if not go to step 9.
8. Run warmer water over the brush, rewetting it, go over the surface of your soap using the soft circle method. If you are using the power scrub tub with loofah, be extra careful.
9. Take your cup of very hot, but safe for fingers, water and

dip brush in for 10-20 seconds. Finger shape your brush.

10. Lay brush flat on a paper towel. Come back in and hour to check the brush. (if you see any color, repeat the cleaning steps)

11. Allow brushes to dry before placing them in your brush cup.

A WARNING ABOUT ARTISTS' BRUSH HANDLES FOR THE ACRYLIC PAINTER

Artists' brush handles are most often made of wood, but can also be made of plastic. Some cheap handles are made of unfinished wood. Higher quality handles are of seasoned hardwood that is sealed and lacquered to water resistance, intended to reduce swelling. This said, there's a lot happening to your brush when you use it. Depending on the water tightness of the seal, where the ferrule meets the handle, you may begin to see cracking and paint chipping along the handle. You may even see the brush head loosening from the handle. After decades of painting I can honestly say brushes are not made for water. My advice to you here is be fastidious. Don't leave your brushes in standing water. Always rinse them out between uses, even during a painting session, and lay them flat. Always always wash and dry after every painting session.

EMERGENCY CARE

I'm sure you have the best intentions to be a good brush caretaker. You may have spent quite a lot of money on your brushes, so you feel motivated to take care of them. But life will happen. You will get distracted by something in your real life that will create the unthinkable situation, your brush standing in water OR your brush left to dry with acrylic paint on it transforming it into a stick...dare I say a very expensive stick.

The first tool to help you save your brushes is rubbing alcohol. Rubbing alcohol will break down acrylic paint allowing you to, with some effort, warm water and good soap return your brush from stick to beloved partner and best friend.

Yes, your brush is your friend. You will get very attached to a good brush who stands by you through thick and thin, through clouds and water, through glazing, scumbling, and sharp curved lines.

The second tool is hot water. Hot water helps in combo with your soap to remove the dried crusty paint that the alcohol loosened. It can also help you tame your brushes bed head. Use hot water (not so hot you get burned). Dip and hold the brush in the water for 10-20 seconds. Remove and reshape it into its former glory. Lay flat and allow to dry. Ready to return to artful duty in your brush bucket.

FINALLY GLUE

If the head of your brush falls off, don't despair, it can be glued right back on. I like Gorilla Glue. Just make sure the handle and the head of the brush are dry. Apply a dab of glue to the handle and press the ferrule back into its seat. Allow to cure and get back to making art!

CANVAS, BOARD, OR PAPER?

CANVAS

Acrylic paint will stick to almost anything. What it won't stick to, there's likely a medium that will let you paint on it anyways. That being said, artists tend to work on stretched canvas surfaces. A stretched canvas surface is basically cotton or linen that is stretched like a drum over wood bars. Most of the canvas surfaces you buy will already be prepared for painting and you won't need to prepare them.

I'm going to be demoing gallery wrapped deep stretcher canvases. This allows me to be finished and ready to hang my art work when the painting is done. The deep sides will be painted to allow viewing from a multitude of angels and is considered a finish state for this type of canvas.

If you purchase canvases with wood stretchers that are less than 1 inch thick, these would traditionally be put into frames before hanging.

BOARD

Artist boards are thin board surfaces that are prepared for taking paint and come in a wide range of qualities. Some are made of compressed paper with a textured gessoed finish but often warp and don't take paint well. They are the cheapest of the art boards. Some are made from mason board and are finished with a cradled surface ready to hang. My favorite artist boards are Ampersands. You should be able to find artboards easily in an 8 by 8 size. The positives of artist boards is they tend to be a little more economical than stretched canvas and they store easily taking up less space while still being very easy to frame.

PAPER

There are several types of paper that are suitable for acrylic painting. The first factor to look at is the weight of the paper;140 lb is ideal. Paper comes in a cold press or hot press surface. Cold-press is rough and hot press is smooth. Many people use multimedia paper which is lighter weight but it will be more prone to warping. What you need to know about paper is that it's thirsty and it's going to suck in your acrylic paint. So ideally you're going to prep it. This can be done by sealing the paper with an isolation coat and then for painting with a coat of gesso. I like a product called GAC 100 as an isolation coat. One or two coats will seal the paper. Once thoroughly dry you can apply one to two coats of gesso for lovely toothy surface.

TECHNIQUES FOR THIS COURSE

TECHNIQUES FOR THIS COURSE

During our 30 days there are several essential techniques that we will be utilizing regularly. Feeling confident in these brush strokes and techniques will help you have a higher level of satisfaction with your overall journey. In art there are a lot of terms. For the purposes of this book, I'd like us to think terms of fine art vocabulary and practical studio vocabulary. We're going to use a bit of both. Some of our terms will be firmly seated in traditional artist thinking. Some of our terms are going to come from my more whimsical teaching style. The following will help you navigate these terms so that you can make them your own and elevate your chances for feeling confident within your projects. What's the number one thing that makes a student feel anxious? Not knowing what to do or how to do it. In my mind this is a very human thing because none of us like to be unempowered. I think the feeling is a little bit like being in a dream where you find yourself in a classroom taking a test you had no idea was happening and that you haven't studied for. But unlike the test of your dreams you can prepare for this. Practicing in art it's actually fun.

DRY BRUSHING -

This technique utilizes less water in the brush and a lighter pressure through the stroke. The goal being to allow some of the surface to show through and the texture of the bristles to be evident. It is an excellent way to create texture or transition in artwork. It's especially important in acrylic because of the way our medium dries. Unlike other artists mediums that can be reactivated and moved once acrylic is dry it's pretty much stuck there. Dry brushing is a great way to continue transitions once paint is dry. It's actually one of my very favorite parts of acrylic painting. Dry brushing is an essential technique to master.

SCUMBLING -

Scumbling certainly has some dry brushing to it but involves a more randomized circular brush stroke. Be careful when you scumble you don't want to press so hard that you break the heel of the brush. In scumbling just like in dry brushing we won't be using a lot of water in the brush. But this time we're going to want to move the brush around in a random and circular motion creating no sense of a particular line or direction.

BLENDING WET INTO WET-

Another way to create transitions from one color to another or one value to another in acrylic painting is by blending colors together with the brush on the canvas while both are still wet. Mastering a blend like this is also essential for acrylic painting. In general blending requires a soft pressure with a bit of urgency because it must be accomplished before the paint is dry. If you are in very dry studio conditions such as air conditioning or dry heating in

winter. Your paint may dry out faster than you can blend it. No worries, there are mediums called retarders that you can add to the paint to slow the drying time.

LAYERING -

This is a very important part of acrylic painting. It can be hard for new artists to understand because it's used in so many different ways. you can layer wet paint over wet paint. You can layer dry paint over dry paint. You can glaze over dry paint to layer also. Layering can help you build texture and depth in a painting. Understanding that techniques are built up in layers will help you move away from the magical brush thinking. What I mean by that is you remember seeing cartoons paint a tunnel in one stroke with a single brush? As regular humans we can't do that to get these effects, We need to layer the paint. Once you embrace this thinking the depth of your painting will improve greatly

GLAZING -

Glazing is taking thin transparent coats of paint over another coat of dry paint. The transparency of the paint allows the color from the paint underneath to affect the paint on top. This is another way for artists to make transitions with acrylic paint. Some paint is naturally transparent because of how the pigmentmented it is. Colors like quinacridone magenta or phthalo blue are very transparent. Opaque pigments can be made transparent using a medium for glazing.

SMOOTHLY BLENDED OR TIGHT PAINTING -

This is when you smooth the paint and try to hide the brush strokes and transitions. When you hear an artist talking about a particular painter being tight, what they're speaking of is the way that this artist is able to hide the medium method of the painting. Acrylic blending is one of the more frustrating techniques for new artists.

LOOSE, EXPRESSIVE AND PAINTERLY -

This is when you paint showing the brush stroke. The painting has a freshly captured feel. This technique gives the impression of capturing a moment in time. It has qualities where the color stroke in texture defines the artwork instead of line.

FEATHERED BLENDING -

When you create a softened edge by gently brushing on the toe of the head of the brush allowing the bristles to feather out visually defusing the stroke.

CONTOUR PAINTING -

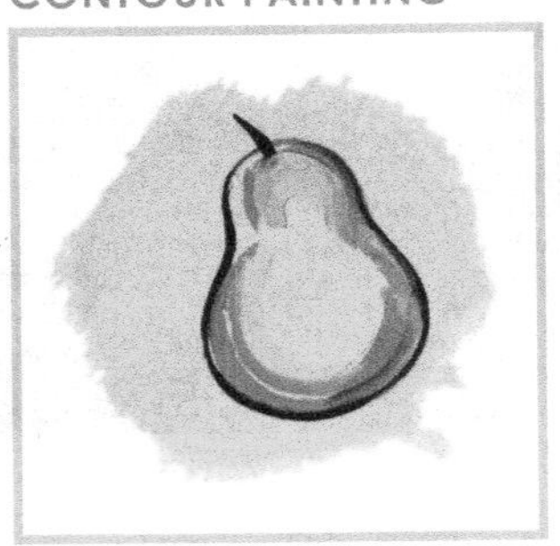

This is where you use the brushstroke to define the outline of the form. The brushstrokes are long and smooth and help us express the form and line of the object.

FINE LINE WORK -

Taking paint that is made more fluid and a fine line brush to create brush Strokes that are delicate and elegant in nature. This is often used for hair, delicate grasses or natural elements, edged highlights.

ARABESQUE STROKES -

When you hear an artist refer to an Arabesque stroke, this is a complex multiple curve stroke with the feel of calligraphy reminiscent of Arabic lettering.

CALLIGRAPHY STROKES -

Using a brush in the manner of a calligraphy pen. These brush strokes can be used in anything from lettering to elegant form expressions.

S STROKES -

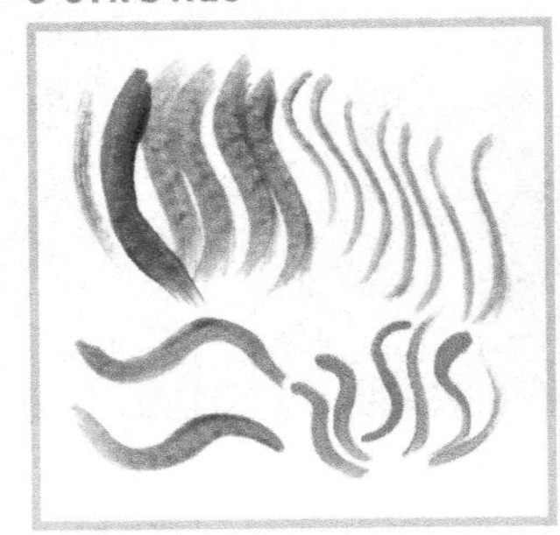

Being able to create compound curves as strokes is a very important technique in painting. Most of the natural world will require your ability to execute it as stroke. It's a good idea to practice making bold S strokes and delicate S strokes.

CURVED STROKES -

Curved Strokes are when you give a gentle angle and curve to the brush as you pull or push out. most often done on the toe of the brush they help us create implied line shape and form. This directionality is very important in our painting. From the inside of a wave, to grass blowing in the wind, and all the clouds in the sky mastering the curve stroke will help you create more elegant images.

THE TOUCH PULL STROKE -

This wonderful brush stroke is great for creating loose expressive flowers and leaves. Begin the stroke by touching the toe of the brush to the surface. As you pull the brush stroke increase pressure, and at the end of the brush stroke release the pressure flicking the brush

GRASS STROKES -

Grass Strokes really involve several other strokes. What is specifically elemental to a grass stroke, is the variance and playfulness of your brush work. Grass Strokes begin firmer at the bottom and release to a tapered point. Grass Strokes cure in many directions implying a wind blowing through them. As a beginner it's good to move away from what I call mowing the grass.This is when all the brush strokes are even and of equal length. Experiment with longer and shorter brush strokes expressing the wild and unruly soul of nature.

LONG STROKES -

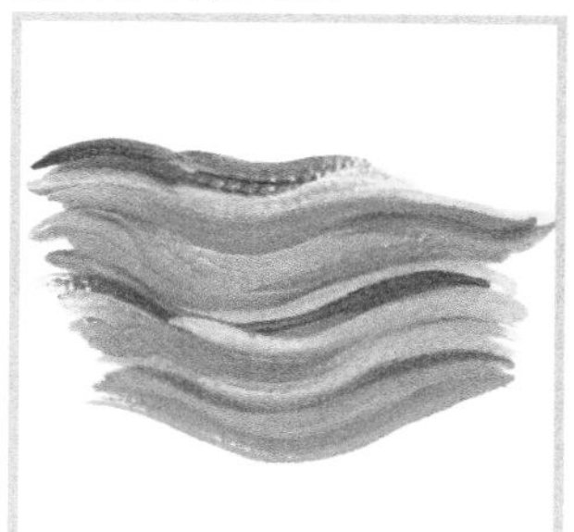

Sometimes it's a good idea to connect the brush to the surface pulling it along with expressive brush Strokes. The effect is smooth and elegant.

SHORT STROKES -

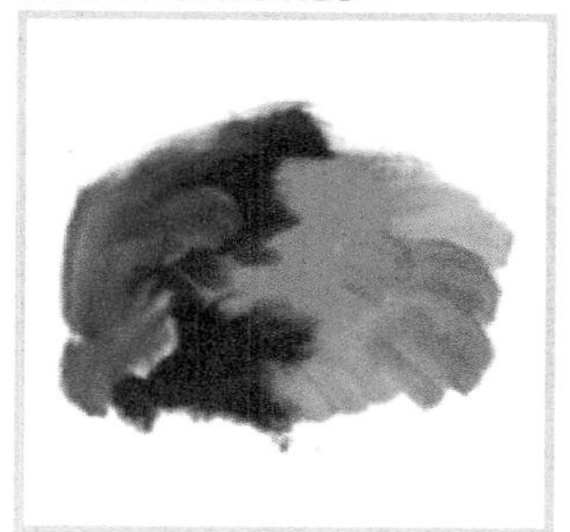

Short brush Strokes are energetic and textural. The brush engages with a canvas for small expressive amounts of time.

SPLATTER -

Splattering is an expressive technique where paint is propelled at the canvas resulting in dispersed, splattered pigment. Splatter generally requires a more fluid paint. You can create splatter by flicking a stiff brush with a finger. Or by whacking two brushes together where the brush closest to the canvas is loaded, or using a tool specifically for splatter.

WASHES AND DRIPS -

Acrylic paint was made to be thinned with water. You can create washes and drips by thinning your paint with water. Check with your paint company to see the amount water they recommend can be added to paint. I find 30% to be a pretty safe rule. If you use a lot more water you may need to allow the canvas to rest as the pigment can take much longer to bind. Too much water and it potentially won't bind

LOOSELY MIXED -

Taking two colors and mixing them together we're both colors are still evident in the mix and brush stroke

THOROUGHLY MIXED -

Taking two colors and thoroughly incorporating them so they make a smooth even secondary color with no sign of the two colors used to create it.

TRANSITIONAL MIXING -

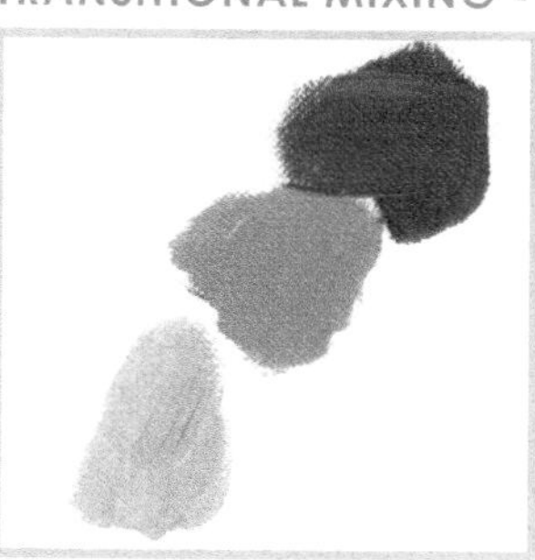

There are many ways to blend acrylic paint creating tonal and value transitions through the hues. When you have two very different colors, you can create hues that are half shades by mixing them together, biasing the mix to create a subtle transition. This is always useful.

TROUBLESHOOTING AND THE GRIDDING METHOD

TROUBLESHOOTING

Removing chalk - When your paint is completely dry you can remove the remaining chalk lines you may have left behind. To do this take a brush dampened with water delicately list the lines off the canvas. Remember to keep your brush just damp you don't want it to be actively wet. And you do want to use a soft brush so it doesn't remove any paint underneath the chalk.

IMPROVE PAINT FLOW

Sometimes you'll find that your paint feels very dry. As if it's scraping across the desert that is your canvas. You will see a lot of the surface showing through and it can feel like it won't cover easily. There are many ways to fix this issue. Go through this checklist to self-diagnose where your difficulties are.

Not enough water in the mix. Loading the brush with one drop of water at a time, we're going to incrementally thin the paint until the flow of the brush over the canvas covers easily without drag or difficulty.

1. Dip you brush in your clean water, dragging off the extra water on the edge. Take your brush to your paint from the edge of your paint. Mix the water thoroughly with a small amount of paint. Now do a test stroke on a test canvas. Did the paint flow easily? Did it feel like your brush was gliding with no drag pulling against it?
2. If your previous stroke was not satisfactory rinse out your brush and repeat step one mixing one more drop into the paint you've already thinned.
3. Continue thinning by adding one drop at a time until the paint becomes too thin.

PAINT DRYING TOO FAST

Are your paint conditions too arid?

1. Try a mister
2. Try a wet palette
3. Try to add a humidifier by your palette
4. Use a retarder to slow drying

SHERPAISMS:

"A TITCH", "A SCOTCH", "A SMIDGE"

This is a small amount of paint. It can range anywhere from the size of a sesame seed to an orange seed. I use this expression of small measurement because some colors are highly staining. It doesn't take a lot of phthalo blue to change the hue of your white. So sometimes it's best to proceed with caution. When you see this unit of measurement that is what I'm referring to.

"WE'RE TALKING ABOUT"

Sometimes I will say to my students as I'm painting "we're going to talk about grass over here." If you think of art as a visual language, every brush stroke is a conversation. When I paint in a particular area of a painting, creating techniques to express my subject, I feel that this is a type of conversation.

THE GRIDDING METHOD

All our images will be illustrated using the gridding method so that you can duplicate the image onto your canvas. The gridding method allows you to dip your toe into drawing without being in the deep end of the drawing pool on day one. For our purposes, the gridding method has been worked out for you. We will work on a 1" scale and everything will be of equal ratio. On your 8" x 8" canvas, you will make a mark using your chalk tool and a T-square ruler at every inch point. Using the guide, draw lines horizontally and vertically this way. The T-square will help ensure that your lines are straight.

1. You will have 1-8 columns at the top. Number them.
2. You will have 1-8 rows on the side. Number them.
3. Find the fist row that the contour line of your image enters and exits. Duplicate only what you see in that one single square.
4. Continue through the entire image, square by square, transferring the contour lines of the subject with chalk onto your canvas.
5. When you have duplicated the subject from your reference to your canvas, you will be done.

In our step-by-step chapters, you can check your work against the "Step 1" example in each chapter.

You can remove chalk easily by taking a soft brush and getting it damp with clean water. Gently brush over the lines you wish to remove and they will lift.

To do the grid your canvas must be dry and its advisable that it is also cool. You can use chalk that is wax or oil free. It must be pure chalk. In this book I'm using a dritz fabric marking tool. I like this tool because it does fine lines easily and removes well from the canvas. There are chalk pencils or you could use chalkboard chalk. While I will always share with you the tools and equipment that I'm using you are welcome to deviate from that anytime you feel is best for you.

Something that I have learned especially with complex images is that it can be easy to get lost in the grid. If you find yourself unsure, go back and check to make sure that the square you're marking on two matches the square in your reference. After you master this method you'll be able to use gridding to transfer any image from a reference to your canvas.

If you want to do a different size, there's a lot of great resources out there that involves math about how to scale. I have decided to skip the math because we're already painting every day for 30 days and that's enough to worry about. Also I don't teach math for a many good reasons I could count them all for you but that would be doing math. The resources out there for that information and those mathematical formulas exist online in copious amounts. If you're choosing to paint different sizes then we're utilizing in this book I highly recommend finding one of those formulas and mastering it. Short of that, buy 8x8 canvas for your 8x8 grid.

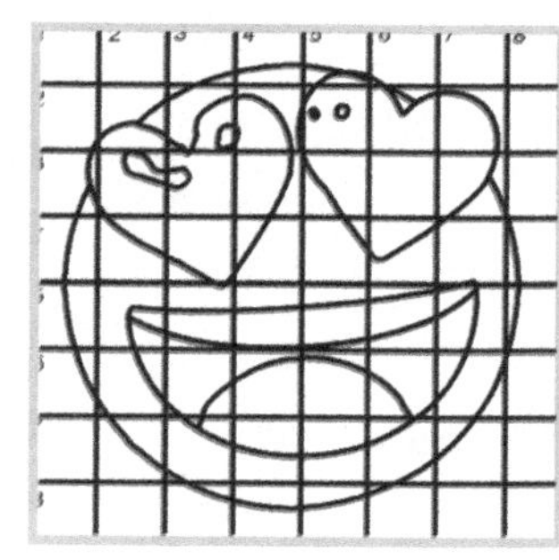

GLOWING SUNSET

COLOR PALETTE:     

Today's color palette is Dioxazine Purple, Quinacridone Magenta, Cad Red Medium, Cad Yellow, and Titanium White. This is your Master Orange mix.

1. BACKGROUND AND GRID

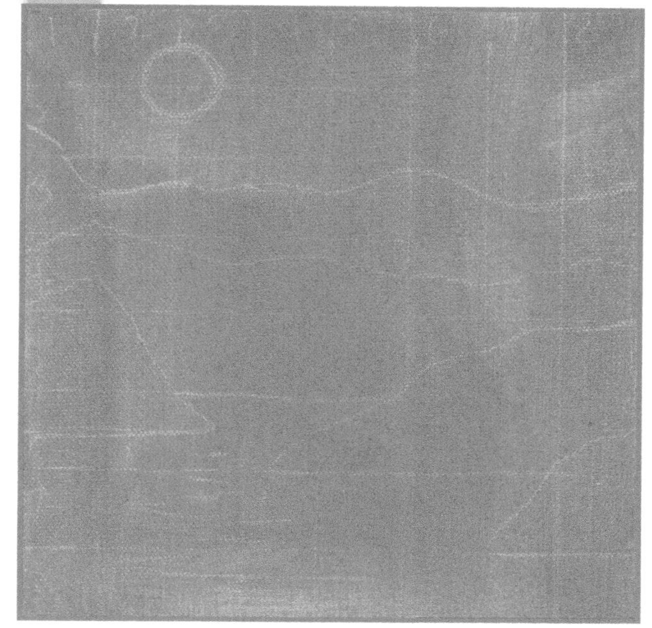

COLOR MIX: Cad yellow with some cad red to make a bright orange, add some white to make it a little peachy. Get some water on your background brush, just enough to help your paint flow. Paint your entire surface. Dry Completely.

GRID: With your t-square and chalk, create a 1" x 1" grid on your canvas. Number the squares across the top 1 - 8, and along the left side, top to bottom, 1 - 8. Duplicate the image exactly as shown in the reference, one square at a time. Only draw what's in that square before you move on.

Take a deep breath and remember, if you have to change any lines, the chalk is removed easily with just a damp brush and clean water.

2. DRAMATIZE THE SKY AND SUN

With your #8 Bright, use your master orange mix and add more cad yellow to make it a lighter shade, and then some white. Using a back and forth motion, paint the sky lighter at the top, getting darker as you move down. Paint around the sun. You can add white to increase the lightness around it. With a dry brush, get into the white, with a bit of yellow, but mostly white, to paint in the sun. A yellow sun would not work here. Use the reference I provide to help you keep on track.

3. ATMOSPHERIC PERSPECTIVE OF A MOUNTAIN LANDSCAPE

To create atmospheric perspective we use color and value to imply distance and shape by creating light, distant mountains which will darken as they come forward. Still using your #8 bright, take the master orange color, but make it one shade darker with a little more saturation of red. Starting at the mountains that appear furthest back, bring this color about half way down this section of sky. Add yellow, and from the bottom of this section, scumble this lighter color up, softly blending wet into wet with the darker top color. This lighter color coming up from the bottom of the mountain will create a misty effect. Before you build in the next mountain, your edges should be dark and the base should have a gentle, warmer glow.

4. 2ND MOUNTAIN RANGE

We are using the same steps in each mountain, darkening each section as we move down the canvas, continuing to create atmospheric perspective. Remember to use the same steps here. Making sure you blend part of the way down with your darker color, wipe off your brush and begin gently blending your lighter color up from the base of each mountain. Add a little white to create the misty base. While the paint is still wet, add a little white to the tip of your brush and blend that mist up with a dry brush. Make sure there is a darker edge to all the mountains.

The mix is still going to be quite orange, but this time take yellow to your red to make a more red than yellow color. As these mountains come down, you will add more yellow into the mix to almost the color we originally painted the canvas. Use your reference to finish painting this next step.

5. MISTY MOUNTAIN MAJESTY

Mix cad red and quin magenta to make the next darker value, and paint in the little mountain on the left. As you come down, add a smidge of white to create the interesting misty effect. Wiggle the brush to create the mist. Go ahead and paint the mountain on the right, because they are very similar. Add just a smidgiest smidge of diox purple to darken these mountains. Use white to make the misty base.

You can come back with cad red and quin magenta with a touch of diox purple at the top if you need to adjust your light and dark values.

6. BABY DARK MOUNTAIN

Our baby mountain will have our darkest color, cad red, quin magenta and a larger amount of diox purple. Paint this smallest rock in, starting at the top with your dark color, and repeat the same steps to create that misty effect at the base.

Make sure there is a darker edge to all the mountains. Use the reference to help you get through this step, and don't forget you can always go back and review the video at any time.

7. CREATE A HORIZON LINE AND A WATER MIRROR

What you have to remember on a landscape is that water, whether it's frothy or not, is essentially a mirror. It refracts light. If you can't see through it, you're looking at the surface of it and it's going to reflect some of the sky. But the trick is that you need to keep a very sharp horizon line, and to do that, I tape it. Make sure your canvas is completely dry. Run a line of low tack tape across the bottom edge of the mountain and use your ruler if you need to to keep it level. Everything below the tape will be water.

With your #8 Bright, come in with the base sky color. Not the lightest, but the base color, and paint in the water. Moving your brush back and forth and even in these brush strokes, staying level, add a little more yellow and put a bit of white into it as you move towards the bottom of your canvas. You want to look for that mirror effect in the sky.

9. SIGNATURE

Sign your name and take a moment to feel great about completing your first painting

8. HIGHLIGHTS AND LOWLIGHTS, DEFINING WATER

Switching to your #4 round, get a very light yellow by mixing your cad yellow and white. On the toe of the brush, with a light feathering stroke, start adding highlights. Zigg zagg your brush across the water. You want to really make sure that you have reflections. On the toe of the brush, feather a bit of yellow and zigg zagg your brush across the water. Add more cad yellow to slightly darken your water as you move toward the bottom of the canvas. Your water should mirror your sky. You might want to add just some small, almost white highlights, just a few, to really help the reflections shine.

Don't forget to add shadows under your rocks. Because solid objects would block the light in water, you'd see a bit of darkening along the bottoms of your rocks.

Mix your quin magenta and cad red, making a nice dark shadow color. Still on the toe of your #4 round, zigging and zagging to create shadows at the base of your first two rocks, make the darker shadows for the darkest rock, mixing quin magenta and purple. Keep zigging and zagging. You want to trick the eye into believing that this is water.

Using the reference here, stand back and really take in your work. Refine, retouch, or change any part of it that you feel needs your attention. Check that your highlights are reasonable to the light source, and that your shadows correspond to something that would block the sun.

SWATCHING PRACTICE PAGE

1. Practice mixing the colors from todays palette and paint in your circles with your colors.
2. Check your values and hue by swatching your paint mixes on the sample images.
3. Do a tiny fast grey scale sketch to help you express light and shadow - use paint or pencil, either is fine.

TRACEABLE

THE ART SHERPA

LADYBUG

COLOR PALETTE:           

Today's color palette is Phthalo Blue, Phthalo Green, Ultramarine Blue, Naples Yellow Light, Cad Yellow Medium, Burnt Sienna, Mars Black, Cad Red Medium, Quinacridone Magenta and Titanium White.

1. BACKGROUND AND GRID

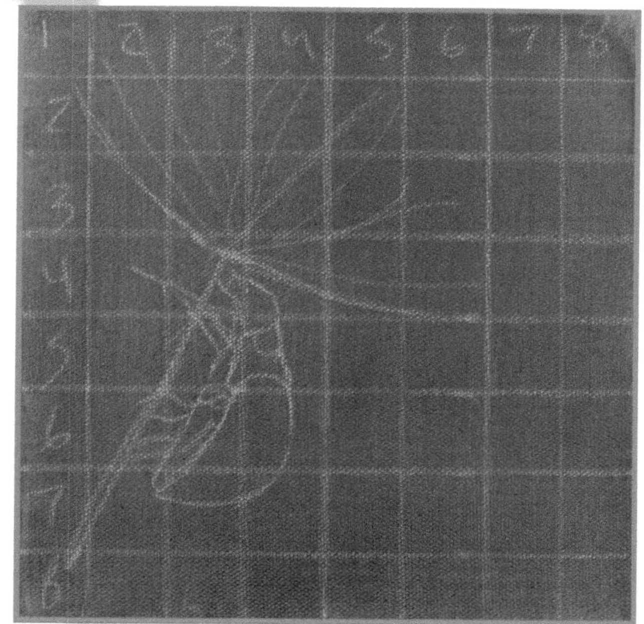

COLOR MIX: Ultramarine blue with phthalo green to make teal. Add a little naples yellow to lighten. Get some water on your background brush, just enough to help your paint flow. Paint your entire surface, allowing it to dry completely.

GRID: With your t-square and chalk, create a 1" x 1" grid on your canvas. Number the squares across the top 1 - 8, and along the left side top to bottom 1 - 8. Duplicate the image exactly as shown in the reference, one square at a time. Only draw what's in that square before you move on.

Take a deep breath and remember, if you have to change any lines, the chalk is removed easily with just a damp brush and clean water.

2. DANDELION STEM AND FLUFF

With your #4 round, mix a bit of your cad red into your cad yellow and paint in the stem. Lighten this mix with white to add the highlight. Mix some burnt sienna and black for the much deeper values of the stem.

Rinse out your brush before moving to the cute little fluff. You're using your color values to knock the white back so that our fluff feels like it could definitely fly! Mix some white and purple to create contrast, ultramarine blue for the shadows and some pure purple for deepest values. Using a very light stroke, add some fluff!

3. DANDELION FLUFF AND LADYBUG

Dry your canvas.

Get pure white and thin it with water and use this to catch those interesting fluffy highlights. Then come back with a yellow and red mix to anchor the fluff to the stem. Still using your #4 round, get some mars black to start blocking in the little beetle body. Don't worry if you get your black into the white parts, you can always come back and reestablish the white. Be sure to do the joints, legs and prongs, which are all very delicate.

Refine anything you feel you need to, and remember that you can always go back to view the video any time you want.

4. REFINING THE LADYBUG & REMOVING THE GRID

Mix a little quin magenta and cad red, leaning toward the quin side. Start to paint in the glowy, bright, vibrant red areas to the ladybug shell. If using student or craft paint, you may have to add 2 coats or paint the area white before painting red to get the brightness.

Let dry.

Take phthalo blue and white to add belly reflections, using more blue for the deepest values, and pop the reflections with your lightest blue.

Let dry completely before cleaning up any remaining chalk. Use a moist brush, more water where necessary, to remove the grid.

5. REFINING THE LADYBUG & HIGHLIGHTS/LOWLIGHTS

Coming back with our red mixes, use quin when it is darker or fuller, cad red when it's a little more in sunlight. Use your naples yellow and white for interesting little reflections. Keep your white values very subtle.

Compare the reference to determine when you are happy.

6. ADDING DOTS, FINISHING TOUCHES AND SIGNATURE

Before you start the dots, dry and cool your canvas and rinse out your brush. Take phthalo blue into black to make a very subtle blue cast and add your dots using the reference photo. Thin some pure white, and wipe to remove any clumps, load the toe of your brush, and then add this highlight color to the shell and these weird highlighty, reflective parts on their legs.

Start catching details by putting back in some of the yellow white and black that you feel needs strengthening. The aim here is to get the features, the focal bits you want to pop out of the canvas.

With your #1 monogram liner, add your signature and please, please, post your finished picture.

SWATCHING PRACTICE PAGE

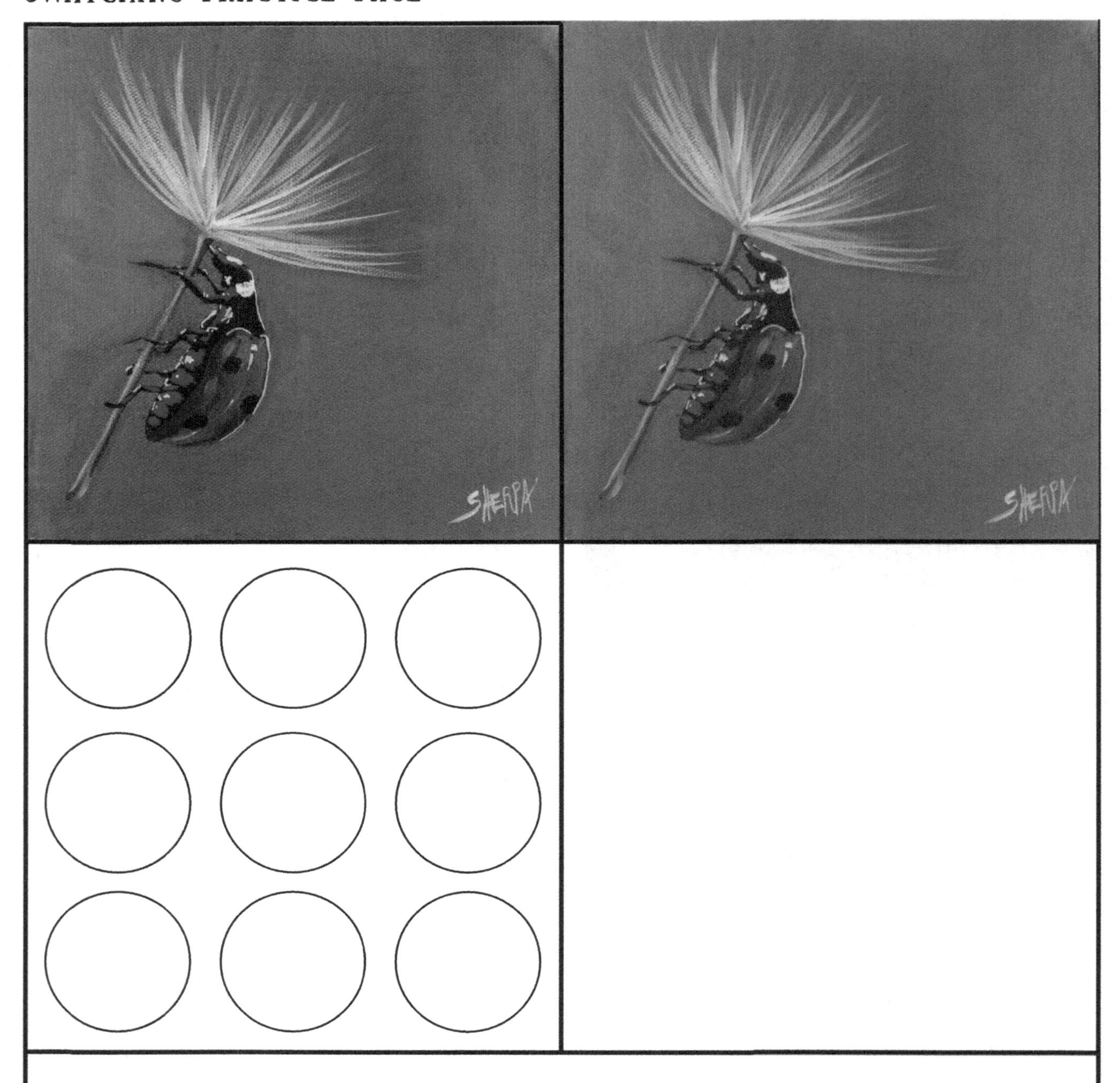

1. Practice mixing the colors from todays palette and paint in your circles with your colors.
2. Check your values and hue by swatching your paint mixes on the sample images.
3. Do a tiny fast grey scale sketch to help you express light and shadow - use paint or pencil, either is fine.

TRACEABLE

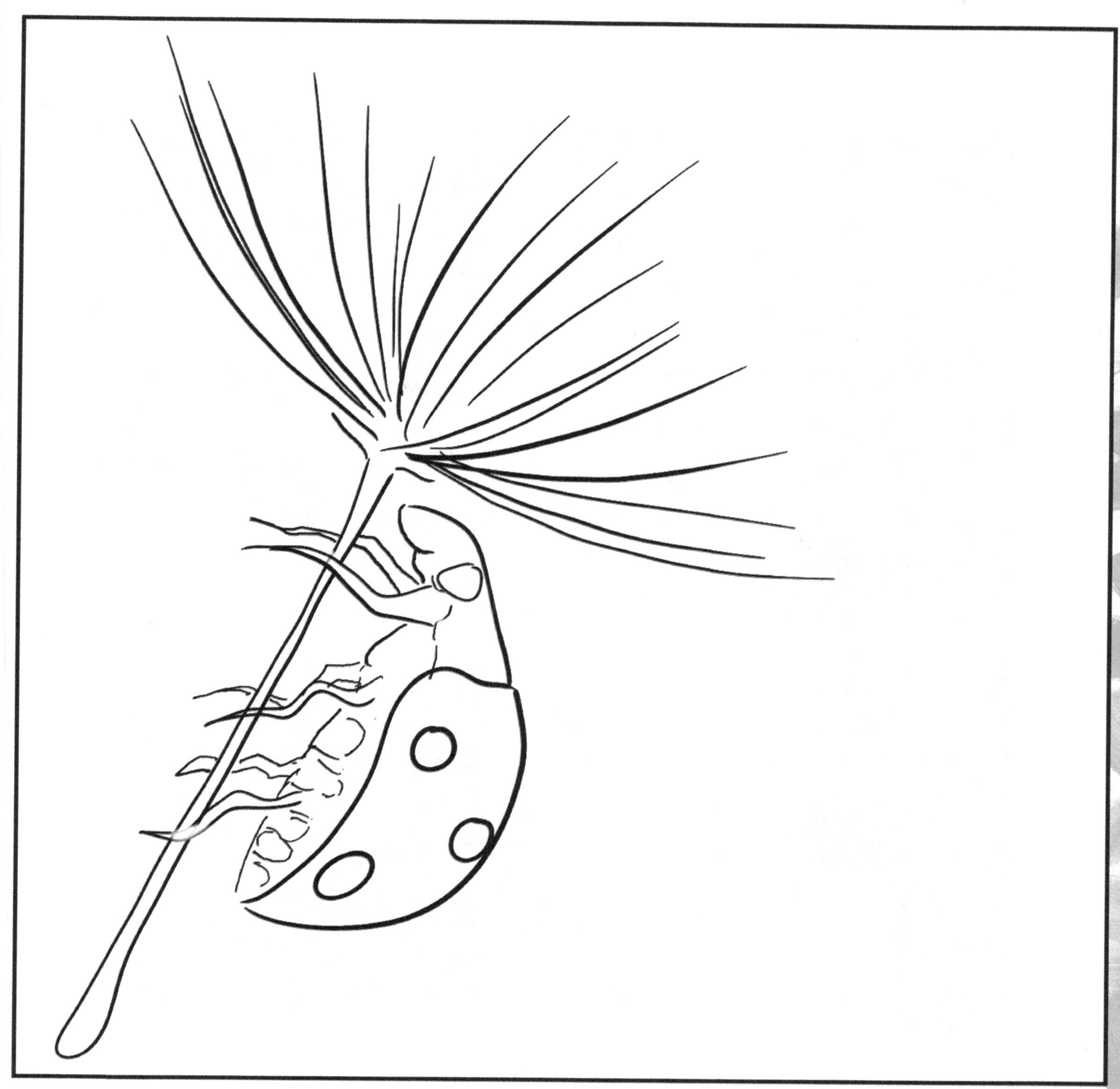

PHOENIX

COLOR PALETTE:      

Today's color palette is Mars Black, Cad Yellow Medium, Cad Red Medium, Quinacridone Magenta, (sometimes called Quinacridone Fuchsia) Titanium White and Phthalo Blue.

1. BACKGROUND AND GRID

COLOR MIX: Mars black. Get some water on your background brush, just enough to help your paint flow. Paint your entire surface. Dry completely.

GRID: With your t-square and chalk, create a 1" x 1" grid on your canvas. Number the squares across the top 1 - 8 and along the left side, top to bottom, 1 - 8. Duplicate the image exactly as shown in the reference, one square at a time. Only draw what's in that square before you move on.

Take a deep breath and remember, if you have to change any lines, the chalk is removed easily with just a damp brush and clean water.

2. CANDLE SHADOWS AND FLAMING THE PHOENIX

With the #8 cat's tongue, grab a little black and mix it with cad red for our candle shading, and don't forget the drip. Use a little bit of this red for the wick. Lay the groundwork for some of the lighter areas of the Phoenix, and to create the feeling of fire, mix a bit of white and yellow together. Remember that the areas that are hottest will be lightest.

Use your calligraphy stroke here to create the sense of flame. Staying on the toe of the brush, paint some plumage coming off his head and at the joint of the wing. Just pulling it all together.

Refer to the reference provided to help you through this step.

3. CANDLE GLOW

Grab the #4 round and let's get some candle glow going. Add a mix of Yellow and a bit of cad red to the candle, especially toward the flame. Catch the little drips going down and brightness coming up that wick. Make a darker value for your shadows with a mix of cad red and quin magenta to cool it down because the further we are from the light, the less glow our candle has.

Next take pure cad yellow, adding titches of cad red to brighten, and use those calligraphy brush strokes on the wing. Keep your paint on the toe of the brush for the flame-like effect. For the little sparks from the wing, mix some red into the yellow. For the candle flame, at the base, add pure yellow. Let it dry and use your reference to compare. Come back with very light values for hot spots.

4. WARM AND COOL FIRE

To create the cooler ranges of fire that might be on his wings, take quin magenta and mix 1 to 1 with cad red for the outer ranges of feathers. Mix cad yellow and cad red and bring that into the feathers, the plume, and belly, just cooling him down. Back to your orange mix, and add some to the wings, building layers out. Get the deeper red values around the eye.

5. CONTINUATION OF WARM AND COOL FIRE

Play with that fire color and check your reference for guidance.

Work his top knot, get the beak and it's shadows, and the tail. Add yellow to white to create the real light highlights, perhaps even at the top of that wax. Highlight that flame again with the red and quin mix.

Highlight your candle glow. Look for small details you may have missed. Does the beak have a highlight and shadow value? Really evaluate here and resolve all steps up to here.

6. HIGHLIGHTS/LOWLIGHTS

Remove any remaining chalk lines with a damp brush.

Mix white with water to get fluid, and look for those yellow places where the center might be hotter, the core of the fire, the candle flame tip.

Get a tiny bit of blue and some white white and add just a bit of light blue to the highlight around the base of your candle flame. This will help make it look real. Keep referring to your reference.

Do you need more shadow values or highlight values? This is the step to get all of those in. When you look at it, does your eye believe there is heat?

7. FINISHING TOUCHES

Time to work the eye detail and create little hot ember spots. Take some quin and cad red and come into the eye and shape it out with your #4 brush. Don't get into the hyper small area, you can always add that back in with a toothpick or a very small brush.

Now grab pure cad red and add to the pupil then add white. Is your stare a little intense? Mine usually is. The more white, the more intense.

Now go back with the #4 round and create those little glows by wiggling your brush, make them float. Vary the size and colors of your embers. The closer to the flame, the hotter they will be.

Dry your canvas, then come back in with yellow and a lot of white to add the centers of the embers.

8. SIGNATURE

With your #1 monogram liner, add your signature and please, please, post your finished picture.

SWATCHING PRACTICE PAGE

1. Practice mixing the colors from todays palette and paint in your circles with your colors.
2. Check your values and hue by swatching your paint mixes on the sample images.
3. Do a tiny fast grey scale sketch to help you express light and shadow - use paint or pencil, either is fine.

TRACEABLE

THE ART SHERPA

COLORFUL PIG

COLOR PALETTE: 

Today's color palette is Cad Red Medium, Quinacridone Magenta, Naples Yellow Light, Cad Yellow Medium, Burnt Sienna, Phthalo Green, Phthalo Blue, Ultramarine Blue, Mars Black, and Titanium White.

1. BACKGROUND AND GRID

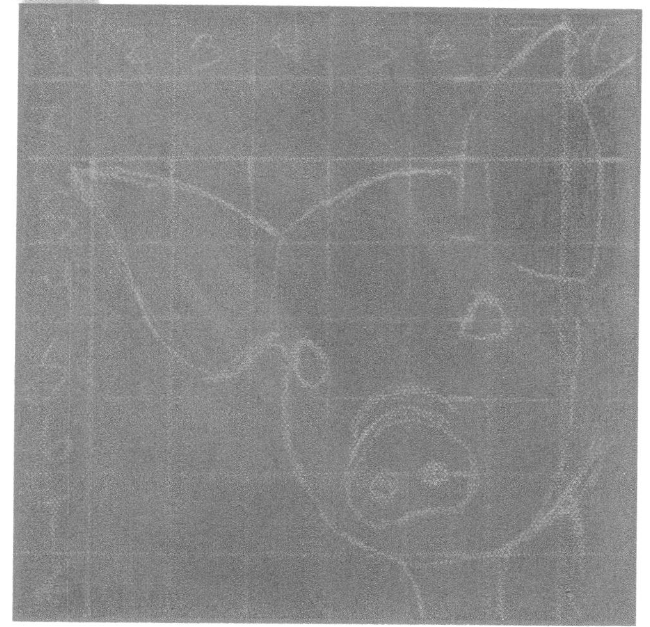

COLOR MIX: With black and white, create a light gray color. You want it dark enough so the chalk will show up against it, but still to the light side. Get some water on your background brush, just enough to help your paint flow. Paint your entire surface, allowing it to completely dry.

GRID: With your t-square and chalk, create a 1" x 1" grid on your canvas. Number the squares across the top 1 - 8, and along the left side, top to bottom, 1 - 8. Duplicate the image exactly as shown in the reference, one square at a time. Only draw what's in that square before you move on.

2. LIGHTEN THE BACKGROUND

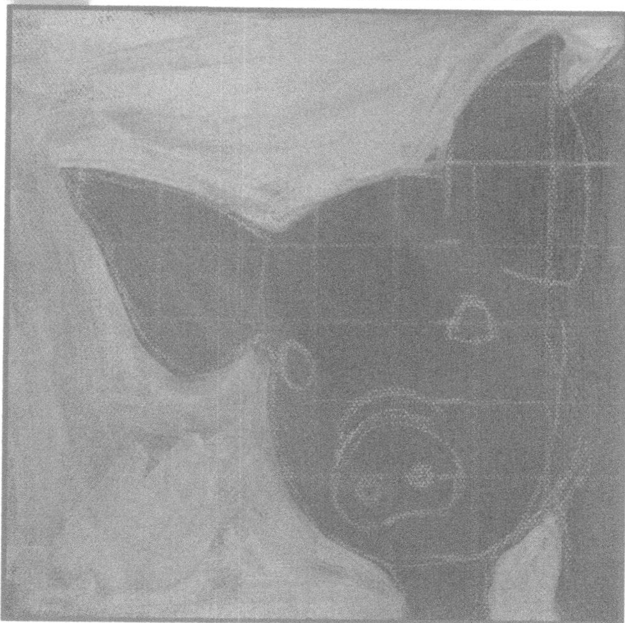

Look at the reference and note the lighter part of the background around the piglet. Take your gray, lighten it with white, and use the reference as a guide to lighten that background. The piglet should stand out.

3. BEGIN THE SHADOW AND SHAPE OF YOUR PIGLET

With a #8 cats tongue, mix the basic pig color, which will be quin magenta and cad red to create a pretty pink tone, add a bit of naples yellow. Begin painting in the ear, leaving some cartilage space. Add water to improve flow as needed. Fill the snout in with basic pink.

Move to the nostrils with pure quin, blending wet into wet, a little redder underneath. Add Shadows under the belly and legs.

Lighten your basic pig color with white and go around the eyes. Use this color on the top edge of the ears. Refer to your reference to determine when you are done with this step.

4. LAYERING SHADOWS

Using your basic pig mix of quin magenta, naples yellow and white, loosely painting in the body of the pig.

Add Quin shadows to the insides of the ears, wrinkles on the neck and snout and around your eyes.

5. FUN COLORFUL HIGHLIGHTS/LOWLIGHTS

You can express your shadows and highlights with the use of unexpected and playful colors. Try mixing phthalo blue, phthalo green and a touch of white to create turquoise. You can lighten your turquoise with naples yellow or white. Add your lightest turquoise under the chin and top of the ears.

Create strokes of the deeper turquoise under the chin and bottom of the right ear. Mixing magenta into the ultramarine creating a purple. You can brighten the purple by adding some white. Create a shadow with this color on the belly and ears. Stand back and refer to your reference to determine if you have completed this step.

6. MORE LAYERING AND DEFINITION

With the #6 bright, continue working the basic pig color mix. Add white or naples yellow for lighter values, and quin magenta for darker values. Step back and evaluate as you need to. Focus around the eyes, nose and ears. Magenta inside the ear. Add some cad yellow to the pink, maybe some white, for the snout. Try naples yellow to lighten the paint up.

Remember, if you allow your canvas to dry between layers, any mistakes can be easily removed with a little bit of water. If you are painting wet on wet, colors will blend better. Mix quin, cad yellow and naples yellow for pink nose colors and with the #4 round, and make the top half of the nose lighter. Add white if you need to, pure naples yellow where you need it. Wipe your brush off if you need to lighten the paint load. Wiggle the brush back and forth for effect. Shape the nose. Define his wrinkles with purple shadows and light pink highlights. Work around light and deep pinks to define the eyes. Take a little black into the brown for the eyes.

7. ADDING HAIR AND HIGHLIGHTS

Add interesting texture you can do is hair by using your bristle brush #8 cambridge and primary pig color mix.

Add a little yellow to lighten and a touch of cad red. Focus on values. Your brush strokes should be a little out of focus and a little rough. Add water to the brush as needed but don't get waterlogged.

Soften around his face and don't forget his little knees.

8. DRAMA AND EVALUATION

Dramatize those eyes with a bit of cad red and cad yellow to an orange color; add some brown. You can always add cad yellow and cad red for a brighter orange for highlights. Maybe some ultramarine and white. If you get carried away, you can always come back with the brown black mix. Deeper black where needed. Naples yellow and quin magenta for that dark rose color. Phthalo blue and ultramarine blue for a dark color, even add a touch of black. Add white for lighter values. Exaggerate the lighting.

We're almost done here. Step back and compare your painting to the reference. Is there anything you feel needs refining and are you ready for the next step? Use your reference for that final check.

9. SIGNATURE

With your #1 monogram liner, add your signature and please, please, post your finished picture.

SWATCHING PRACTICE PAGE

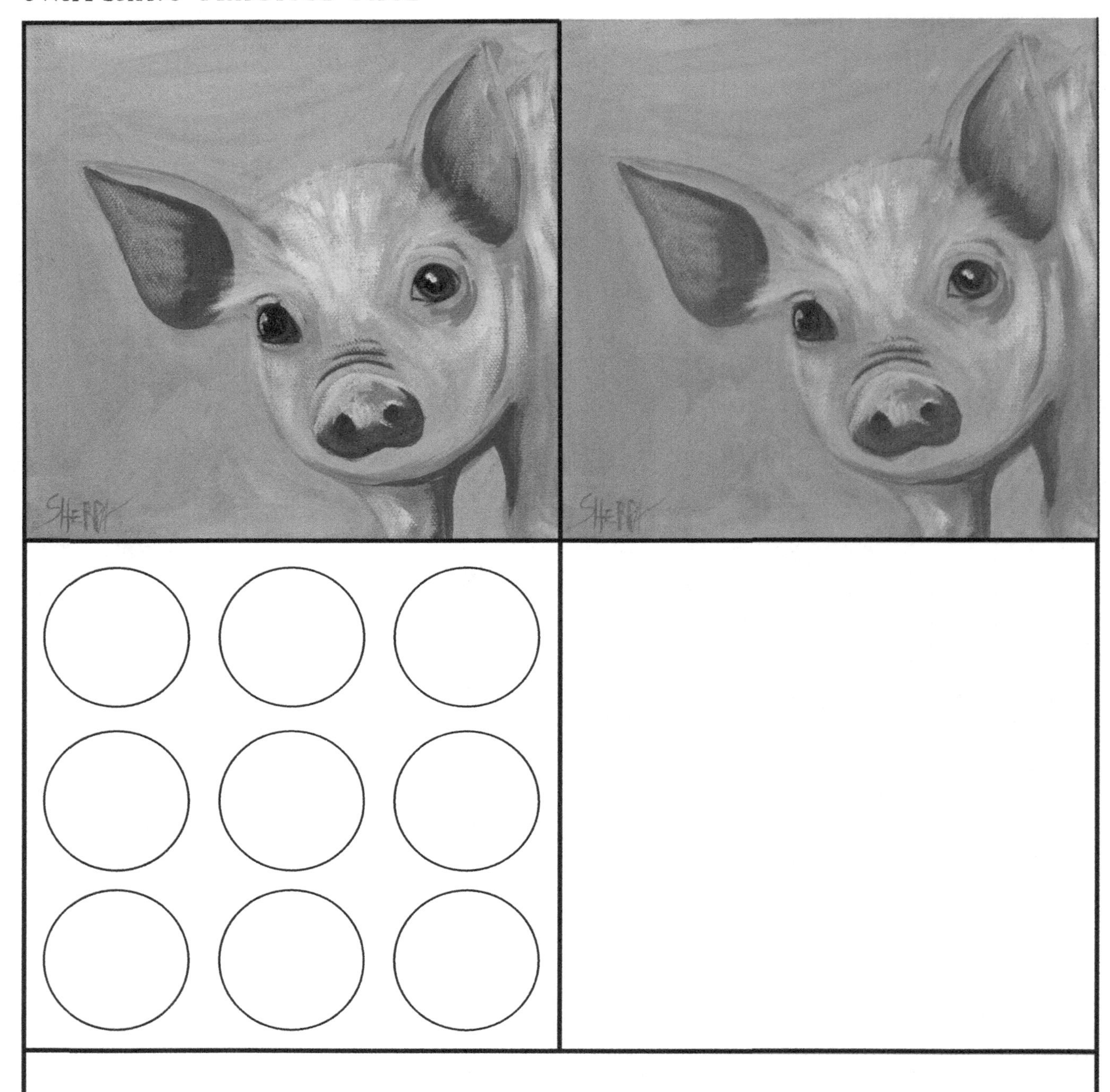

1. Practice mixing the colors from todays palette and paint in your circles with your colors.
2. Check your values and hue by swatching your paint mixes on the sample images.
3. Do a tiny fast grey scale sketch to help you express light and shadow - use paint or pencil, either is fine.

TRACEABLE

COLORFUL BUBBLES

COLOR PALETTE:        

Today's color palette is Mars Black, Phthalo Green, Phthalo Blue, Quinacridone Magenta, Cad Yellow Medium, Cad Red Medium, Dioxazine Purple, and Titanium White.

1. BACKGROUND AND GRID

COLOR MIX: Mars black. Get some water on your background brush, just enough to help your paint flow. Paint your entire surface, allowing it to completely dry.

GRID: With your t-square and chalk, create a 1" x 1" grid on your canvas. Number the squares across the top 1 - 8, and along the left side, top to bottom, 1 - 8. Duplicate the image exactly as shown inthe reference, one square at a time. Only draw what's in that square before you move on.

2. THE FURTHEST BUBBLE

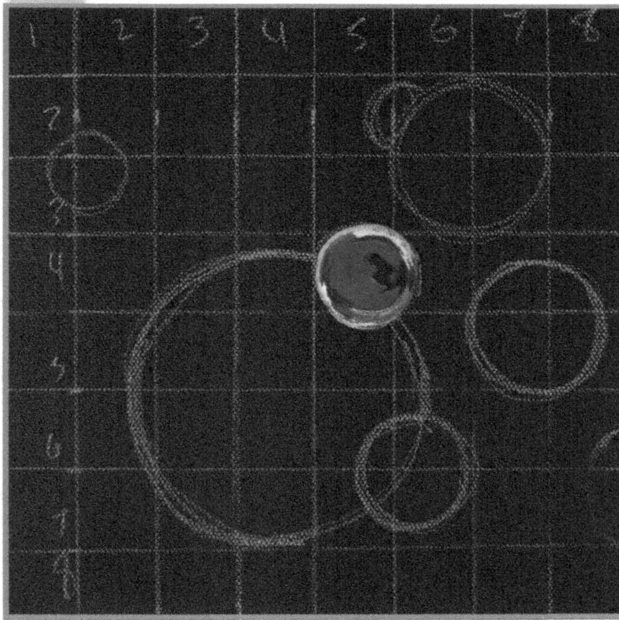

With a damp #6 bright, starting on the furthest back bubble, get yellow and a smidge of cad red and outline the outer edge. Mix quin magenta and a bit of white, not too much, in a couple of places. Rinse out.

Work some quin magenta in between the yellow and pink. Phthalo blue and just a touch of white, even into the purple, for the center. Maybe add some pure yellow, slivers of color, and bright pops of color.

You're just looking for those bright, bright colors that are reflecting off the surface of the bubble. Refer to your reference to determine if your back bubble is complete.

3. FOCAL BUBBLE

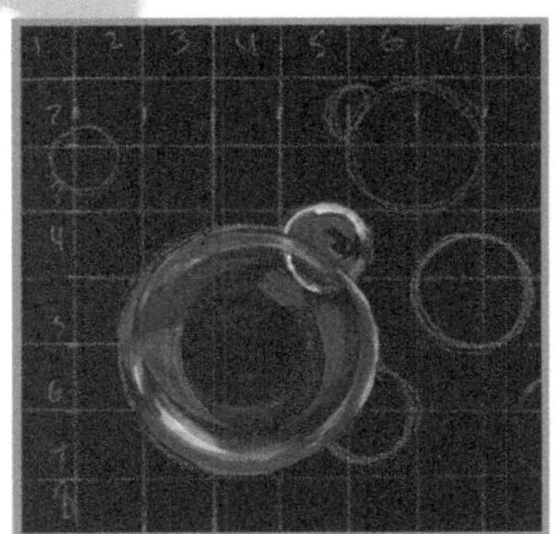

Let your canvas dry completely.

To work the focal bubble, get your #6 and mix phthalo blue and phthalo green together for phthalo turquoise, take it into the outer circle, lightly dry brushing over the back bubble. Add a little yellow pulled around like curved lenses. Leave the see-through part of the back bubble and let it peek through a little.

Let dry.

Mix white into to quin magenta to add pops of color. Add a little yellow in the mix and quin around the outside edge. A triangle down for a reflection of structural light. Add Quin and purple highlights.

4. LITTLE FRONT BUBBLE

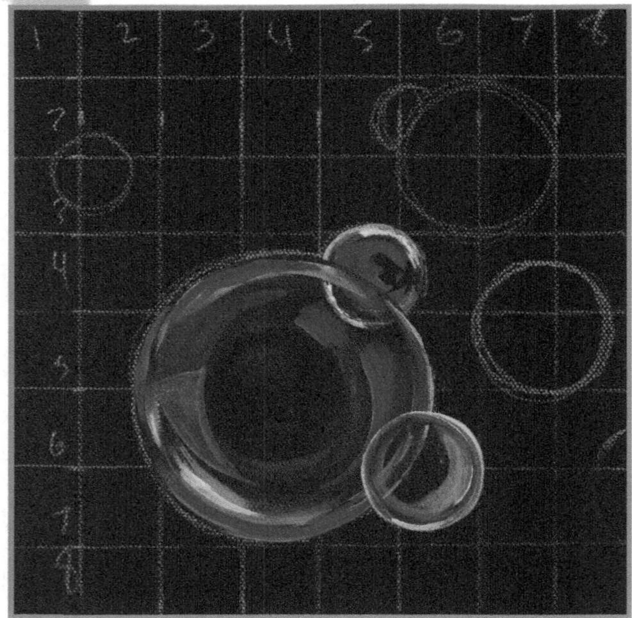

With the #4 round, get yellow with a little white, but to the yellow side, and let's add another little bubble just in front of the last. Come in next to the yellow with a mix of magenta and white, adding water to improve flow when needed. Mix some quin and cad red for super hot highlights.

Add a bit of phthalo turquoise to the inside. Add some white to the turquoise, Curve strokes to help show the edge of the circle. Come back with any colors you need to reinforce all three bubbles before stepping back to compare it to your reference.

If you painted something out, just come back in and add it in when you can. No worries.

5. BUBBLES BUBBLES BUBBLES

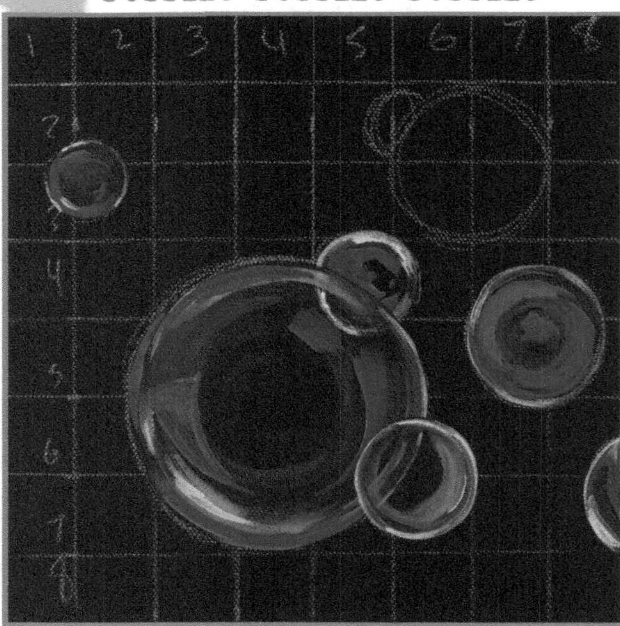

Before we do the compound bubble go ahead and use the same techniques to paint in the other bubbles. Remember your mixes, yellow and then add a bit of white for the highlights. Mix quin and cad red to add in a couple of places. Work those aquas, blues and purples in the center. Phthalo blue and a bit of pure diox purple for your deepest value. Getting that glow!

Use your yellow and white to add hotspots in a couple of places. Use your reference photo as a guide. Evaluate. Would a little phthalo green highlight that center?

6. COMPOUND BUBBLE, CHALK REMOVAL

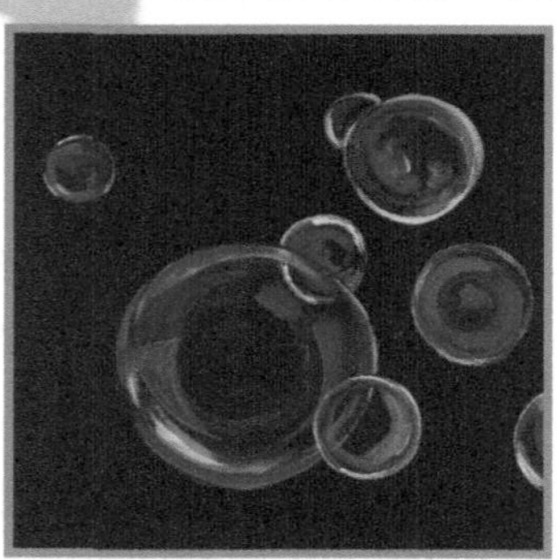

Starting with yellow outline the compound bubble, take note of the counterbalance of the colors between the two joined bubbles. This bubble is in light, so I want a very bright yellow. Get some quin magenta and a little yellow. Pop in some pink. A little cad red and cad yellow for a wiggly reflection. Blend some blue in. Don't forget purple for those dark areas.

Dry your canvas and clean up your chalk marks with a damp brush.

Use your reference photo to determine if you are happy with your progress so far and make any adjustments you need to make. I used my #8 cats tongue and black to reinforce the black areas and remember, foremost, all bubbles are not round. Bubbles wobble.

7. BUBBLICIOUS HIGHLIGHTS

Using a #4 round get some white and highlight the bubbles with curved light strokes. Catch the little area between the compound bubble. You will need to refer to your reference a great deal in this step. It's impossible to point out all the potential for highlights. Step back periodically and compare to the reference.

Go back and review the video for more detailed instruction about placement.

8. FLARE REFLECTIONS

Grab the t-square and #1 monogram liner. Thin your highlight color with water and dot some spectacular highlights. Dot, dot, dot. Play with those dots, refer to your reference.

Use your ruler to put sparkle reflections by lining all the way through some of the dots creating an X axis, cleaning the ruler off between bubbles.

If you'd like to soften a glow on your layer, come back in and dust with a dry brush. Don't hesitate to add a bit of dry brush to the hotspots to make them appear more featherly.

9. SIGNATURE

#1 monogrammed liner and sign your name to your incredible painting and please share it with the community. You should be very proud of yourself.

SWATCHING PRACTICE PAGE

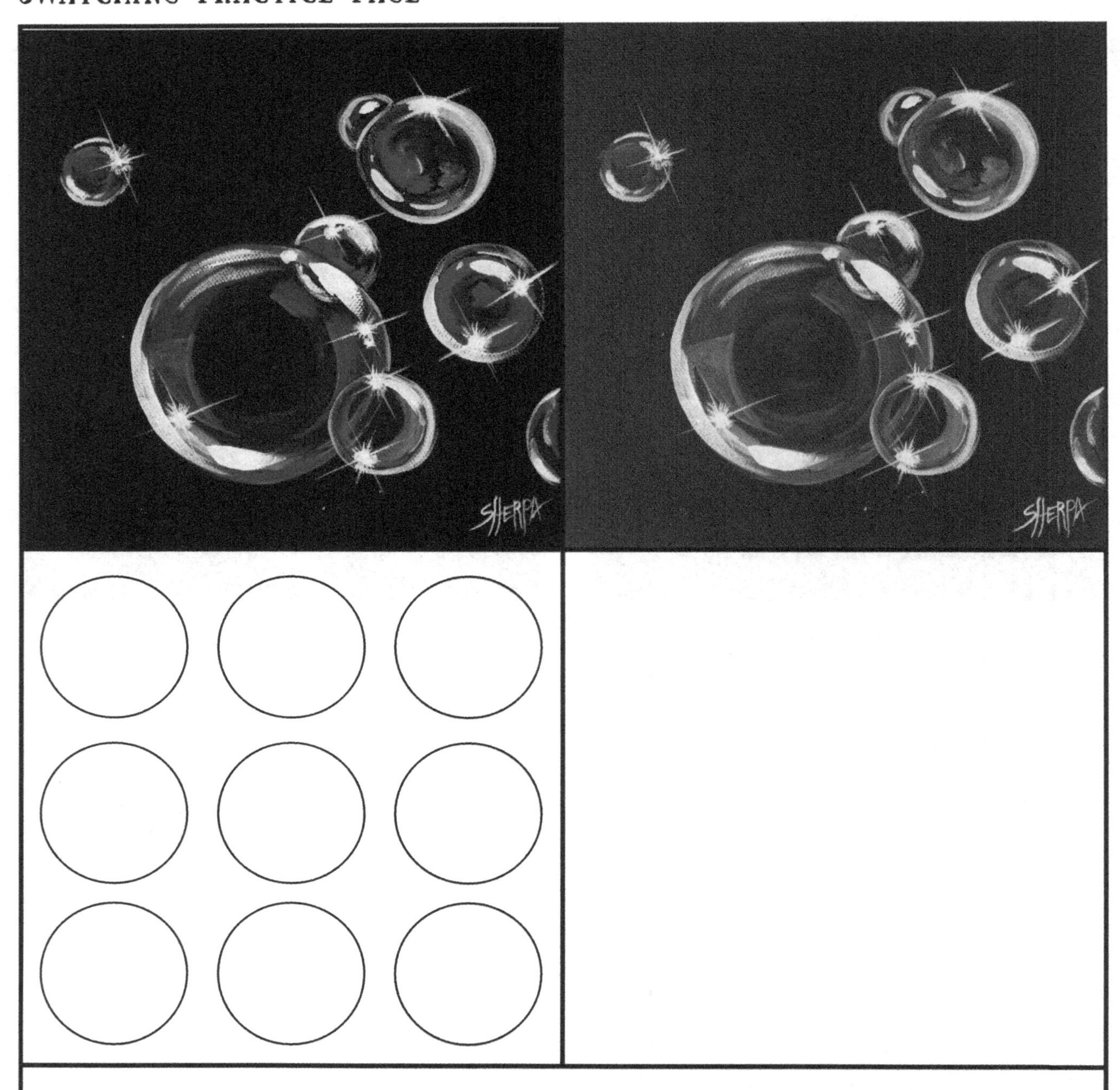

1. Practice mixing the colors from todays palette and paint in your circles with your colors.
2. Check your values and hue by swatching your paint mixes on the sample images.
3. Do a tiny fast grey scale sketch to help you express light and shadow - use paint or pencil, either is fine.

TRACEABLE

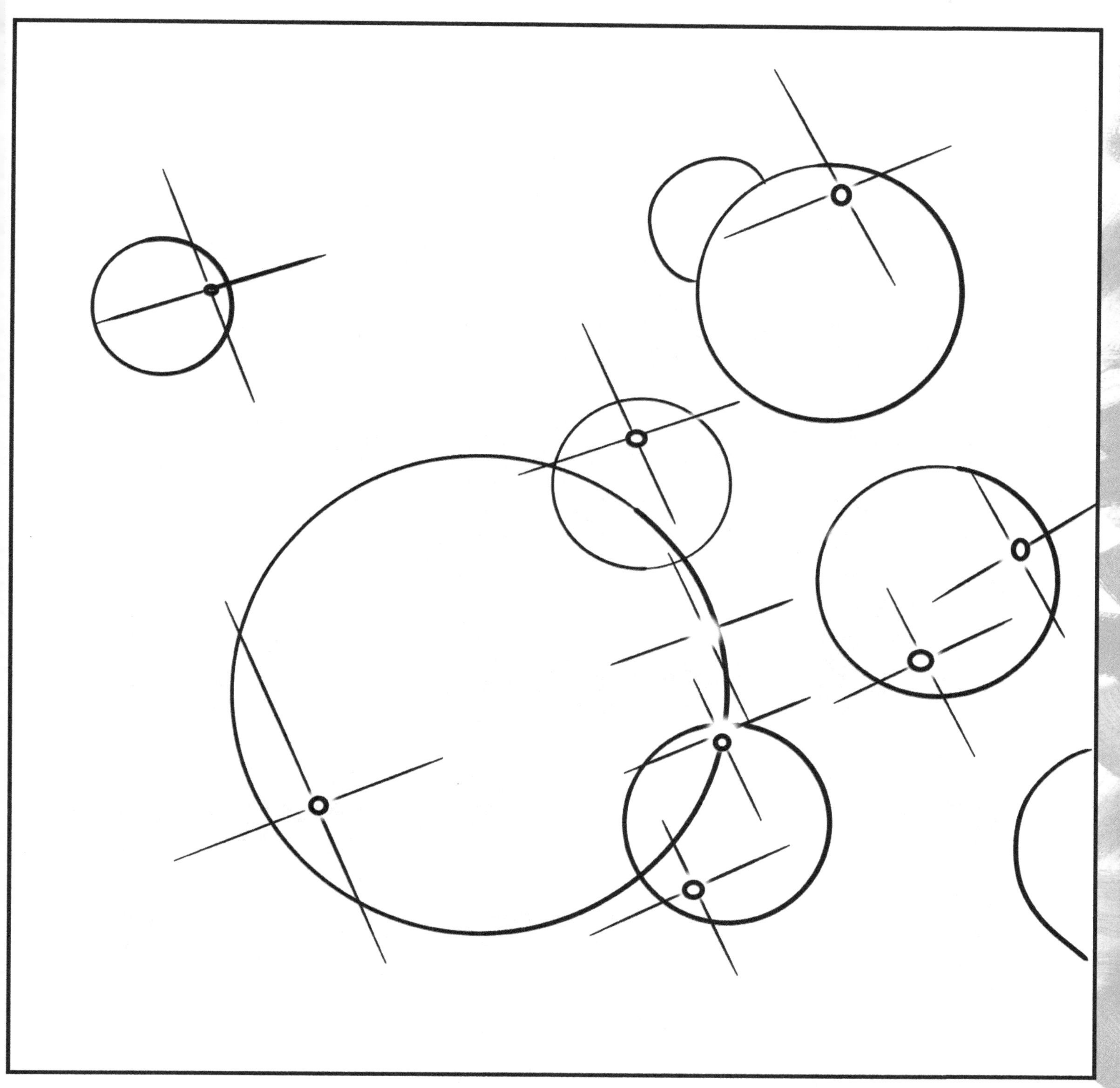

THE ART SHERPA

ZEN STONES CANDLE

COLOR PALETTE:        

Today's color palette is Phthalo Blue, Phthalo Green, Burnt Sienna, Cad Yellow Medium, Cad Red Medium, Mars Black, Naples Yellow Light, and Titanium White.

1. BACKGROUND AND GRID

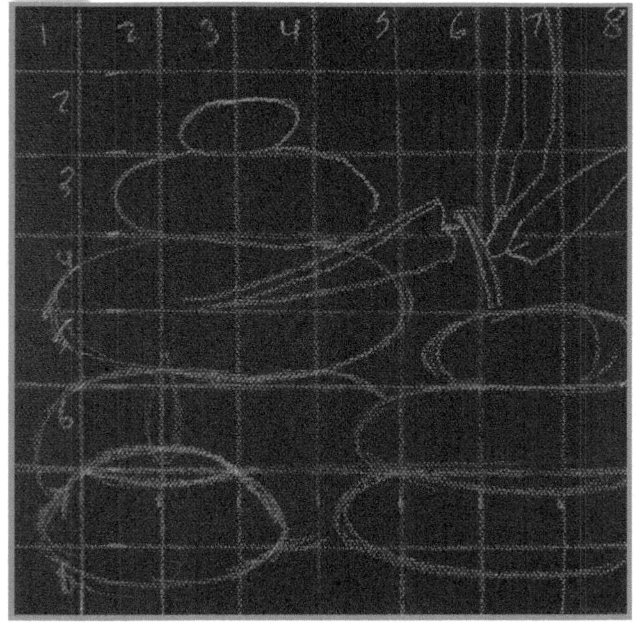

COLOR MIX: Mars black and burnt sienna, very loosely. Get some water on your background brush, just enough to help your paint flow. Paint your entire surface. Dry completely.

GRID: With your t-square and chalk, create a 1" x 1" grid on your canvas. Number the squares across the top 1 - 8 and along the left side, top to bottom, 1 - 8. Duplicate the image exactly as shown in the reference, one square at a time. Only draw what's in the square before you move on.

2. BLENDED BACKGROUND

With your #8 cats tongue, or a round, take a little cad red into Naples yellow and get a warm peach color. Paint this color from the outside in so that it gets darker and moodier. Paint around the contours of the objects and then paint the spaces around those contour lines using loose strokes.

Add a little yellow where you think it needs to be, and get some burnt sienna, maybe a little red for a nice deeper color. The line between 6 and 7 is our horizon line, so your background won't go past that. For that ground, some black with a little burnt sienna, loosely mixed. Contour around the stones again.

Remember your horizon line, tape it off if you need to. Refer to your reference before you move to the next step.

3. BLOCKING IN THE STONES

Take a little bit of black and some blue and work the darkest stone shadows. Try to imitate those convex areas. Add a little more blue into your blue-black mixture and work those portions of the stones that the candle is lighting, but still in shadow, where light might be partially blocked.

Add some white to the mix for the gray that is the natural color of the stones. Use broad strokes to get the stones in. A little more white for a middle gray to work on our stones.

Refer to your reference and don't forget that you can always go back to rereview the video. These are stacked stones, so lots of shadow; if you happen to paint out a shadow, it's ok, just dry and go back and fix it.

4. STONE TEXTURE

Time to capture the stone texture, accomplish that with dry brushing and scumbling. Start with a #8 Cambridge, take cad red and cad yellow with a skosh of brown. Scumble that in for warmth. Continue working in the stones using your references as a guide. You can wiggle textures with the corner of your brush. Put in highlights as well as shadows.

Rinse out your brush between dark and lighter tones if you need to. Yellow and black make a wonderful yellow gray which adds a lot of interest. Don't hesitate to add pure cad red where you want to indicate heat. Mix cad red and cad yellow, more to the yellow. Add a little naples yellow, and maybe white for a compound mix that is excellent for bright highlights.

5. REFINING STONE SHAPE

The purpose of this step is to add sharper, more defined edges to our stones and help pull them into very distinctive shapes. Use your #4 round, get it damp, and come back with black and a touch of blue, under the stones, for that very deep shadow range.

Take your basic stone gray and add white and a touch of Naples yellow to add depth. Touch in those little reflections. Are your stones feeling stoneish? Stand back to critique your progress against the reference.

6. BAMBOO

Time for that calming, zennish, beautiful bamboo. Begin with your #4 Round, mix the darkest green value, which is phthalo green and burnt sienna. paint in the bamboo with the tip of your brush. Let your brush wander up to the delicate little leaf with the pretty pointy end. Come back with yellow and burnt sienna and pull that into the leaf. Blending wet into wet. Work the stem with perhaps a little more black and burnt sienna to tone it.

The shadow is not where you think it's going to be because of the stones. Find the shadow and add it, check the base of the stems. Lighten the bamboo with cad yellow, right into the deep green. Surprisingly enough, add a little cad red for highlights.

Refer to your reference and remember that you can always go back to my video at any time for additional support.

7. CANDLE AND GLOW

I just love candle glow. Mix a medium orange using cad yellow and cad red. Make some of it brighter with more yellow, and deeper with a bit of red. From top to bottom create an ombre glow. The candle wax glows brighter nearest the flame and the glow deepens and darkens the further away it is. Dry, and now you can go back with brighter highlights near the top. Make sure the area around the wick is the brightest Add more white or yellow to vary the values. Work the mid orange, blending down that glow.

For the glow reflection under the candle, take yellow and red to make a yellow-red, more bias to the red. Work your dry brushing technique. A little naples yellow and white on the outer edge. Yellow and white where they need to be. A little black for the wick. We're almost done here.

Step back and compare your painting to the reference. Does your water need changing? Is there anything you feel needs refining and are you ready for the next step?

8. LIGHT THAT CANDLE

Rinse your brush and start with white, add that to the hottest part of the flame, little curves, a bit of a halo.

The smallest amount of light blue at the base of the flame will help give it a realistic look. Naples yellow to make sure we have a bit of a light aspect around it. White on the outside edge. A bit of orange at the tip of the wick. A bit of cad red to signify an ember. Is your flame softly diffused.

Stand back and assess your progress. Refer to your reference. Revise and refine anything that you feel you need to.

9. SIGNATURE

Sign your name to your incredible painting. You should be very proud of yourself.

SWATCHING PRACTICE PAGE

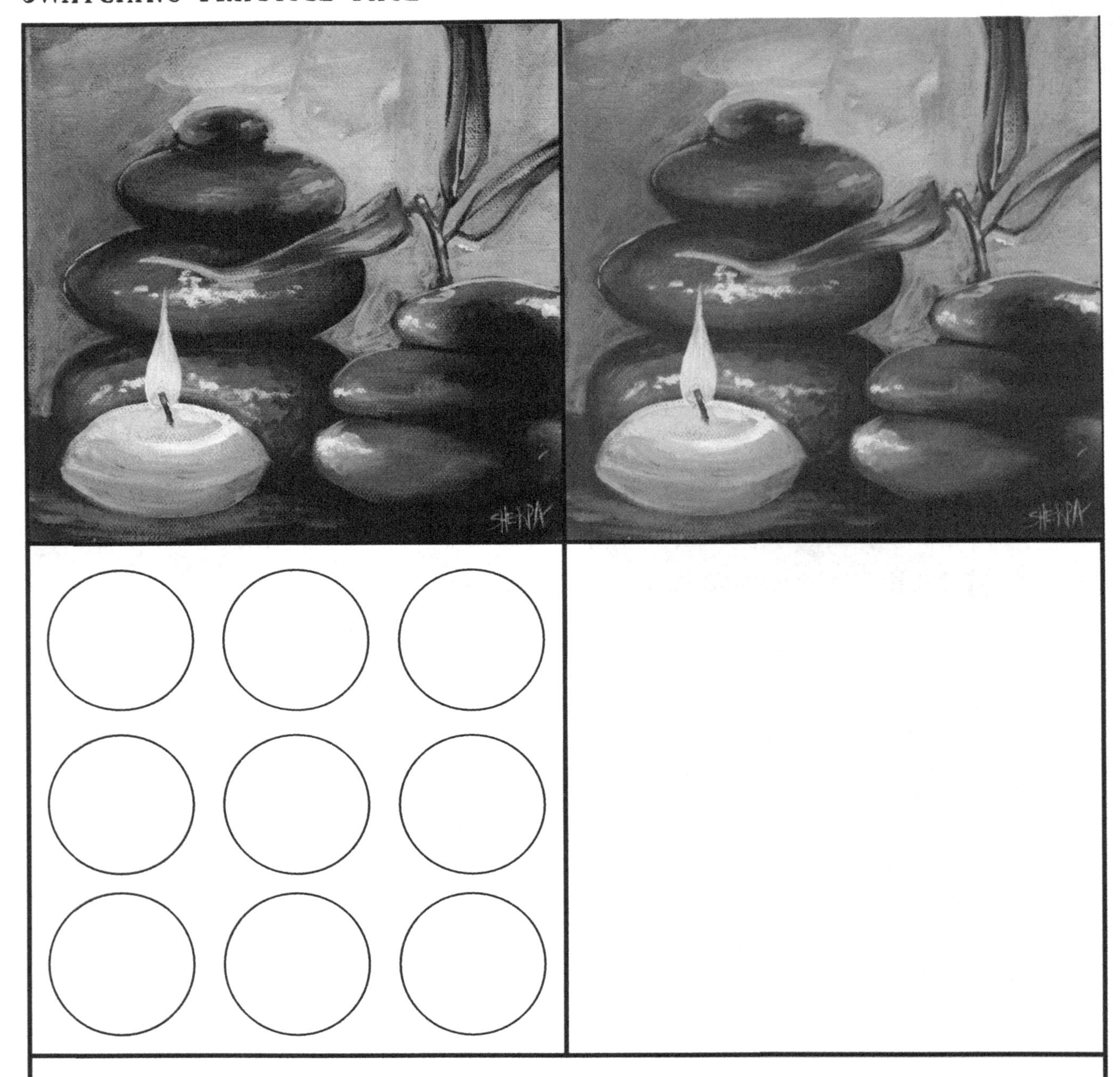

1. Practice mixing the colors from todays palette and paint in your circles with your colors.
2. Check your values and hue by swatching your paint mixes on the sample images.
3. Do a tiny fast grey scale sketch to help you express light and shadow - use paint or pencil, either is fine.

TRACEABLE

THE ART SHERPA

WINE AND POUR

COLOR PALETTE:         

Today's color palette is Cadmium Yellow Medium, Cad Red Medium, Naples Yellow Light, Quinacridone Magenta, Dioxazine Purple, Phthalo Blue, Phthalo Green, Mars Black, and Titanium White.

1. BACKGROUND AND GRID

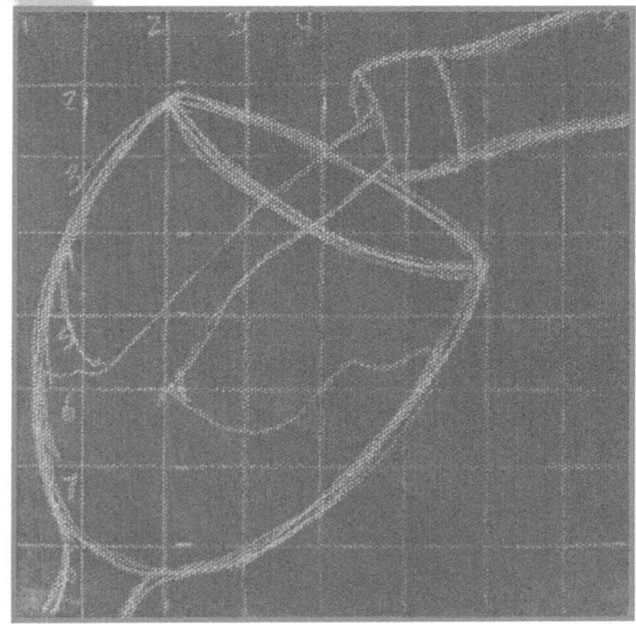

COLOR MIX: Quinacridone magenta with some naples yellow to make a rose color. Get some water on your background brush, just enough to help your paint flow. Paint your entire surface. Dry completely.

GRID: With your t-square and chalk, create a 1" x 1" grid on your canvas. Number the squares across the top 1 - 8 and along the left side, top to bottom, 1 - 8. Duplicate the image exactly as shown in the reference, one square at a time. Only draw what's in that square before you move on.

2. DEFUSED BACKGROUND

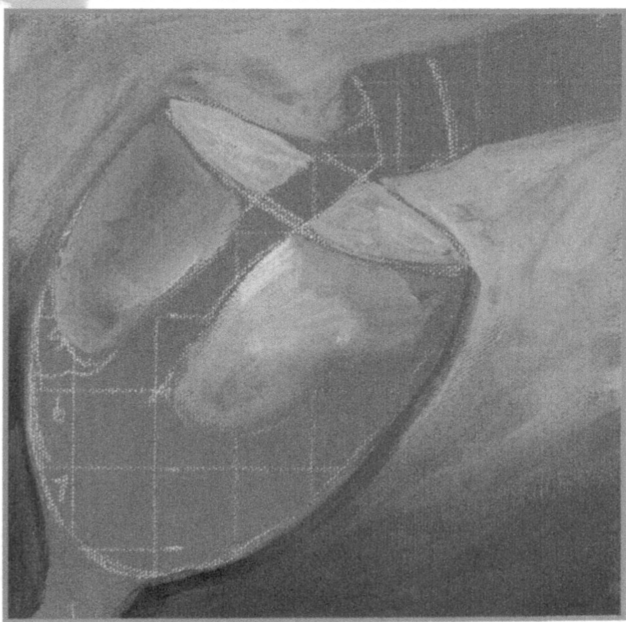

We will be working varying tones to create our diffused, soft background. With a #8 cats tongue, get some purple and start with your darkest values, adjust by adding quinacridone and a titch of yellow to soften. On the toe of your brush, bring this up contour sketching around the glass. Take some quinacridone and add some naples blending wet into wet, lighten the value with white. As you move away from the glass.

Leave some background color in the center. Wet your brush to make the paint flow easily. Use your references to help you with placement and don't hesitate to rereview the video.

3. POUR THE WINE

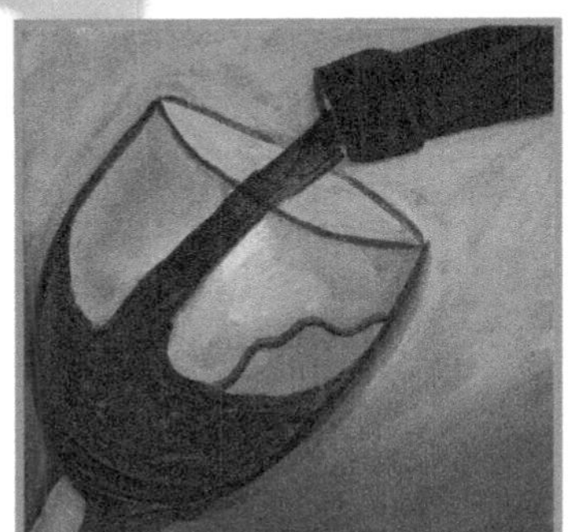

With the #4 round, grab some phthalo blue and purple for the glass dark value. Put in your glass dark values using your reference, add a little purple for the glass bottom edge. We are painting the light we see on the object.

Blocking in the bottle, get some green then add some phthalo blue, but keep it to the green side and paint that in with some nice broad strokes. You're getting depth of color; bring that up the neck with quin and cad red, a bit of purple to create that deep plum of the wine and fill the glass. Don't forget to outline that little splash up the side of the glass. Come back with your quin and naples to any areas that might need reemphasizing. Blending wet into wet, refer to your reference.

4. POP THE BOTTLE

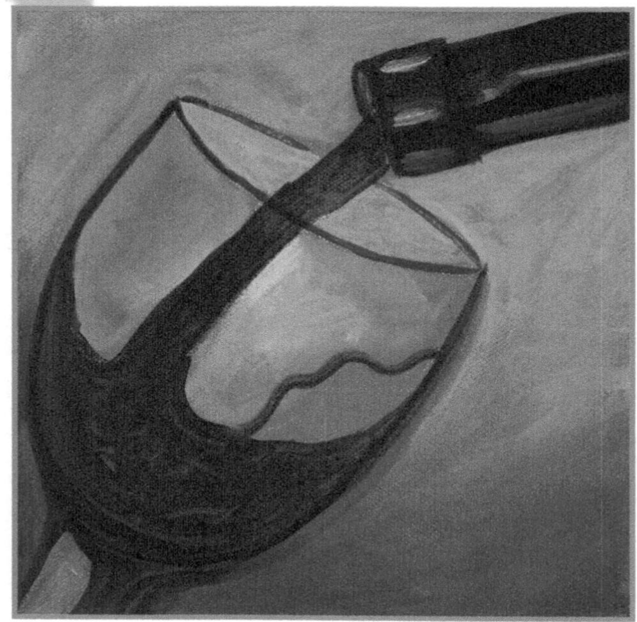

The wine spout coming from out of the picture implies that there is a world we don't see, but have been invited to view. Mix some green with a little cad yellow for the first layer of highlight, make some nice strong bright green lines where shown. Tone with more yellow and maybe a little white for a lighter green and come back along the same lines.

Now, mix magenta with your green for a unique deep tone, add that dark line beneath your central highlight going up the bottle neck, work the values down the front pulling it into the shadows. For the glow and some of the lightest reflection effects, mix a super smidge of white into phthalo blue and come along the underside of the bottle and atouch to the opening.

5. VALUES OF WINE

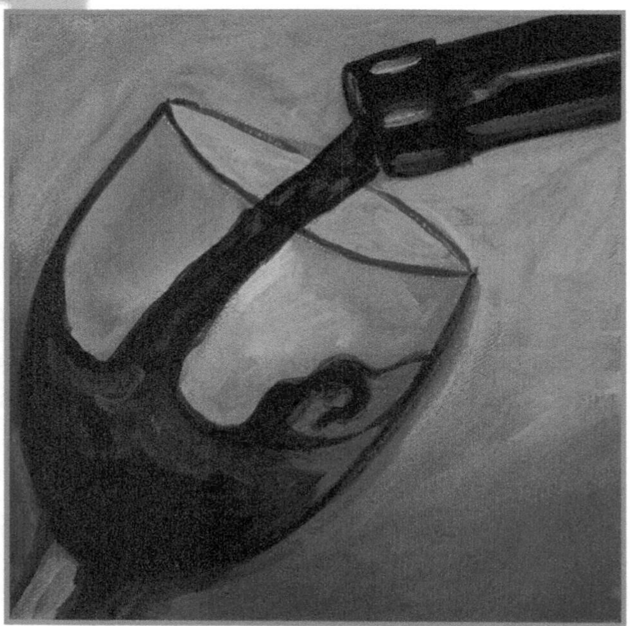

With the #4 round, take some quin into the cad red and add little bits of highlights, those brighter values of red. The curves would have some lighter values.

To add deep darker wine values you want purple and magenta, perhaps a little cad red. Take this dark tone into your wine to the bottom of the glass, and wiggle a bit, into the pouring and splashing areas adding depth. Get your plummy color and add some shading in the wine splash going up the sides.

Stand back with your reference and compare. Watch the video for more visual assistance in helping you place those highlights and lowlights.

6. BRIGHT WINE REFLECTIONS

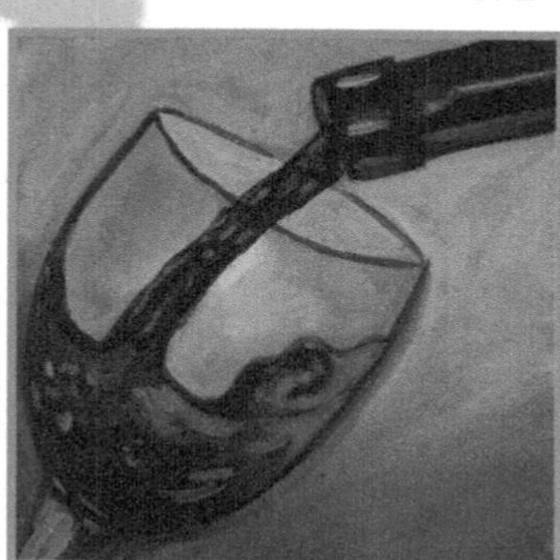

Now to add the gem-like tones of wine that will be our bright reflections in the wine.

A bit of cad red and cad yellow to start making it a bit warmer, adding little bits of reflection, using a reference is very helpful to find where the light will be getting caught. Some maybe on the outside of the glass, down the stem not a lot just a hint. Take a little magenta and add some white to a bright pink, warm it with a bit of yellow for a beautiful highlight.

Add a little blue, and there's another reflection color. Refer to your reference and remember to breathe and to clean your brush water from time to time.

7. GLASS SHADOWS AND MIDTONES

With the #6 bright, dipped in water, let's put in some reflections. Add a smidge of purple into the quin and you have a naturally transparent hue perfect for glazing, add this to the glass as seen.

Grab some white on a dry brush with light pressure, and add some highlights. With your #4 round add a little purple and quin to the rim of the glass.

Dry the canvas.

Grab some Naples yellow and add some beginnings of highlights to the rim and stem to the outer edge of the bottom of the glass.

8. WINE THAT SHINES

With your #4 round, and clean water, thin some white. Reflections in the shiney dark glass are so terrific, use the reference to find the hot spots on the bottle and glass. The pouring wine also has reflections, add a few wiggles of white there. A delicate touch for swirling wine. Less is more.

Use your reference if you need help determining where you should be putting your frosting.

9. SIGNATURE

Sign your name to your incredible painting.

SWATCHING PRACTICE PAGE

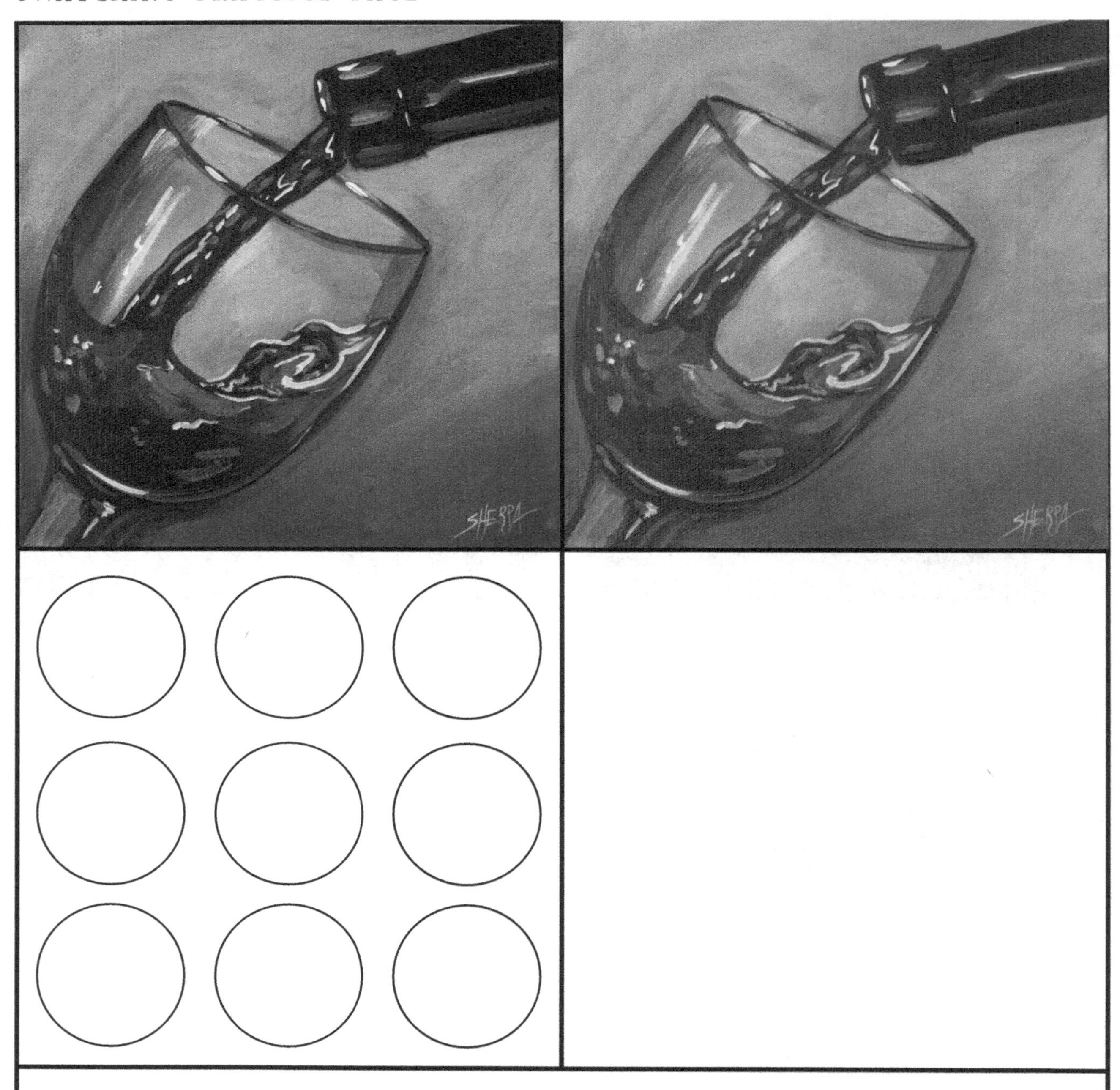

1. Practice mixing the colors from todays palette and paint in your circles with your colors.
2. Check your values and hue by swatching your paint mixes on the sample images.
3. Do a tiny fast grey scale sketch to help you express light and shadow - use paint or pencil, either is fine.

TRACEABLE

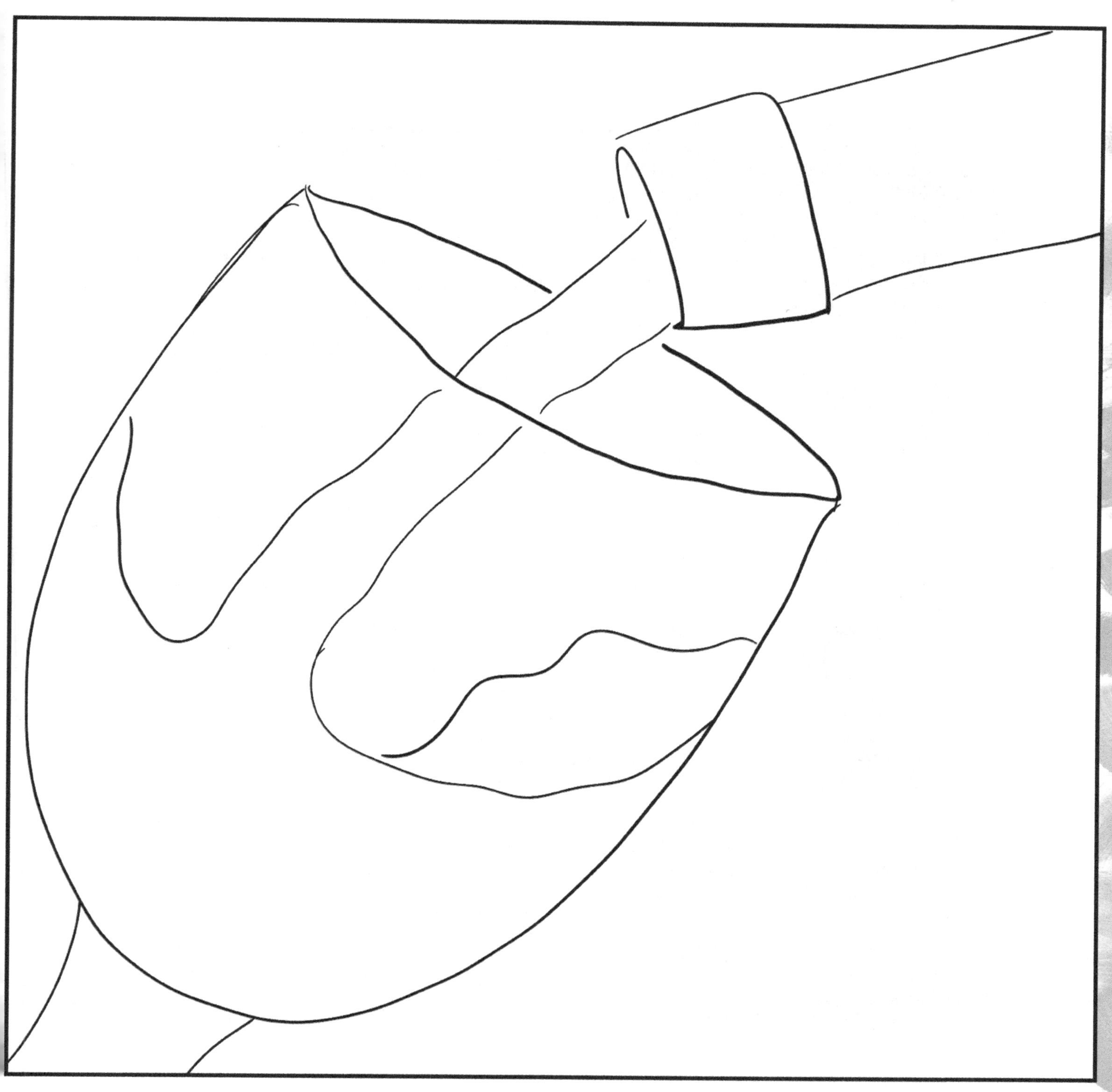

ROBINS EGG NEST

COLOR PALETTE:        

Today's color palette is Phthalo Green, Ultramarine Blue, Phthalo Blue, Mars Black, Burnt Sienna, Cadmium Yellow, and Titanium White.

1. Background and Grid

COLOR MIX: Black and burnt sienna, a loose mix of both. Get some water on your background brush, just enough to help your paint flow. Paint your entire surface. Dry completely.

GRID: With your t-square and chalk, create a 1" x 1" grid on your canvas. Number the squares across the top 1 - 8 and along the left side, top to bottom, 1 - 8. Duplicate the image exactly as shown in the reference, one square at a time. Only draw what's in that square before you move on.

2. Nest Shadows

Dip the #8 cat's tongue in the water, drag off excess water, mix burnt sienna, cad yellow and add a smidge of black. Start at the base of the nest and work the nest effect around adding black when you need to get darker because it darkens as you continue. Be loose!

Now mix burnt sienna and black and remember to curve the brush strokes as you go around the nest. As you come up the nest, more burnt sienna, yellow and white because nesting material has color. Check reference to see where to place the tones.

3. Refine the Nest

To refine the nest and add highlights and shadows, black and phthalo blue for a cool recessive value. Go into the deep shadows underneath the grasses where the light is blocked. Define those deep shadows and use your reference if you have difficulty finding them. Don't forget that highlighted areas will still have definable shadows. You are trying to capture that the nest sloops around.

Did you notice that some of your grasses have a red hue to them? Keep using and mixing your brown, black, yellow, white, and blues to make those wonderful nest values. Your reference is going to your best friend.

Step back and look, are you happy with what you have refined on this step, do you see the stronger upper edge?

4. REFINE HIGHLIGHTS AND GRASSES

Switch to a #4 round to refine highlights mix brown and blue for gray and add some white. Keep changing up your values as the nest goes around. You do want to see some blues in the nest, burnt sienna and phthalo blue for the twig elements, little implied structures. As you work these values, don't hesitate to add more sienna or black to the mix.

For the grasses yellow highlights, add some white for lighter values. Come back with any colors you need to reinforce any area you need to before stepping back to compare it to your reference.

5. DECORATIVE ELEMENTS

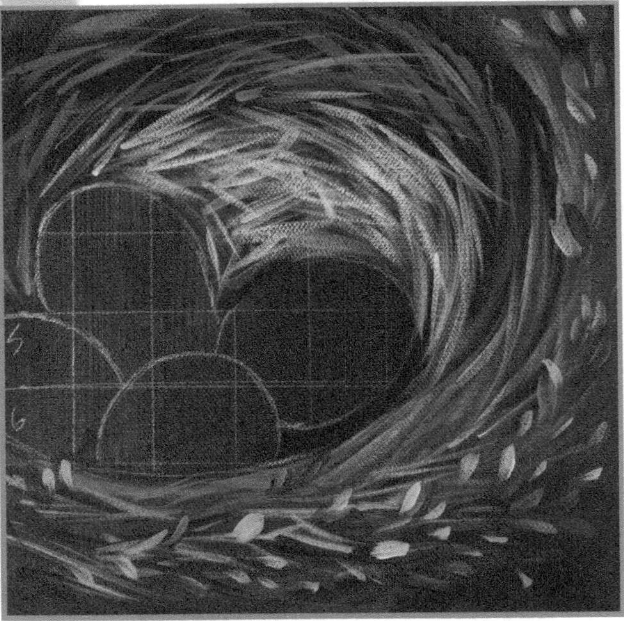

Let's create little decorative elements. Mix burnt sienna and phthalo green for a very deep, deep green. Begin to create plant texture. Add cad yellow for mid-tone green in a couple of places. Bits of implied leaves. Add some white and maybe extra yellow, but not bright yet. If you get too bright, tone back with burnt sienna. Get that little collection of spring greenery. Curve your brush to get those little leaf curls.

Use your reference photo as a guide.

6. EGG SHADOWS

With the #4 round, mix black into phthalo blue for the egg shadows. The shadows should represent the roundness of the eggs. A touch of white for lighter blue highlights and be sure to blend. Eggs teach you some important aspects about lighting. They have a matted surface, They really let you see the ranges of light and how form is created through light and shadow.

Dry and before moving to the next step.

Refer to your reference and remember that you can always go back to my video at any time for additional support.

7. Eggs and Hot Spots

Make phthalo turquoise by mixing phthalo blue and phthalo green for the darker value. Paint your darker value first and remember to shape the eggs. While still wet, add another layer with more white. Very loose, almost dry brushing with light pressure. White makes the color much more opaque.

Step back and compare your painting to the reference. Is there anything you feel needs refining and are you ready for the next step?

8. Spots and Mottling

Mottling and spotting will be a mix of burnt sienna and ultramarine with a bit of black. Be sure to vary the size and vary the hue by adjusting the brown and blue. Wiggle the brush. Don't make patterns and put some spots off the edge of the egg. Do your speckles vary in size? Are they non-symmetrical and random?

9. Final Touches and Signature

To add the final touches, get cad yellow and burnt sienna, using the reference, add this to your nest, sweep a bit over an egg to establish foreground.

You can imply the flora with blue and white, maybe a little brown if it gets too bright. Come through the leaves and touch bits of white around the edge. Let the brush help make the petals much like you did with the leaves. Add a skosh of yellow to your off-white, this will highlight the petals.

Sign your name to your incredible painting and please share it with the community.

SWATCHING PRACTICE PAGE

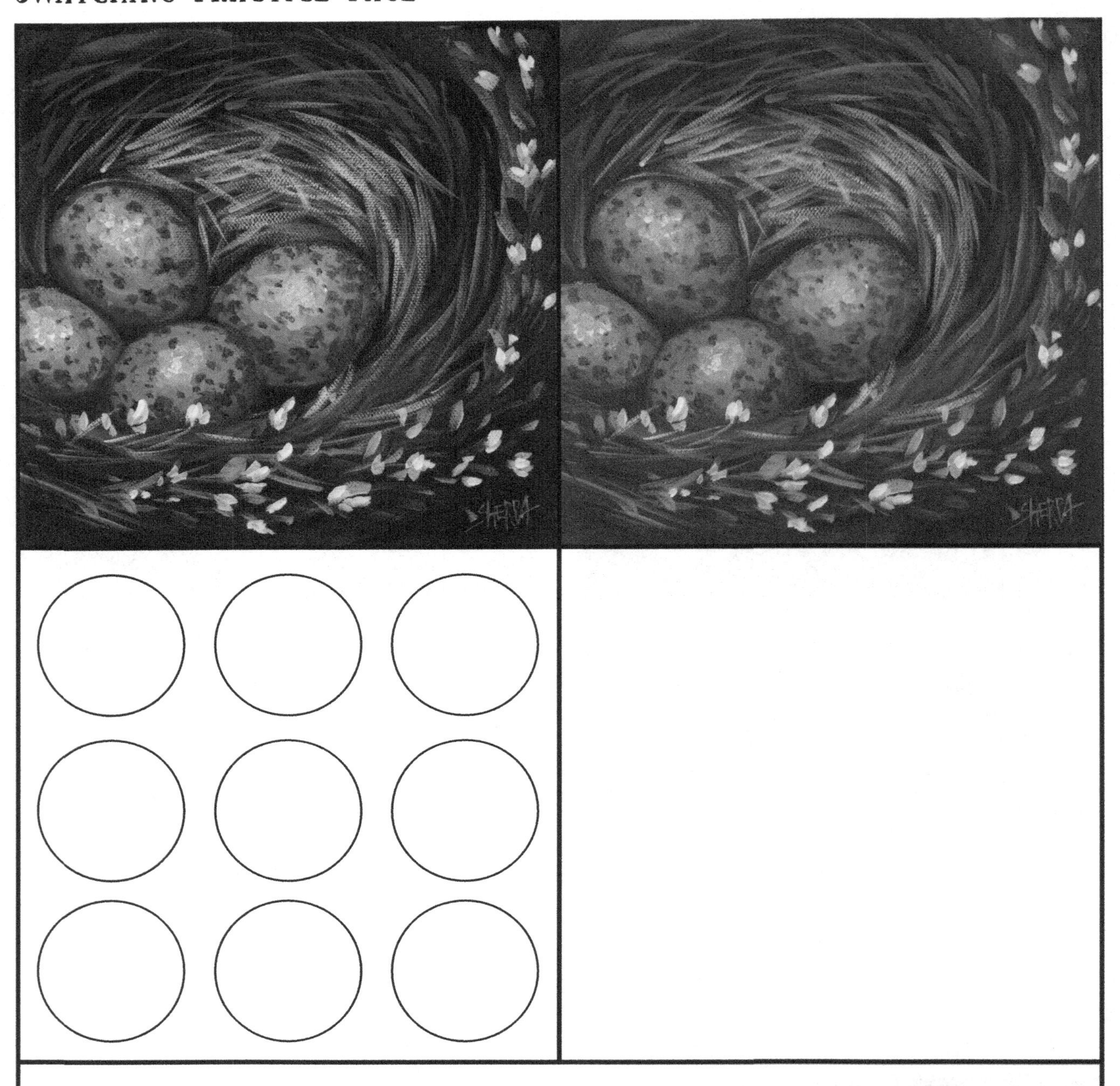

1. Practice mixing the colors from todays palette and paint in your circles with your colors.
2. Check your values and hue by swatching your paint mixes on the sample images.
3. Do a tiny fast grey scale sketch to help you express light and shadow - use paint or pencil, either is fine.

TRACEABLE

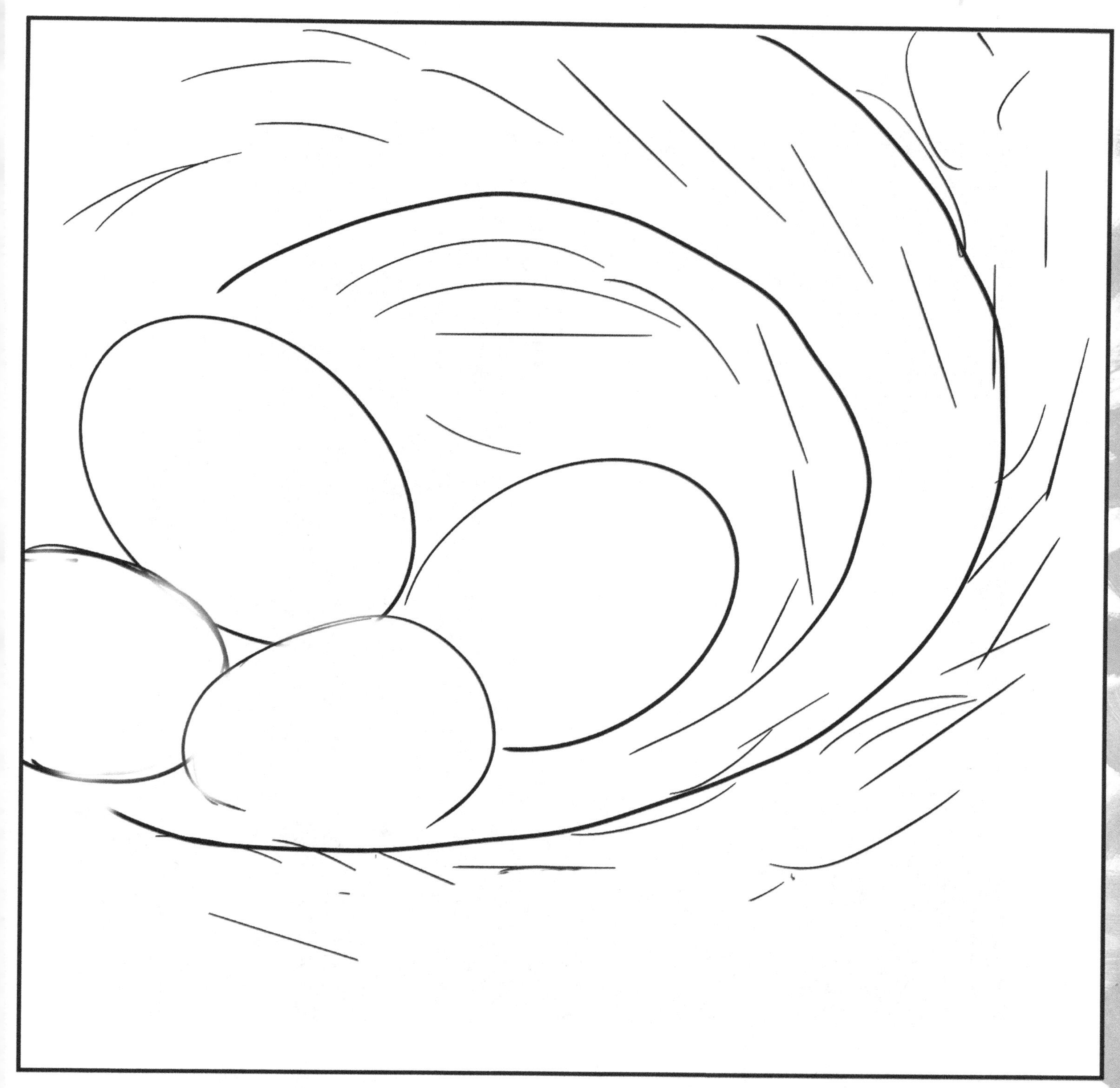

FLUFFY BABY CHICK

COLOR PALETTE:           

Today's color palette is Burnt Sienna, Ultramarine Blue, Quinacridone Magenta, Cad Red Medium, Naples Yellow Light, Cad Yellow Medium, Phthalo Green, Phthalo Blue, Mars Black, and Titanium White.

1. BACKGROUND AND GRID

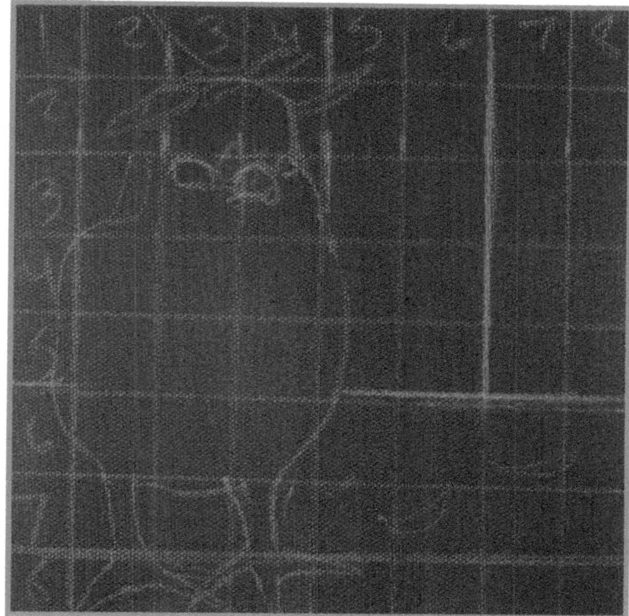

COLOR MIX: Burnt sienna. Get some water on your background brush, just enough to help your paint flow. Paint your entire surface. Dry completely.

GRID: With your t-square and chalk, create a 1" x 1" grid on your canvas. Number the squares across the top 1 - 8 and along the left side, top to bottom, 1 - 8. Duplicate the image exactly as shown in the reference, one square at a time. Only draw what's in that square before you move on.

2. WEATHERED WOOD

With a #8 Cambridge ,slightly damp, mix burnt sienna, ultramarine blue, and the tiniest bit of white. Dry brush that color with light pressure to create our wood. You want the texture of old barn wood. The challenge here will be to go around your chick with the wood color and not seem like it's going around the chick. Long straight strokes playing with the tones. I attempted to keep a 2" diameter width on those wood planks. For the baseboards, add more blue to imply shadow.

You will probably lose a bit of your chicks feet but that's easy to sketch back in with the traceable or freehand. You can also re-grid if you prefer.

3. WOOD HIGHLIGHTS AND LOWLIGHTS

Keep dry brushing to create highlights and shadows of the wood. Phthalo blue to ultramarine blue, semi-dry brush, a little brown if you need to tone back. Long and short brushstrokes to vary the texture. Get some brown into the brush and add white to "gray out" the wood. Blend the wood.

Switching to your #6 bright using the corner of your brush, mix a bit of black and brown, add the shadows between the boards and some to the boards to weather them further. Your reference will help you figure out where the shadows might be. Imperfect wood is just beautiful.

4. CHICKEN FEET AND FLUFF

You might want to sketch your chicken back in, because that is where we are going to start. With your #4 round mix some cad red and cad yellow with a touch of burnt sienna for our deeper value to block in the legs. Add just a bit of black for the shadow inside of the leg. Wet the brush for paint flow if you need to.

Using a #8 for your fluff, grey some cad yellow with a titch of black then grab a smidge of red for our deep chicken fluff color. painting where it is darkest with the barnyard dirt. Flicking the brush for the fuzzy effect.

A touch of naples yellow and white for our fluffy fluffs.

5. FLUFFER-NATION

Cad red and quin magenta with a touch of naples, and we get a pink to start the beak with. Pay attention to the overall shape. Add some yellow along the top. Lots of small highlights and lowlights will make this beak happy. A little pink around the eyes will exaggerate them, then black and brown for the pupils.

Dark values on the underside of the beak. Use your reference to where to add brown, red, yellow, pink, and white hues as you need to. There is a highlight on the inside front of the leg and at the back of the leg.

You need to really refer to your reference on this step to get all those critical highlights and lowlights in place. Do you need clean water? Do you need a brush rinse out? Step back and evaluate and redefine or enhance as you feel appropriate. Breathe.

6. FLUFF UP AND DEFINE THE EYES

Get naples yellow, using the #8 Cambridge, dry brush fluffiness as you feel fluffiness would exist. Use the corner of the brush and try to be loose. You can always come back with cad yellow if you need to. Look for nice shadows and play with little color hue changes as you add the fluff layers.

Now, add white to the brush and come just above the beak. Mix black and brown and a touch of ultramarine and come under the feet to help with that dark value, creating little shadows. Yellow and white for the little claws. Add a little reflection to his eyes with the gray-blue color.

Refer to your reference to determine when it's time to stop "fixing" and remember that you can always go back to video my video at any time for additional support.

7. FLOWER CROWN

For the flower crown, mix burnt sienna into phthalo green with the #4 round. Bring the stem off at an angle, flair the stem out. Add some cad yellow into that, wet on wet. Mix cad red and quin magenta, add a little naples, for a coral-pink color that is wonderful for the petals and don't forget to curl them. Petals are uneven. Add quin magenta for the underside value. Add some white for the light value. Wet your bush for flow if needed.

Fuss with his fluffiness around the flower crown, play with it, wet on wet. Are you happy with it? Balance it out by putting a petal on the ground that has dropped. We're almost done here, use your reference for that final check.

8. SIGNA-

Sign your name to your incredible painting and please share it with the community. You should be very proud of yourself.

SWATCHING PRACTICE PAGE

1. Practice mixing the colors from todays palette and paint in your circles with your colors.
2. Check your values and hue by swatching your paint mixes on the sample images.
3. Do a tiny fast grey scale sketch to help you express light and shadow - use paint or pencil, either is fine.

TRACEABLE

REALISTIC STRAWBERRIES

COLOR PALETTE:           

Today's color palette is Cad Yellow Medium, Phthalo Blue, Phthalo Green, Ultramarine Blue, Burnt Sienna, Cad Red Medium, Quinacridone Magenta (sometimes called Quinacridone Fuchsia), Naples Yellow Light (sometimes called Nickel Titanate or Titanate Yellow) Mars Black, and Titanium White.

1. BACKGROUND AND GRID

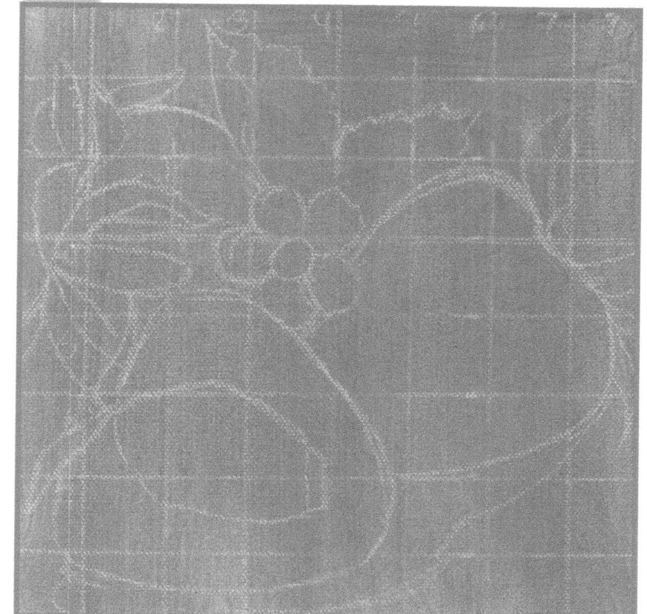

COLOR MIX: Mix phthalo blue and phthalo green, to create phthalo turquoise. Add white until you achieve the color of the background in the reference. Get some water on your background brush, just enough to help your paint flow. Paint your entire surface. Dry completely.

GRID: With your t-square and chalk, create a 1" x 1" grid on your canvas. Number the squares across the top 1 - 8 and along the left side, top to bottom, 1 - 8. Duplicate the image exactly as shown in the reference, one square at a time. Only draw what's in that square before you move on.

2. CONTOUR THE OBJECTS

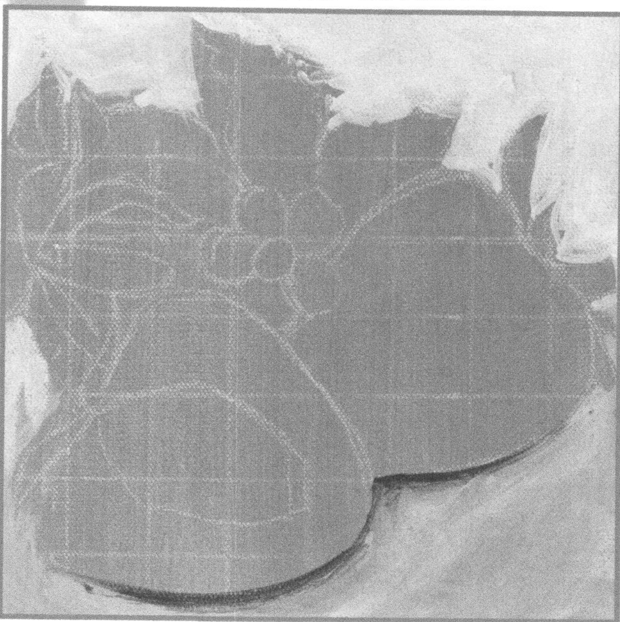

With the #8 cats tongue, take the background color and mix white and make a very light color, much lighter than the background color. Paint around all the objects keeping the contour lines intact. Don't be too precious about it. You just want to know where your objects are. To add depth and interest, wipe off your brush and mix naples yellow with your white. Loosley blend some of this color across the top and in the two top corners.

Refer to your reference to find other places where this beautiful yellow might exist.

To add shadow at the bottom, take ultramarine and white and put in some shadows. While still wet, come back with ultramarine and a smidge of quin magenta to make an even darker shadow color and come underneath the strawberries with the toe of the brush, blending soft lines.

3. REFINING AND BLOCKING IN

As we refine these objects and block them in, we will capture the value of the colors in a loose, expressive way. Start with your #6 bright, dipped in water. Get some quin magenta with a smidge of cad red. More quin magenta if you need to deepen it. I am starting with the dark shadow I see just under the flower, in the middle and start to block in that area. As you work this step, you may wish to rereview the video because there is a lot going on with strawberries. Keep working your shadow areas, referring to the reference if you need, until you are happy.

The brighter version of this red has more cad red than magenta. You can add ultramarine to your shadow color to deepen it. You might want a darker edge to your strawberries just to define the shape. Remember that to lighten red, you won't add pink. You want to add a little cad yellow.

For that brightest red, add some of your napales yellow to your red mix. Use the colors mentioned above and bring your painting through the step using all the references you need to do to do so.

4. LEAVES

Paint your leaves using various greens mixed from, phthalo green, burnt sienna, and cad yellow. For your darkest deepest green, mix a little phthalo green with burnt sienna. First block in shadows around the edges and where you see them on your reference. For your lighter greens, rinse off your brush and add some yellow to your green-brown mix and add some lighter green values. Find the places where that mid-green value would exist. More cad yellow and naples yellow for the lightest values and highlights.

Ask yourself where the light is coming from and how it reflects on the leaves? Where are they the darkest? where are they the lightest?

Come back with any colors you need to reinforce your progress before stepping back to compare it to your reference. If you painted something out, just come back in and add it in when you can. No worries.

5. RESOLVING AND REFINING - FLOWER

We will resolve more of the strawberries, start to put in the flower and refine elements of the composition. Start with the #6 bright, and get some quin magenta with a bit of cad red, and white, perhaps a touch of naples yellow, and come into the center of the strawberry. Blend in some of the green with a soft dry brush effect, adjusting the shape of the strawberry.

Get back into the white for that light pink hint value, and on the toe of your brush tap in the little red veins and elements of the strawberry. You can make tiny value adjustments by gently tapping in those darker and lighter values with the corner of your brush.

For the Flower, get your #4 round. Take a titch of ultramarine into white and paint in the petals. Remember the brush strokes move outward in the direction it grows. A little ultramarine and quin magenta for a deep purple around the edges of the petals to contour them, and the shadows between them. For the center, mix a little bit of orange and mute it with a bit of bright yellow green, because there's always a little bit of chlorophyll. Go around the center with a light yellow green, pulling little strokes out from the center

Use your reference photo as a guide. Evaluate.

6. REFINING VALUES, SEED PODS

For the whiter center, quin magenta, cad red, and cad yellow, then add some white for the thin whitish vein spaces. Try to avoid stripes. Lightly on the toe of your brush, wiggle and make natural looking vien shapes.

Use your reference to help you determine where the highlights and shadows are. The highlights and shadows are important to help us see the divots with seeds.

Take ultramarine, Cad Red and Quin Magnenta to mix a dark wine color. Paint in the depression that holds the seeds with this color. For the seed pod, you don't have to do every seed. Use the darkest mixes colors first, then come back with the wonderful orange. Create your seeds using a mix of cad red and cad yellow. You can add a skosh of green and/or white and pop these seeds in. Make little marks. Be random in your placement. When they are dry, you can come back in with the shadowed ones and glaze them back with a wine mix of your colors. This glaze should be a tint not a covering.

Take a deep breath, relax your shoulders, clean out your water if you need to, or have a sippy sippy moment. Remember that you can always go back to the video at any time for additional support.

7. RESOLVE THE FLOWER

Let's resolve our focal point, the flower. The flower pulls the eye and brings balance to the painting. With naples yellow and white, from the outside of the flower petals, lighten the petals working from the outside edge toward the center. Work the inside with yellow and it's ok if the yellow has bits of the orange and other colors in it. Add little center dots. Add some little orange bits. Get some white on the toe of your #4 round, add white highlights to the petals. Mix in some yellow for other highlights.

Refer to your reference to help you see where to adjust your highlight values. Focus and try to let yourself relax into it.

8. DEEP SHADOWS AND BRIGHT HIGHLIGHTS

Deep shadows and bright highlights are what will make our objects stand out and pop against each other. Use your #4 round. Shadow colors mixes are phthalo blue or green with a touch of black, to get those deep, dark values. Use your reference if you need help determining the light source and where the shadows might be. The seeds actually have delicate shadows of blue and black. Phthalo blue and black for the super deep shadows.

Let's pop some seeds with blue and white for a light reflection. Dip your brush in water and work the paint to help flow if needed. Use your reference if you need help locating highlights. With the yellow-green and some white, add some bright highlights. Maybe more yellow on those leaves? With just the tip of the brush pop in some highlights with a fine subtle broken line, catch the highlights along the top of the lower strawberry.

We're almost done here. Step back and compare your painting to the reference. Is there anything you feel needs refining? Use your reference for that final check.

9. SIGNATURE

Sign your name to your incredible painting and please share it with the community. To coin a rather great guy, I'm so glad we had this time together.

SWATCHING PRACTICE PAGE

1. Practice mixing the colors from todays palette and paint in your circles with your colors.
2. Check your values and hue by swatching your paint mixes on the sample images.
3. Do a tiny fast grey scale sketch to help you express light and shadow - use paint or pencil, either is fine.

TRACEABLE

THE ART SHERPA

TROPICAL SUNSET

COLOR PALETTE:           

Today's color palette is Naples Yellow Light, Cad Yellow Medium, Cad Red Medium, Quinacridone Magenta, Mars Black, Phthalo Blue, Phthalo Green, Ultramarine Blue, Dioxazine Purple, and Titanium White.

1. BACKGROUND AND GRID

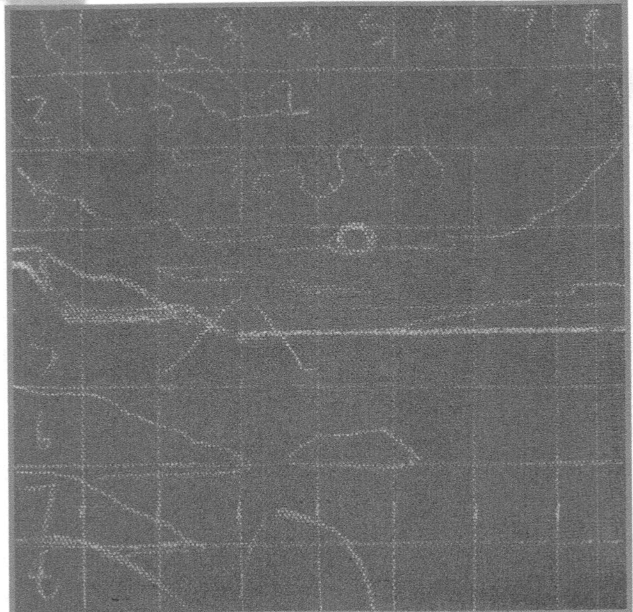

COLOR MIX: Quin Magenta - I chose that color because it's the most harmonious to all the colors layering on top and won't gray out my vibrant colors. Get some water on your background brush, just enough to help your paint flow. Paint your entire surface. Dry completely.

GRID: With your t-square and chalk, create a 1" x 1" grid on your canvas. Number the squares across the top 1 - 8 and along the left side, top to bottom, 1 - 8. Duplicate the image exactly as shown in the reference, one square at a time. Only draw what's in that square.

2. SUNSET FOUNDATION

Dampen your #8 Cambridge, start with the lower section of the sky with cad red and cad yellow in a bright orange. If you paint out rocks or objects, don't panic. Add more naples yellow to lighten, blending on the canvas with a slight curvature of the brush to bring energy and motion into the clouds.

Rinse out, add cad yellow and naples yellow to those places you feel need them and let dry. The sky color is a bit of phthalo green, phthalo blue and a touch of white. Fill in the sky area varying this mix. It's OK if some of your magenta shows through. Refer to your reference for assistance.

3. DRAMATIC CLOUDS

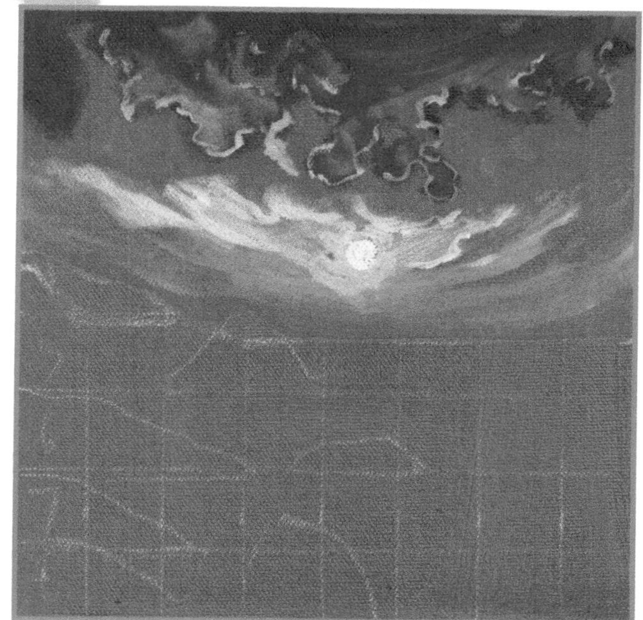

For the dramatic sunset clouds, Still using your #8 cambridge mix some quin magenta with some cad red, maybe some naples yellow into a peachy color. Avoid too much water in the brush, wiggle back and forth and start constructing the basic foundational cloud shapes. Randomly scumbling them in and avoiding repetition of shape.

Come back with the #4 round, naples yellow and cad yellow and add highlights around the sun. Come back with some magenta, white and yellow and highlight the cloud tops. Not every one, just those that catch the light. Less is more. The sun is done in pure white.

Don't hesitate to use your reference to help you identify those highlights.

4. WATER & HORIZON

Start with a damp #6 bright and our orange color to put in the horizon line. Use a ruler if you need to, but you want a straight line. Add more magenta into the orange as you move along, and then phthalo blue into a purple. Blending forward, with a back and forth motion. Naples and quin create a warm pink that you may want to use. As you continue, don't hesitate to use some pure quin magenta.

5. ROCKS

With black and a bit of blue, let's start laying in our rocks with their shadowy sides. You won't "see" some of the rocks until we add in the lighter colors. If you prefer, you could paint all the rocks this color and add highlights later. Get the #4 round and a little yellow into the cad red for highlights on the front of the rocks. Some yellow in places where there is light. Rocks also have hot spots. Use your reference to help you with shadows and highlight placement.

For the rough watery marks, a little diox into the ultramarine and add some white for violet. If you need to add magenta to get the tone you want, that's fine. Paint loosely and create that feeling of a waves crashing. Play with the waves, adding darker tones where you need to, lighter highlights where you need to. Magenta in some places. Bring the splash up the rocks as you continue to resolve your dramatic tropical sunset.

Use your reference photo as a guide. Evaluate.

6. OBJECT RELATIONSHIP THROUGH ADDITION OF SCALE

Distant hills and plant life will add scale through object relationships and visual textural interest. With the #4 round, thin some black with drops of water to improve flow, and add some delicate little palm tree trunks with the toe of the brush. Maybe some sea grasses. Your palm trees need fronds but avoid uniformity. Kind of feather them down. Sometimes palms are very sparse, sometimes very solid. Lastly, take your violet color and add an ample amount of magenta to warm it up. Add little rock highlights. Maybe some yellow highlights. Resolve your rocks.

Now stand back and assess your progress against your reference. Are you surprised at how this piece is coming together?

Remember that you can always go back to video my video at any time for additional support.

7. WATER SPLASHES

Let's splash a little more water with the violet mixture lightened with a bit more white up on the rocks. For deeper values, add ultramarine or even a bit of phthalo blue and ultramarine. Find your low lights as well as your highlights. Play, play, play, splash, splash, splash.

We're almost done here. Step back and compare your painting to the reference. Is there anything you feel needs refining and are you ready for the next step? Use your reference for that final check.

8. HIGHLIGHTS & LOWLIGHTS

We need to create some very bright highlights and reflections on the water. With some cad yellow on the #4, add some distant bright yellow reflections far away. Come in with naples yellow for some highlights. See how the cool yellow and the warm yellow play against each other and create pop. Add some cad red to the cad yellow on the tip of the brush and wiggle up an interesting little water shape. This is not dissimilar to clouds. Where is something catching the light? Put some dot splashes in the air, maybe some light coming down the corridor. Rinse your brush and come back with naples to define outer edges and get that glow.

Step back and refer to your reference. Are you happy with your progress?

9. SIGNATURE

Sign your name to your incredible painting and please share it with the community. You should be very proud of yourself.

SWATCHING PRACTICE PAGE

1. Practice mixing the colors from todays palette and paint in your circles with your colors.
2. Check your values and hue by swatching your paint mixes on the sample images.
3. Do a tiny fast grey scale sketch to help you express light and shadow - use paint or pencil, either is fine.

TRACEABLE

LAVENDER FIELD SUNSET

COLOR PALETTE:   

Today's color palette is Naples Yellow Light, Cad Yellow Medium, Phthalo Green, Ultramarine Blue, Phthalo Blue, Burnt Sienna, Dioxazine Purple, Quinacridone Magenta, Cad Red Medium, Mars Black, and Titanium White.

1. BACKGROUND AND GRID

COLOR MIX: Quinacrodone Magenta. Get some water on your background brush, just enough to help your paint flow. Paint your entire surface Dry completely.

GRID: With your t-square and chalk, create a 1" x 1" grid on your canvas. Number the squares across the top 1 - 8 and along the left side, top to bottom, 1 - 8. Duplicate the image exactly as shown in the reference, one square at a time. Only draw what's in that square before you move on.

2. SKY, CLOUDS AND SUN

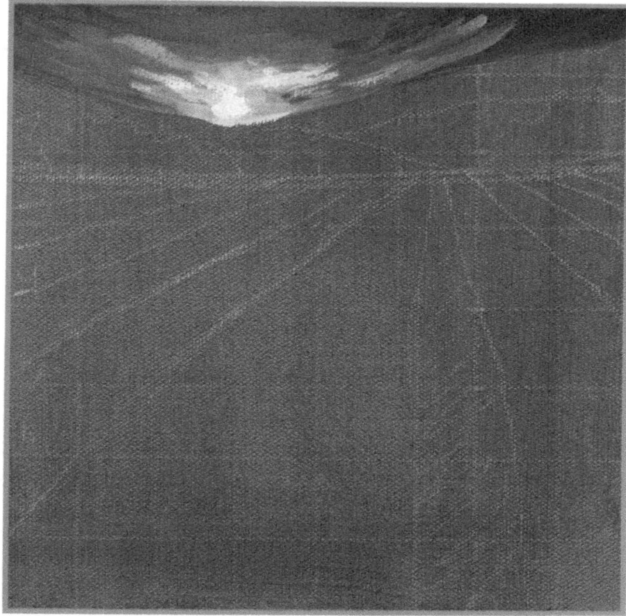

With the #8 cat's tongue, mix ultramarine blue with quin magenta to a purple and add a little white. This is a bit transparent and adds a glazing effect. Refer to the reference for where the sky should start and take this all the way to the top. Now a bit of quin and cad red with a touch of white for the far edge of the mountain line. Blending that in. Layering. Maybe adding some naples yellow light for an incredible pink. Wispy and thoughtful, rinsing when you need to. Mix cad red to cad yellow for orange and blend that in. Maybe some orange along the mountain line. Continue to brighten as you come forward, wet into wet. Create a little hombre of glow. Get that bright orange and pop it in on the toe of the brush and add distant clouds floating in. A bit of cad yellow and naples yellow for a half tone. Wiggling in a spot of light.

You can always repink up the sky. Rinse out. Yellow and white for a gorgeous little glowing keyhole as the focal point of the sun is glowing out.

3. LANDSCAPE HIGHLIGHTS AND LOWLIGHTS

Our distant, far away, purply mountains are magenta into our mix, and naples yellow for warmth. You have not rinsed out your brush. Add more naples yellow where you need warmth. Highlights where the sunlight falls with naples yellow. Imply some slopes that have caught the light. The mountains will get darker and darker as they come forward. Quin magenta into ultramarine for the darker color. Ultramarine and diox for the darkest mountains. Notice that as I come forward, they are backlit and darker. You are creating distinct ranges. Highlights on those impacted by the sunset with a bit of pink. Add white where the light is really hitting. That which moves away would be cooling and not as bright.

Refer to your reference.

4. TREES AND GREENERY

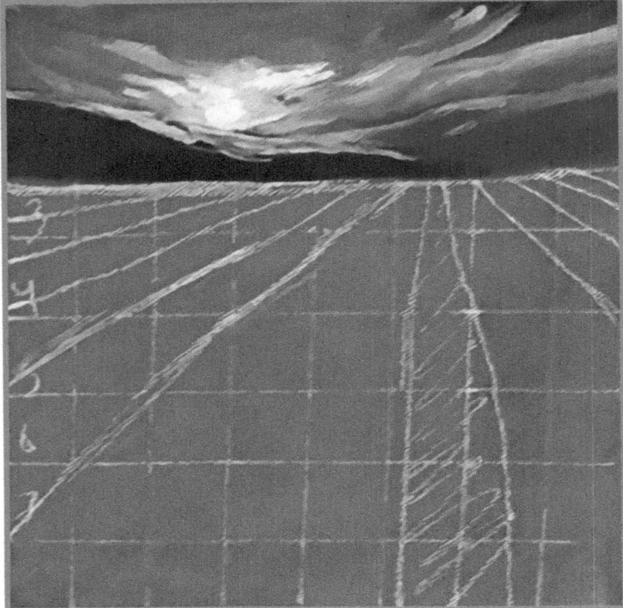

Continue with the # 8 cat's tongue. Get green and burnt sienna and mix a dark deep green. Wiggle this dark color across making uneven shapes of distant trees. Add a little cad yellow and lighten to green along the top lines of the trees. Pick some leaves to make yellow, add cad yellow or naples yellow into the green to touch a few highlights. A little burnt sienna to the green, for a stronger bias of green, add some yellow, and put in the field or grasses. A little naples yellow and cad yellow into the green to make things brighter as we finish our background.

Come back with any colors you need to reinforce your progress before stepping back to compare it to your reference. If you painted something out, just come back in and add it in when you can. No worries.

5. LAVENDER FIELDS FOUNDATION

We start the lavender fields with rows of dirt which our flowers will grow over, so begin with burnt sienna and ultramarine and paint this coming forward, narrowing as you go. It gets browner as it comes forward. Your dark values will be ultramarine and diox for that distant line. Place all your dark values that you can identify, and use your reference to help you determine appropriate placement.

Use your reference photo as a guide. Evaluate.

6. REFINING LAVENDER FIELDS

To refine our dirt, let your canvas dry. With the # 8 Cambridge, get some diox, quin, and a little white. Go up and down on a soft edge, just scribbling the lavender in, allowing the dark values to appear through. Use water to improve flow as needed and try to stay loose. It's ok to allow some of your pink to show through.

Rinse out and get some burnt sienna and ultramarine with a bit of white to catch the sides under the flowers with this brown color. Wipe you brush, and get some sienna to just tap down to make irregular little dirt marks. You can also grab a little red and yellow to add some highlights in the dirt marks. It's distant, it's grayed out, so don't go overboard.

Refer to your reference and remember that you can always go back to video my video at any time for additional support.

7. LAVENDER FLOWERS

Let's paint some lavender flowers. With a #6 bright, let's pull a little purple and a lot of quin magenta, some white. An up-down stroke, turning the brush to the side. Pure diox for the dark values. Ultramarine and phthalo blue is a great lighter shadow color which implies distance. Go for contrast and refine distant spaces. Rinse your brush as necessary. Phthalo blue and diox to refine and shape the shadows. The lavender will be diox, quin, and white.

Rinse your brush and get some phthalo blue and white, a fairly dark blue for a little bit of shadow in the rows.

Step back and compare your painting to the reference. Is there anything you feel needs refining and are you ready for the next step? Use your reference for that final check.

8.

Add more quin to the diox, but don't mix, get some naples and add a bit of that to the distant row.

Now phthalo green into the blue for turquoise, add some white, and then a little brown to a sort of green for shadows on the ground. Get some clean water and take quin and cad and mix to the quin side, a little naples, sometimes more quin or naples as needed to add highlights to the tops of the flowers. Add some turquoise highlights. Does a bit of green peek out? Cad red and cad yellow for drama on the ground. This is all about the drama.

Use your reference and go back and review the video if you need additional assistance in completing this step. It's a big one. The end result is a lavender field in very dramatic lighting with light kind of skipping across the flowers and catching in a few places, making you feel the warmth of that sunset.

SIGNATURE

Sign your name and please, please, please, post your finished picture.

SWATCHING PRACTICE PAGE

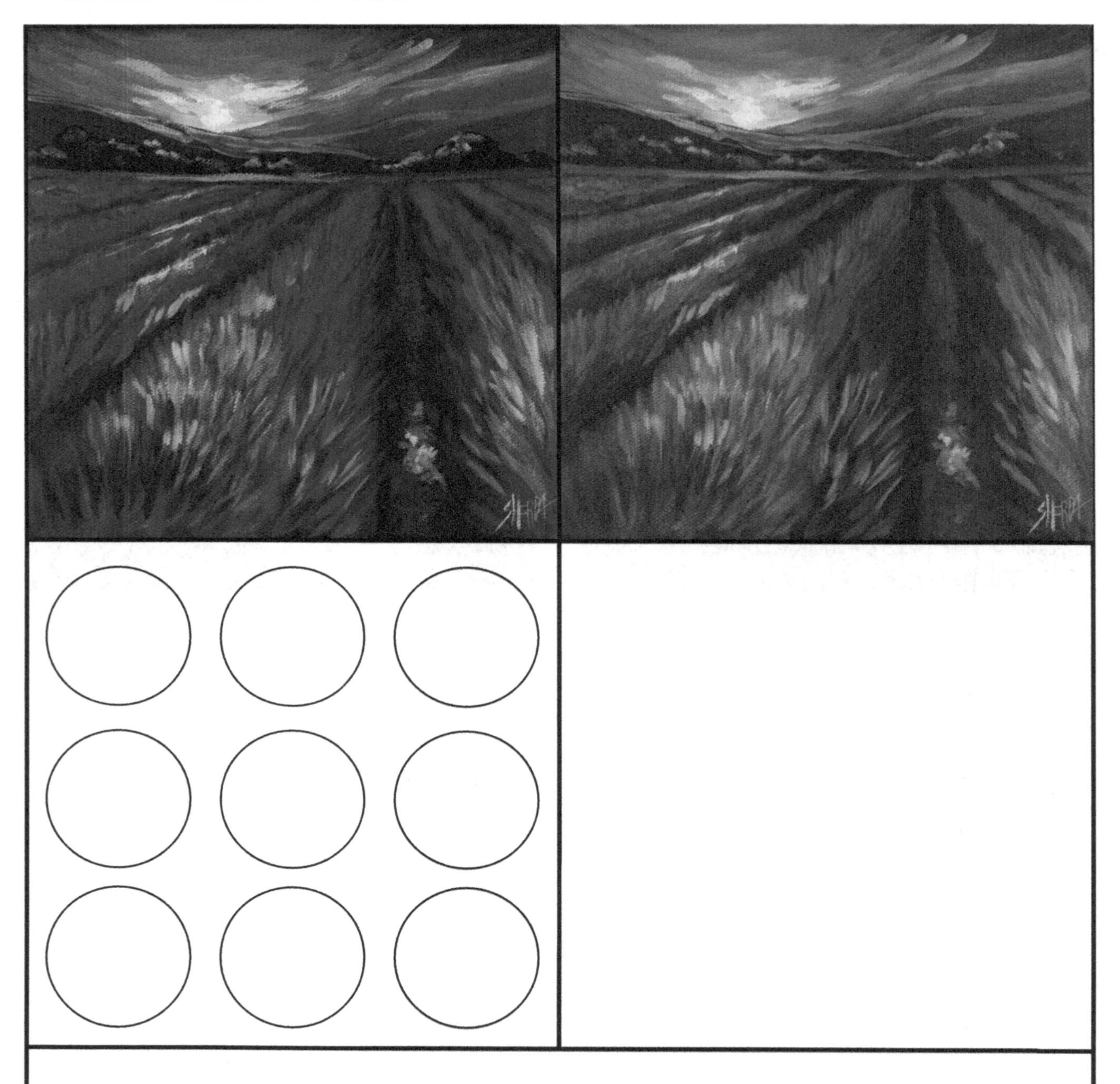

1. Practice mixing the colors from todays palette and paint in your circles with your colors.
2. Check your values and hue by swatching your paint mixes on the sample images.
3. Do a tiny fast grey scale sketch to help you express light and shadow - use paint or pencil, either is fine.

TRACEABLE

A PAIR OF BIRDS

COLOR PALETTE:       

Today's color palette is Mars Black, Cad Yellow Medium, Burnt Sienna, Phthalo Blue, Phthalo Green, Cad Red Medium, and Titanium White.

1. BACKGROUND AND GRID

COLOR MIX: White and Phthalo blue. Get some water on your background brush, just enough to help your paint flow. Paint your entire surface. Dry completely.

GRID: With your t-square and chalk, create a 1" x 1" grid on your canvas. Number the squares across the top 1 - 8 and along the left side, top to bottom, 1 - 8. Duplicate the image exactly as shown in the reference, one square at a time. Only draw what's in that square before you move on.

2. DRAMATIZE THE BACKGROUND, BRANCHES AND HIGHLIGHT THE BIRDS

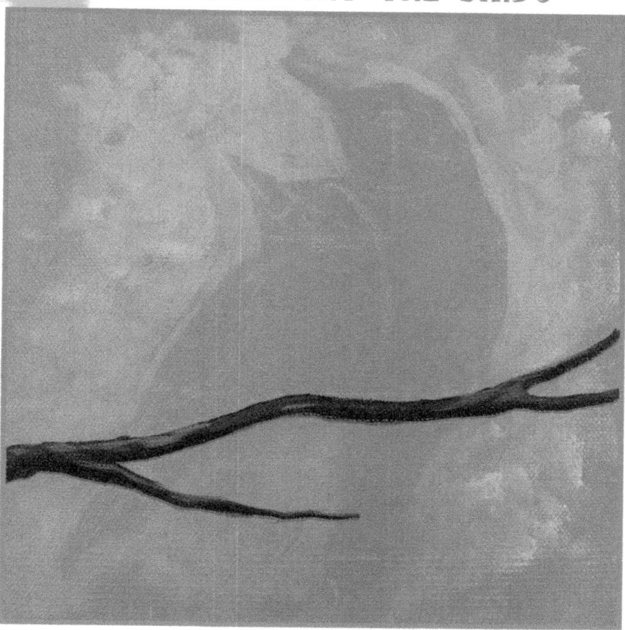

Using a #8 cats tongue and a little phthalo blue, just slightly lighter than the sky, thin out with water, and loosely wiggle the brush on it's edge to get irregular shapes to represent clouds or something fuzzy in the background the birds. Super light pressure.

Switch to the #4 round and mix black, brown, and a bit of green for the branches. Branch highlights are a mix of cad red, cad yellow, and burnt sienna. Add yellow to lighten more; add black to the mix for shadows. Work on the toe of the brush to add shadows under where the birds would be blocking the sunlight.

3. BIRDS BASIC SHAPES & VALUES

With your #6 bright, mix phthalo green and phthalo blue to make a deep value turquoise, and block in the darkest value areas using the reference. Think about your brush strokes as you layer, leaving brush marks a bit like feathers. Come in with just phthalo blue where you see the need.

For the cool orange color, mix cad red and cad yellow, add a bit of burnt sienna to tone, and add to the birds per the reference; wings, head. Use the corner of your brush. Don't forget the little beak. Add brown into the mix, and a bit of black, for the base of the wing and to touch up any part of the branches that you need.

4. BLOCK IN THE FACES

Mix yellow and cad red and add to the neck, top of the heads, chin. Mix an off white with brown into your yellow mix and add a lot of white, to highlight. Use your brown and black mixture for shadows around the neck and eyes. Using your reference, work the beak with the darker value first, and then highlight with the lighter value. You could add some off white for the brightest highlights. Add brown to your yellow mix and white until you get gray to add to the tails. You can always add these colors at the branches if you'd like.

If you paint something out, just come back in and add it in when you can. No worries, you can always go back to the video to review it, as well.

5. VALUES AND FEATHERS

With your #6 bright, continue to block in the values in these wonderful birds. With your cad yellow and cad red mix work the wings with this beautiful orange, play with this mix to change hues. You can always add a smidge of white. Refer to your reference and don't forget the tips of the wing feathers. Back into yellow values for the top of the head. Brown and black For the shadows under the wing.

Rinse out, thoroughly before going back to turquoise, take it to the green side, or the blue where you wish, and add white or yellow to it to lighten. Use it to highlight feathers that are catching light.

6. CLEAN UP, HIGHLIGHTS/LOWLIGHTS

With a clean #6 bright or you can use your #4 round, putting back in some of the white and yellow and black if you feel it needs strengthening. The aim here is to get the features, the focal birds, to pop out of the canvas. Check your values and adjust as needed.

Change to the #4 round, mix white and a bit of blue, for that weird little eyebrow, the eyes, and for a pop of color on the feathers. Add a little white to the top of the beak where it is tilted up to define shape. Use brilliant orange for the eyes. Imply shape with a brighter highlight in the upper right. Refine everything you can and use the reference as a guide.

7. FINDING COLORS & HIGHLIGHTS, REFINING

Staying the the #4 round, layer more feathers using all your color mixes and values, find those features that need more definition. Don't miss those little spots on the chest that are lighter.

Are your dark feathers dark enough, are your light feathers popping? Do you have highlights where the sun would be hitting and shadows where the light would be blocked? Does the orange on the wings draw the eye? Add highlights to the joints of the branches and strengthen any parts that may have been painted out.

8. BIRD FEET AND LAST TOUCHES

With #4 round mix a bit of black into your phthalo blue and add the little bird feet per the reference add pupils, adding little white to this mix to highlight the individual toes of their feet. Use a blue-gray color to start the highlight in the eyes coming back with pure white to reinforce the highlight.

Using the reference, stand back and really take in your work. Refine, retouch, or change any part of it that you feel needs your attention.

9. SIGNATURE

Sign your name and enjoy your finished picture.

SWATCHING PRACTICE PAGE

1. Practice mixing the colors from todays palette and paint in your circles with your colors.
2. Check your values and hue by swatching your paint mixes on the sample images.
3. Do a tiny fast grey scale sketch to help you express light and shadow - use paint or pencil, either is fine.

BOAT AND RED UMBRELLA

COLOR PALETTE:         

Today's color palette is Cadmium Yellow, Burnt Sienna, Phthalo Green, Ultramarine Blue, Phthalo Blue, Quinacrodone Magenta, Cad Red Medium, Mars Black, and Titanium White.

1. BACKGROUND AND GRID

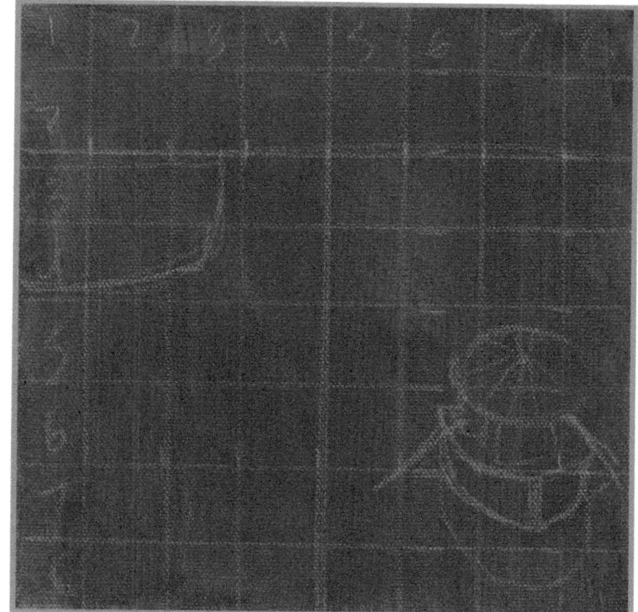

COLOR MIX: Ultramarine blue and phthalo green. Get some water on your background brush, just enough to help your paint flow. Paint your entire surface. Dry completely.

GRID: With your t-square and chalk, create a 1" x 1" grid on your canvas. Number the squares across the top 1 - 8 and along the left side, top to bottom, 1 - 8. Duplicate the image exactly as shown in the reference, one square at a time. Only draw what's in that square before you move on.

2. FLOWING RIVER AND BACKGROUND VALUES

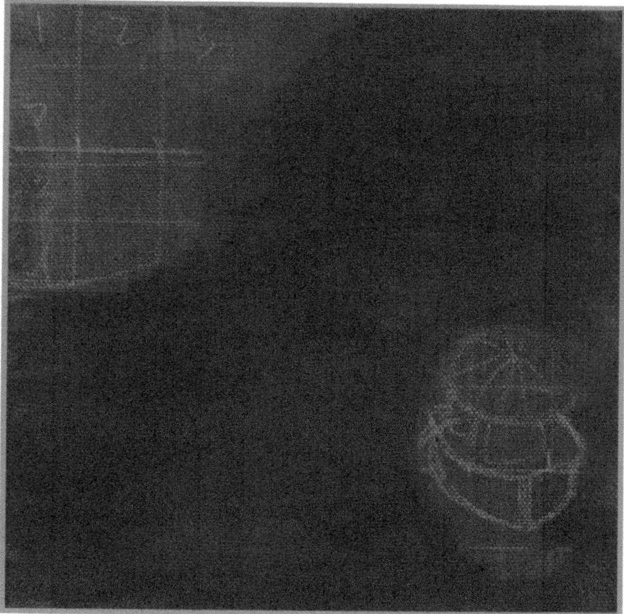

With the #8 Cambridge, dip in water, and take a bit of phthalo green, burnt sienna, and a dab of ultramarine to block in the river with a back and forth stroke. Play with these color mixes to adjust the values to create shadow tones and check the reference for placement.

3. BLOCKING IN FEATURES

Mars black and burnt sienna for the stones that are peeking through. A little burnt sienna, phthalo green, and a smidge of cad yellow to block in the green space.

Rinse out and get a little quin magenta and cad red mixed for the umbrella. A little phthalo blue into your red mix makes a dark blue for shadows on the boat add a touch of white to catch the highlights. Phthalo blue for the shadow under the boat. Don't hesitate to move to your #4 rounds if you need to.

Burnt sienna, phthalo green and yellow for our figure. We've made a lot of mixes and covered a lot of ground. Step back with your reference and compare. It still looks rough, but are you content with your progress? If not, go back and refine anything you need to. Don't forget, you can always go back and review the videos any time you want.

4. STONE WORK

With #8 Cambridge mix a little bit of black and phthalo blue, lighten with white to start blocking in the stones. Without rinsing, grab a little brown for a neutral stone color. Vary the colors and tones for a natural look.

Maybe add some yellow to go green, but not bright, it will help weather the stones. Come back with any colors you need to reinforce your progress before stepping back to compare it to your reference. If you painted something out, just come back in and add it in when you can. No worries.

5. WATER REFLECTIONS & SHADOWS

Reflections and shadows on the water to bring this world to life. Paint the light reflections on the surface of the water with ultramarine and a bit of phthalo green, some brown, and a touch of white, for a blue-gray. Closer to the embankment would be darker. You can go darker with your colors by adding blue, and it's ok to have some green show through. Stay on the tip of the brush. Wiggling the brush to imply rippling water dancing around the boat a darker shadow underneath it.

The trees would have a bit of green shadows, maybe a touch of yellow. Darken places with phthalo green and brown. Get all those dark value places and make them well defined. Catch that embankment. Don't over imply. Rinse your brush out when you need, see if you need clean water. Take a breath and stand back and use your reference to assess your progress.

6. DEFINING REFLECTIONS, STONES, BOAT SHADOWS, PERSPECTIVE

Switch to the #6 Ruby Satin. Find some highlights, by lightening your blue-grey mix. This soft brush can be wiggled, wiggled, wiggled, a very important skill. Come back and break up any lines you feel the need to adjust. Sharp edges are helpful. More blue for deeper reflections in the water toward the top. A little black and blue along the water's edge under the stones.

Mix quin magenta and cad red into phthalo blue for the very dark shadow under the boat Adjust the perspective of the boat with highlights and shadows. Wipe out your brush and paint the brightest reflections white. Refer to your reference and remember that you can always go back to video my video at any time for additional support.

7. UMBRELLA, BOAT SHADOWS

Start with the umbrella, and redefine it with chalk if you need to. Locate the top of it and take cad red on a clean #6 bright to catch the back of the umbrella about half way down, the bottom side is a little more shaded. With cad red in phthalo blue with a touch of white to grey. Catch your highlights on the implied second person in the boat, and you can always switch to the #4 round to help with control.

You're trying to catch perspective using tone values. The oars are lightened phthalo blue, add quin magenta for shadow. The front of the boat is a little darker because it's more in shadow. You want nice clean lines on the boat. White toned with cad yellow for the brightest highlight.

We're almost done here. Step back and compare your painting to the reference. Is there anything you feel needs refining and are you ready for the next step? Use your reference for that final check.

8. UMBRELLA PATTERN, PEOPLE, FLOWERS

With the #4 round and green and burnt sienna, imply the right bit of elbow and under the umbrella with darker green. Add more yellow for fabric and it's reflection. White and ultramarine for a nice off-white for the flowers on the umbrella, Dark dots to the center will help imply that they are flowers.

Phthalo into the turquoise to pop those water reflections of the oars. Catch the ribbing on that umbrella. Retouch anything you might have mistakenly painted out. Refer to your reference and make any changes you want to make before going on to the last step.

9. FLOWER SHADOWS, TEXTURE, TREES

The first layer of flowers will be a shadow tone, using a thick paint application called impasto, tap your canvas with your off white mix using your #8 cat's tongue or #4 round. Blue and white to brighten for highlights. Tap, tap, tapping in color. Catch any contrast might be missing on the oars. Does this tree allow a little bit of the river to peek through. Rolling and turning the brush a lot to not make obvious distinctive shapes. Does your tree have a shadow? Use your reference to catch shadows and highlights.

10. HIGHLIGHTS, ASSESSMENT, & SIGNATURE

With cad yellow and white load the tip of your brush create the flower shapes with a thick impasto style. Highlight branches in your tree, bring that tree to life by capturing the feeling of it. Does your picture share the feeling of shape on the trees?

This is your last step. Stand back and breathe. Use your reference. What do you feel like needs to be fixed? Do you feel the perspective of space? Do you think your highlights and shadows reflect the source of light?

11. SIGNATURE

Sign and I hope that you share your picture in the Facebook group. I know it is just lovely.

SWATCHING PRACTICE PAGE

1. Practice mixing the colors from todays palette and paint in your circles with your colors.
2. Check your values and hue by swatching your paint mixes on the sample images.
3. Do a tiny fast grey scale sketch to help you express light and shadow - use paint or pencil, either is fine.

TRACEABLE

BLUE BUTTERFLY

COLOR PALETTE:           

Today's color palette is Phthalo Green, Diox Purple, Burnt Sienna, Phthalo Blue, Ultramarine Blue, Quinacridone Magenta, Cad Red Medium, Cad Yellow Medium, Naples Yellow Light, Mars Black, and Titanium White.

1. BACKGROUND AND GRID

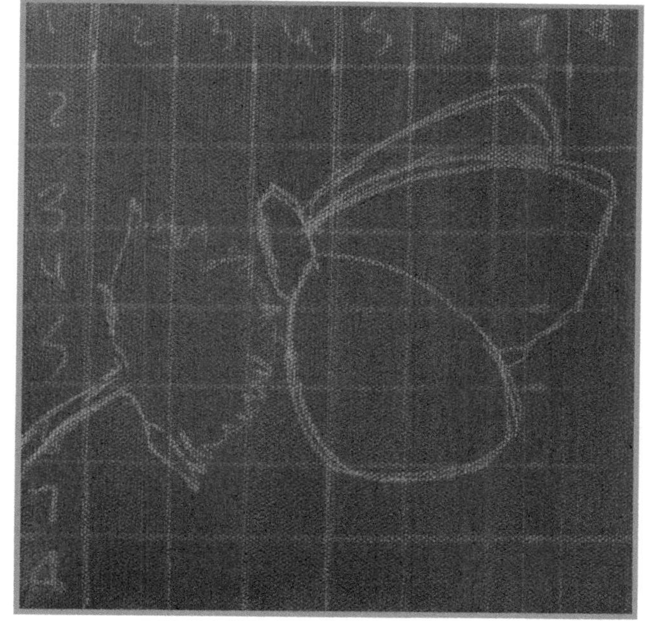

COLOR MIX: Phthalo green. Get some water on your background brush, just enough to help your paint flow. Paint your entire surface. Dry completely.

GRID: With your t-square and chalk, create a 1" x 1" grid on your canvas. Number the squares across the top 1 - 8 and along the left side, top to bottom, 1 - 8. Duplicate the image exactly as shown in the reference, one square at a time. Only draw what's in that square before you move on.

2. OUT OF FOCUS BACKGROUND

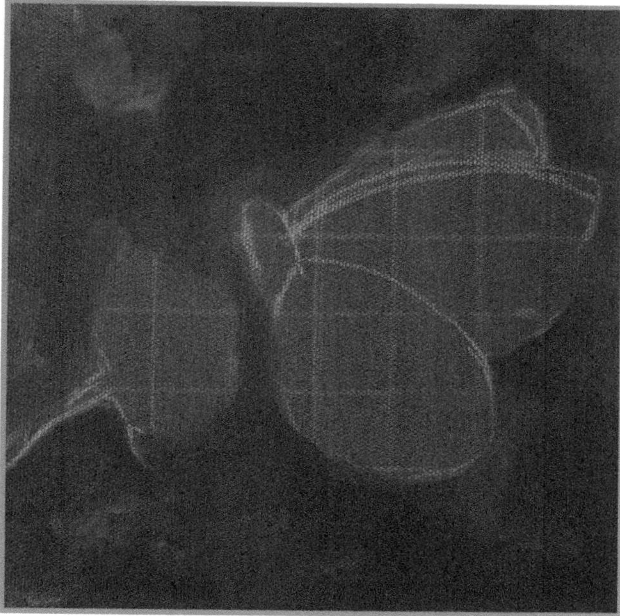

The butterfly is our focus, so come in with the #8 Cambridge and let's start with dark and light values in the background. Take diox and mix with phthalo green to scumble in dark shadows that are out of focus and in the distant bushes. Be loose and let the color act as a glaze.

Rinse very thoroughly and get burnt sienna and phthalo green, maybe a touch of cad yellow, for a bright green to wiggle in. The motion and style of the brush help diffuse the edge lines so they are soft.

3. CLOVER

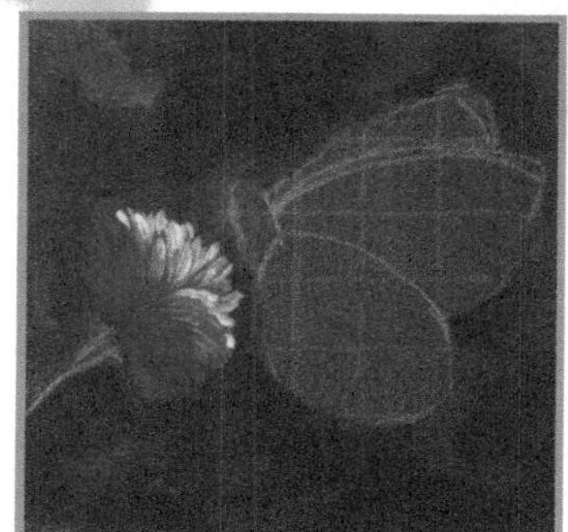

Start with your #4 round. Mix quin magenta and naples yellow, to the quin side. For the little clover petals, Start with the top light petals. Get darker in color as you move down and they run out of light. A bit of cad yellow in there for bright, intense highlights. Ultramarine blue and quin magenta to darken some of our magenta areas into shadow. Blend those little petals in and find those highlights. The brightest highlights should be naples yellow and white.

Refer to your reference to help you with highlight shadow placement if necessary.

4. FLOWER

Our flower needs a stem, so cad yellow and phthalo green to a value that does not disappear entirely into the background. You can always add a bit of phthalo blue for a darker green to stand against the lighter value. Wipe your brush out as needed to keep your brush from carrying a too heavy load of paint. Get some yellow and white to start creating the light values of the stem and highlight at the top.

5. EMBERS

The little embers are cad red and cad yellow with a touch of brown on the #4 round, some little bits of dust that got caught in the sunlight, a sense of magic, place them as seen around your figures. Rinse out. Mix cad yellow and cad red and put this in the center. Bright little dust notes happening around the butterfly, help create an atmospheric effect, drama, and depth.

6. BUTTERFLY BODY

With a clean #4 round and a base of phthalo green and phthalo blue with a small amount of white, paint in the little body. Feather your strokes and let the bristles separate on the brush. Little dark eyes, a little halo hair. Add a bit of black near the wing and strong black for the legs. You may need to thin the black to get the bug legs and feet and antennae so don't be afraid to experiment. Refer to your reference and remember that you can always go back to video my video at any time for additional support.

7. BUTTERFLY WINGS

With the #4 round, mix ultramarine and phthalo blue with a touch of white for the wings. Paint the top wing, beginning from the outer edge brushing toward the body. This helps imply wing texture. Mix in more pthalo to darken and blend in wet-on-wet along the outer edge create Shadows. Add some white to blend in those lighter highlights, lightly blending wet into wet. Do the same on each wing. Notice that farthest wing is the darkest and how they lighten as they get closer. Mix lighter values for the closer wings.

8. VEINING THE WINGS

Veining will be orange with a little brown to warm it, and quin magenta and perhaps a little brown. If you need to lighten, add some naples yellow. You will certainly want to add water to improve the flow for the veining. Come back with black in the veining and don't hesitate to use your reference to help you with that placement.

9. FINAL TOUCHES

Let's start with quin and naples yellow and pop bits of that in as highlights. Dry brush a few places. Add some turquoise, which is our phthalo green and phthalo blue. Add some naples to it to get an interesting effect. Very lightly dry brushing right over the surface to mimic the little scales on butterfly wings. The top of the wing is quite light compared to the bottom. Catch those little value sets and you should start to get some real iridescence going. Grab some yellow and play with those values to make the wings start to shimmer.

We're almost done here. Step back and compare your painting to the reference. Is there anything you feel needs refining and are you ready for the next step? Use your reference for that final check.

10. SIGNATURE

Thin some white and with the #1 Monogram Liner, add little dots of highlights that insects tend to have. Delicate but critical to the eye. Add this wherever you think you need delicate lighting. It really pulls it all together.

Make your signature whenever you are ready and please post your finished picture in the Facebook group.

SWATCHING PRACTICE PAGE

1. Practice mixing the colors from todays palette and paint in your circles with your colors.
2. Check your values and hue by swatching your paint mixes on the sample images.
3. Do a tiny fast grey scale sketch to help you express light and shadow - use paint or pencil, either is fine.

TRACEABLE

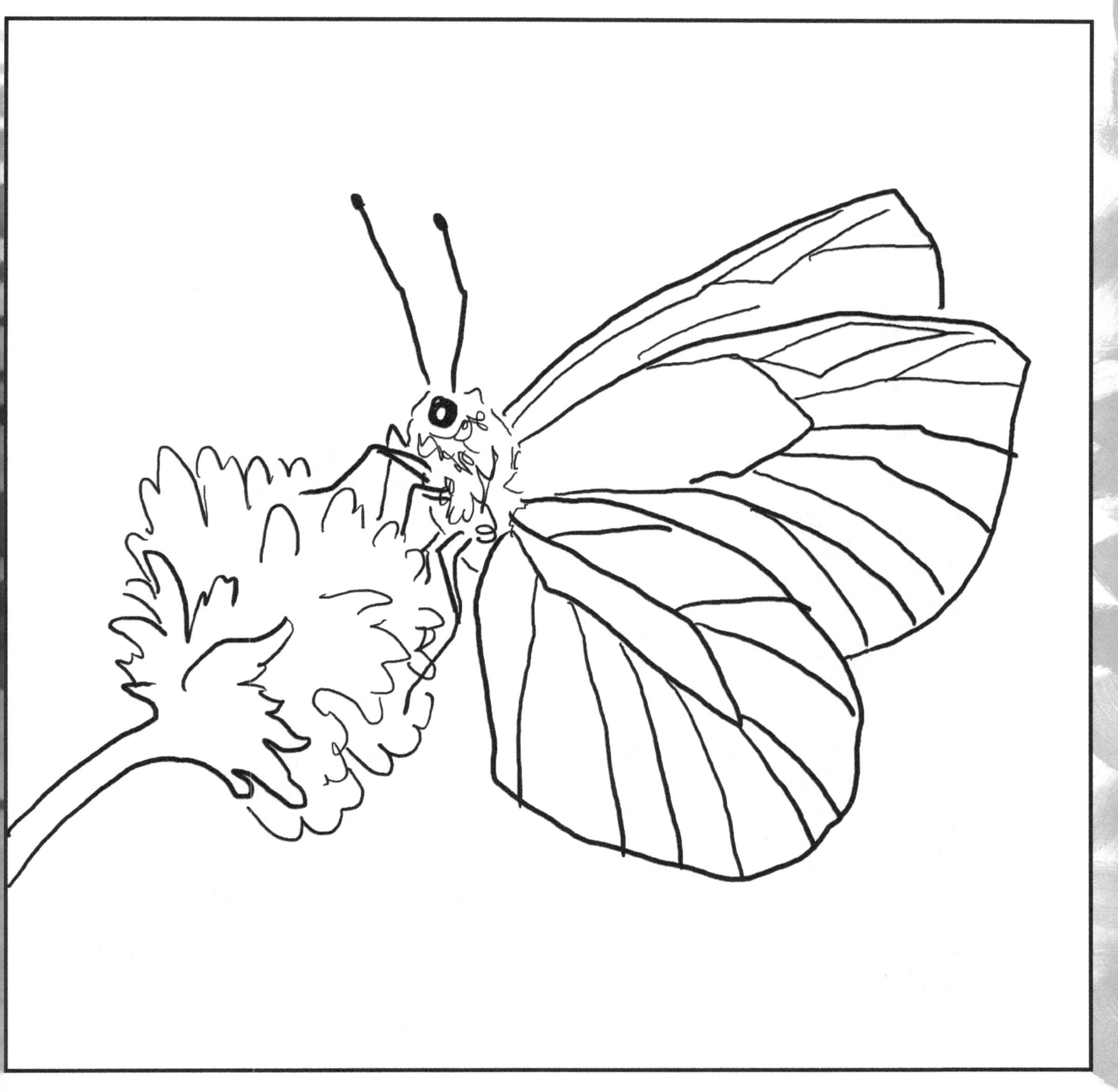

THE ART SHERPA

MOON ON WATER

COLOR PALETTE:        

Today's color palette is Quinacridone Magenta, Cad Red Medium, Cad Yellow Medium, Naples Yellow Light, Phthalo Green, Phthalo Blue, Dioxazine Purple, and Titanium White.

1. BACKGROUND AND GRID

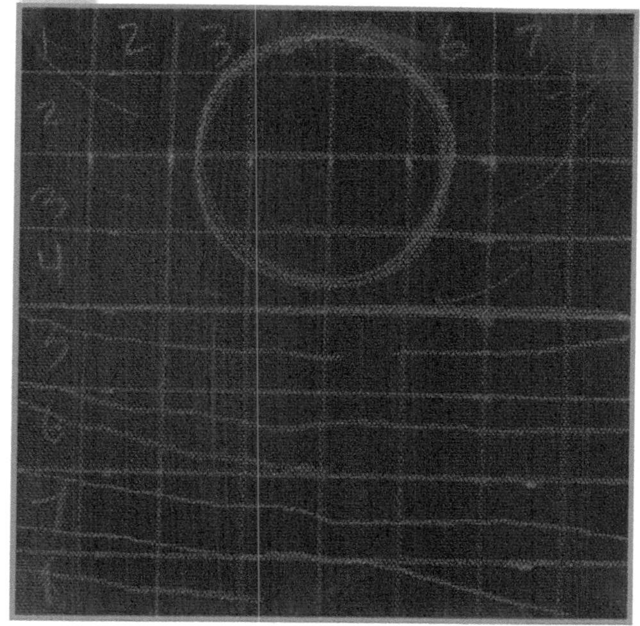

COLOR MIX: Diox Purple. Get some water on your background brush, just enough to help your paint flow. Paint your entire surface. Dry completely.

GRID: With your t-square and chalk, create a 1" x 1" grid on your canvas, number the squares across the top 1 - 8 and along the left side top to bottom 1 - 8. Duplicate the image exactly as shown in the reference, one square at a time. Only draw what's in that square before you move on.

2. SKY AND CLOUDS

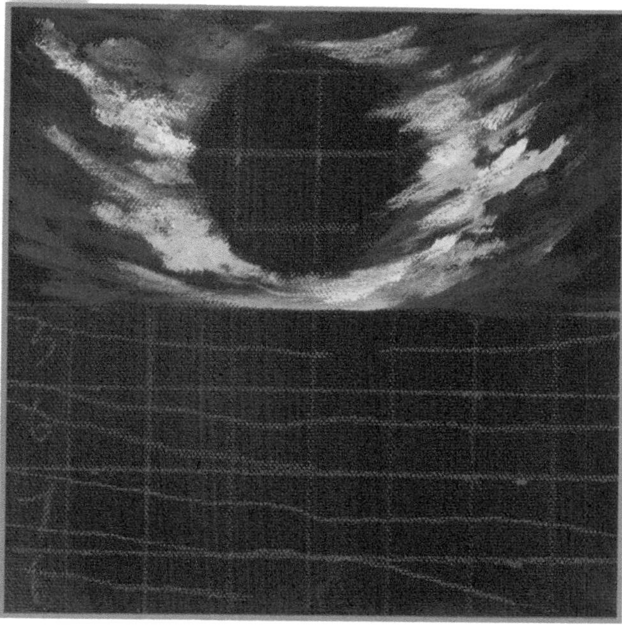

Start with your #8 Cambridge and the dry brush technique. Mix phthalo blue and a smidge of white and speak about the distant little cloud spaces, blending the phthalo blue into diox purple a bit, for a dramatic sky, with a sweeping motion. Using your reference, get some cad red, magenta, and naples yellow for the next amazing color and bring that into the clouds, even coming over where the moon will lie, because clouds should be in front of the moon, yet the moon is never in front of clouds. My moon was intentionally drawn smaller than I might have to allow it to expand over clouds.

Do your clouds have both light and darker values? Do you see some orange variations, maybe some green hues, pinks, and yellows? Clouds are interesting and dynamic, so use your reference to help you create yours. Magenta would be a great dark value for the clouds, naples yellow and cad for a mid-tone, add white for the lightest bits.

3. MOONSCAPE

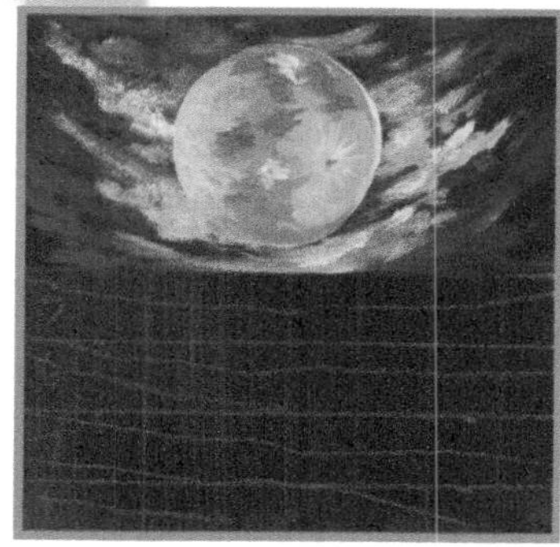

The moon will start with a #8 cat's tongue and a mix of yellow and white. Don't be afraid to use something to help you make the moon round, like a mason jar, or a lid. Don't be afraid to pick up bits of purple from the canvas. Paint the surface and make sure your water gets changed when needed. Dirty water impacts the look.

For the moonscape, mix cad red and yellow, wiggling the brush, Does your moonscape have both light and dark values? Yellow and white is a wonderful light value. Just carving out that emotional moonscape, white in those places where it needs lightening up. Come back and put a few clouds in front of the moon. The moon has craters, maybe with the darker value orange.

Take a breath, stand back and assess using your reference. Allow or dry your canvas entirely.

4. DRAMATIC CLOUD LAYERS

With the #8 Cambridge, scrumble in some dramatic cloud layers. Start with phthalo green and phthalo blue to phthalo turquoise for the darkest layer of clouds. Less is more. Now some magenta and white for the next layer of clouds. Don't be afraid of pure naples or white for the light parts. With #4 round, get turquoise, maybe some yellow, not all the way to green, but bright, add white, and wiggle that color in to capture a halo. Add in a tiny bit of yellow and white for light tones where the moonlight is catching the cloud on the edge. Quin, naples, and white for little wisps of dramatic color. Remember that clouds are all different from each other, they are not symmetrical or uniform.

Come back with any colors you need to reinforce your progress. Step back and compare it to your reference. If you painted something out, just come back in and add it in when you can. No worries.

5. OCEAN

Our ocean is next and we will need to create a corridor of light so that will mean yellows in different reflections in the water. With the #8 cat's tongue, mix a dark turquoise, with a little white, keeping the horizon line level, and leaving the white lines for your waves visible, enforcing the shadow. Keep water brush strokes light and cause the water to flow as gravity pulls it and wind affects it. Imply those ripples in the water with that turquoise. Dark and light values.

Step back and evaluate your progress and make any improvements you feel are necessary.

6. OCEAN VALUES

Still with the #8 cat tongue, come in with pure blue, and maybe purple, for the dark tones and to enforce those little wave lines that you left in.

Rinse your brush between dark and light values and add white to the turquoise to lighten values. Just layering your ocean, implying movement, and using your reference to help you when needed. Naples and white and dry brush that little corridor of light created by our moon. Very rough, this is the foundation.

Refer to your reference and remember that you can always go back to video my video at any time for additional support.

7. REFINING OCEAN COLORS

To refine our ocean colors and reflections, we want to begin to taper the reflection with turquoise, with a little white. Short brush strokes as you come along the wave. Don't take out the wave. Relax through this stage because subtle changes make big differences. Be introspective about your water. Remember to taper towards the center. With turquoise and naples, more yellow or white as you feel necessary, feathering the waves, picking up little water highlights and sheen. Don't paint out all your shadows.

We're almost done here. Step back and compare your painting to the reference. Is there anything you feel needs refining and are you ready for the next step? Use your reference for that final check.

8. CORRIDOR OF MOONLIGHT ON WATER

Bring your yellow down as you move towards the center of the corridor of light created by your moon. Yellow should move to white towards the center as it gets closer and closer to the moon. Lines are uneven and irregular. Some yellow and a smidge of cad red to darken and warm. Naples and cad yellow, touch of white, for a lovely highlight and can be woven out into the yellow a bit. Work on the toe of your #8 cat's tongue. You can also use your #1 monoliner to add some white to the water waves. Use your reference as you finish your project.

9. SIGNATURE

Sign your name to your incredible painting and please share it with the community. You should be very proud of yourself.

SWATCHING PRACTICE PAGE

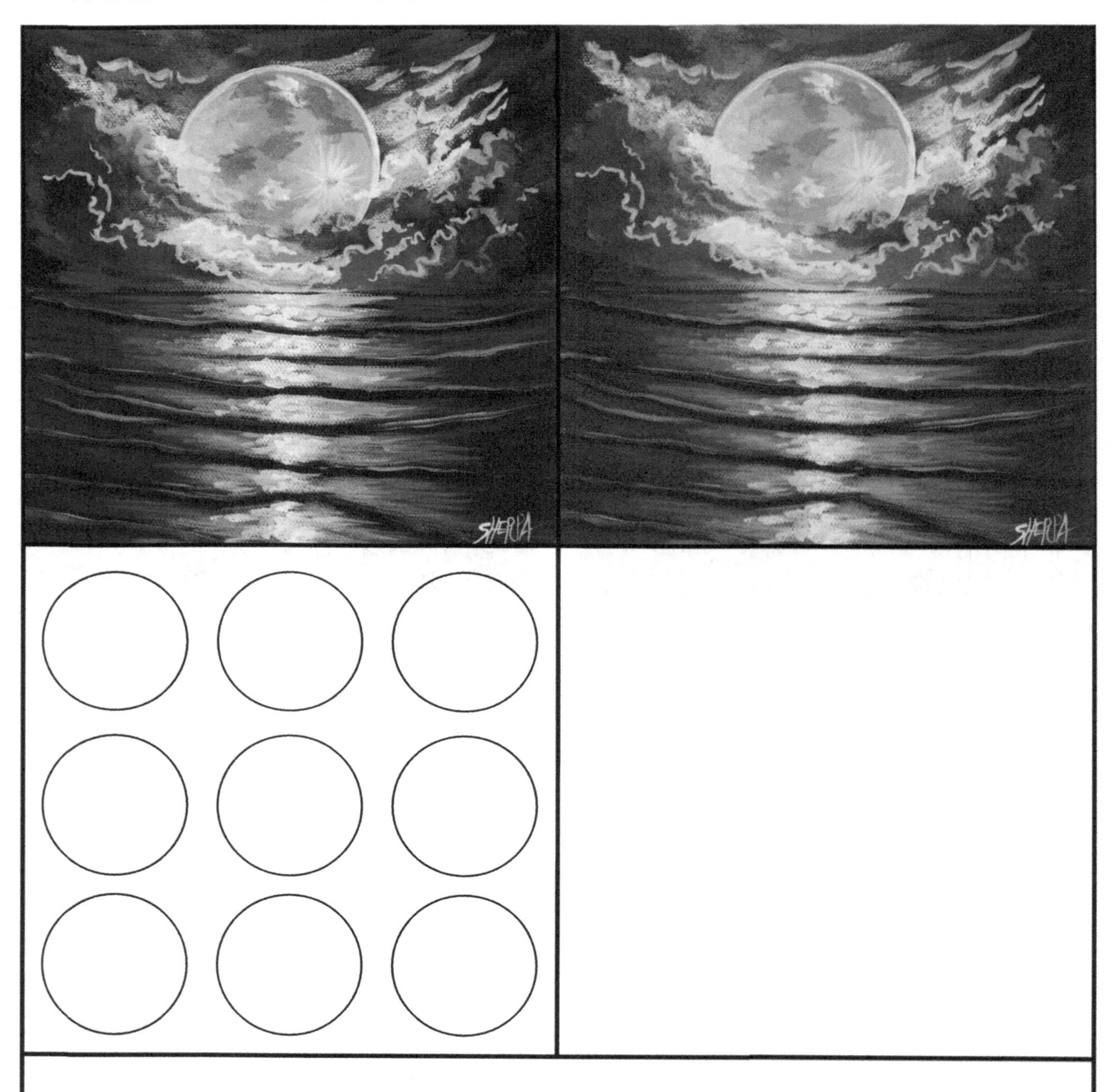

1. Practice mixing the colors from todays palette and paint in your circles with your colors.
2. Check your values and hue by swatching your paint mixes on the sample images.
3. Do a tiny fast grey scale sketch to help you express light and shadow - use paint or pencil, either is fine.

TRACEABLE

THE ART SHERPA

LIONFISH

COLOR PALETTE:         

Today's color palette is Titanium White, Mars Black, Phthalo Green, Phthalo Blue, Ultramarine Blue, Burnt Sienna, Cad Red Medium, Cad Yellow Medium, and Naples Yellow Light.

1. BACKGROUND AND GRID

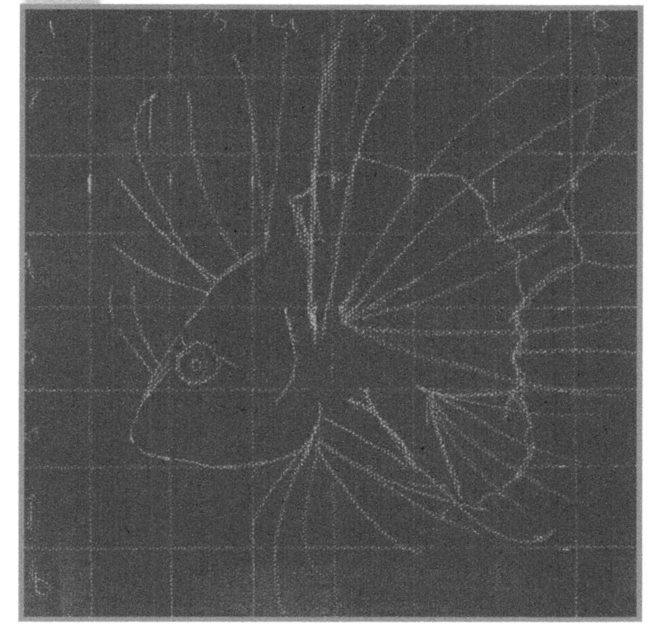

COLOR MIX: Phthalo blue and ultramarine blue. Get some water on your background brush, just enough to help your paint flow. Paint your entire surface. Dry completely.

GRID: With your t-square and chalk, create a 1" x 1" grid on your canvas. Number the squares across the top 1 - 8 and along the left side, top to bottom, 1 - 8. Duplicate the image exactly as shown in the reference, one square at a time. Only draw what's in that square before you move on.

2. FISH STRIPES AND FINS

Dip your #4 round into water, take your background mix and add some white, lots of white. Start painting in the light little lines that are our fishey's striped back fins. Not too bright because they are in water. Some stripes curve upward and others curve back. Now get some red and a little burnt sienna and add little dabs the mix, maybe a smidge of phthalo to darken it.

For the main tail stripes, rinse out and go back to the blue-white, only with more white, so brighter, just a little bit of blue for the marks. Feel free to add the white spots from your reference. Dry and get some fresh water and clean your brush.

3. BLOCKING IN THE FISH AND BOTTOM FAN TAIL

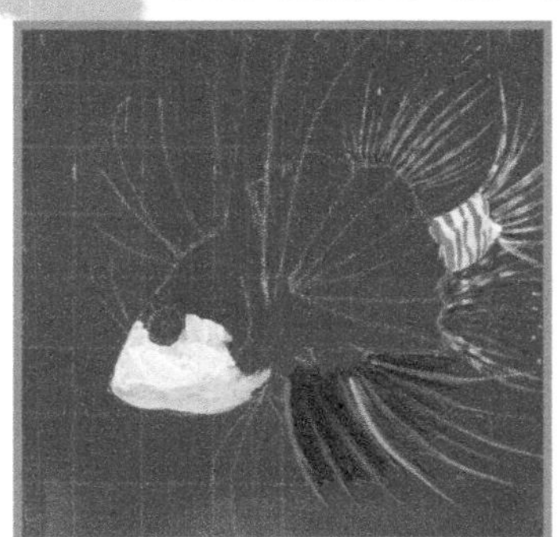

TIPS TO REMEMBER:
This is about layers and values. Always remember you can add water to improve flow if you need too. Be sure to rinse and or wipe your brush when needed. You can use what brush you are most comfortable with. Be sure to let an area dry before you go back and add striping etc. Check your references often and remember you can always go back and view the video.

With your #8 filbert or #4 round paint in the tail with a smidge of cad yellow and a smidge of naples yellow and a bunch of white. Come in with some naples, and then maybe some ultramarine to green it up a little, giving the tail some shadow. Get back into the yellow and white and paint in his face and around the eye. For the stripes on the tail, cad red and cad yellow, maybe more into the red for a bright orange. The stripes are not even, they are thick and thin and have a bit of an angle. Capture that uniqueness.

Bottom fan fin. Bring a touch of phthalo to your orange to get a muted dark orange. Small light strokes from the center and create the scalloped shape. Add a little more phthalo blue to your red to make the darker value. The scallops will define the thorns. Rinse out and make sure your brush has a nice point. Drag out fine little fin lines. Fine fin bones. You might want a darker yellow and red for these.

4. FISH, CONTINUED

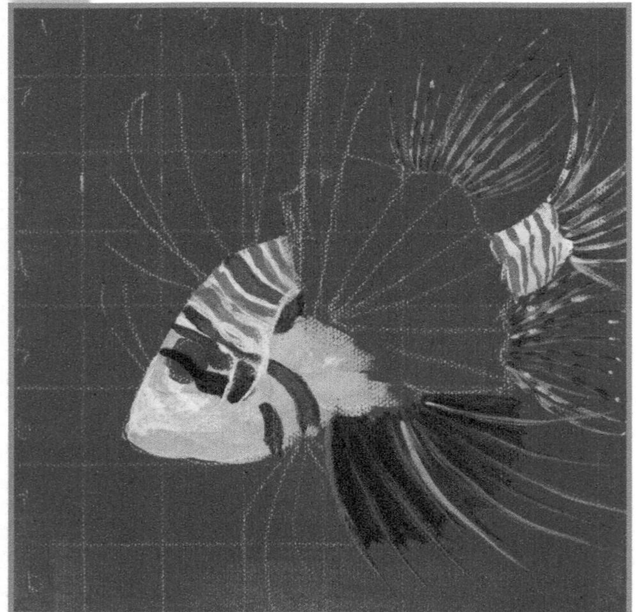

Mix phthalo blue and phthalo green, some naples and some white to make a vintage mint. Paint in the body with this color, adding a little blue to give some varying colors. It's ok to leave some of that light layer showing through around the head.

Start adding stripes. Red and burnt sienna for the center, the really noticeable spine and stripe. Add ultramarine and burnt sienna to darken things. There is a forward facing very dark stripe, another that is a bit off center and a little white fin. Grab some blue for dark values. Switch to the #4 round and grab some blue for dark values. Get more orange in the spaces, yellow in red for other stripes. Be playful and use your reference. Little spots and highlights in white. Tone your cad red with black for some of the spots on the darker areas.

Come back with any colors you need to reinforce your progress before stepping back to compare it to your reference. If you painted something out, just come back in and add it in when you can. No worries.

5. FISH, IT'S ALL ABOUT THE FISH

Let's address the spines that come off top. Naples yellow and cad red for a beautiful coral. Pull some long curved stripes off his back. Check your reference and add some spots to his body. Use phthalo blue and phthalo green for turquoise and a bunch of white for the brighter flag spines, and feather it back on the fin. Get all those little spines, blending orange in where you need to.

Use the dry brush technique if you want to allow the canvas to show through, because fins and spines might be more transparent, right? Brown in places for darker values. Lots of stripes serve as warning flags to predators that "I'm poisonous...leave me alone" Use your reference photo as a guide. Evaluate.

6. WARNING SIGNS

Mix red and yellow to orange and start to blend out the large forward fin. Begin by blending from the body and towards the spines. Fill in between the spines and lighten your orange with yellow and white for those areas that might be illuminated. Phthalo turquoise with a little red for a dark value to tap in some strips. Rinse out your brush regularly to help keep your color bright. Be irregular in your patterns. Your reference is going to be your best friend as you define your lionfish. Play with those reddish brown values to build layers. Grab your round brush any time you feel the need. Turquoise and naples and a bit of white for the highlights in between the spines. Cad yellow and a lot of white for the long floating spines. He's very visually busy but don't pet him.

Remember that you can always go back to my video at any time for additional support.

7. REFINING WITH SHADOWS AND HIGHLIGHTS

Mix a very light turquoise with lot of white to make a very light value, feathering in those little pops of color between the spines that send that warning message. Then with your darker turquoise put in a shadow right next to it. Remember to rinse out your brush to keep your colors fresh and bright. Try to capture the distinctive structure of the fin. They are like little sails in water. Look at the reference often. Mix a little black in to blue for those little dots. If you need to add another stripe, turquoise and white, maybe a highlight around the dot. Stripes in stripes. Breathe. Relax. Assess him close up. Stand back and assess him. Refer to your reference, are you happy? If you were a predator, would you want to take a chance with all those warnings?

We're almost done here. Step back and compare your painting to the reference. Is there anything you feel needs refining and are you ready for the next step? Use your reference for that final check.

8. THE EYE, FINAL TOUCHES AND SIGNATURE

Mix ultramarine and green to teal and paint in the round eye using the toe of your round brush. Add naples to the mix, and catch those reflections and his eye. Thin the dark paint for that wild fish eye. Grab some white for those little dots. Check your reference to help you create this fantastic eye.

Sign your name to your incredible painting and please share it with the community. You should be very proud of yourself.

I hope you're feeling amazing about your painting.

SWATCHING PRACTICE PAGE

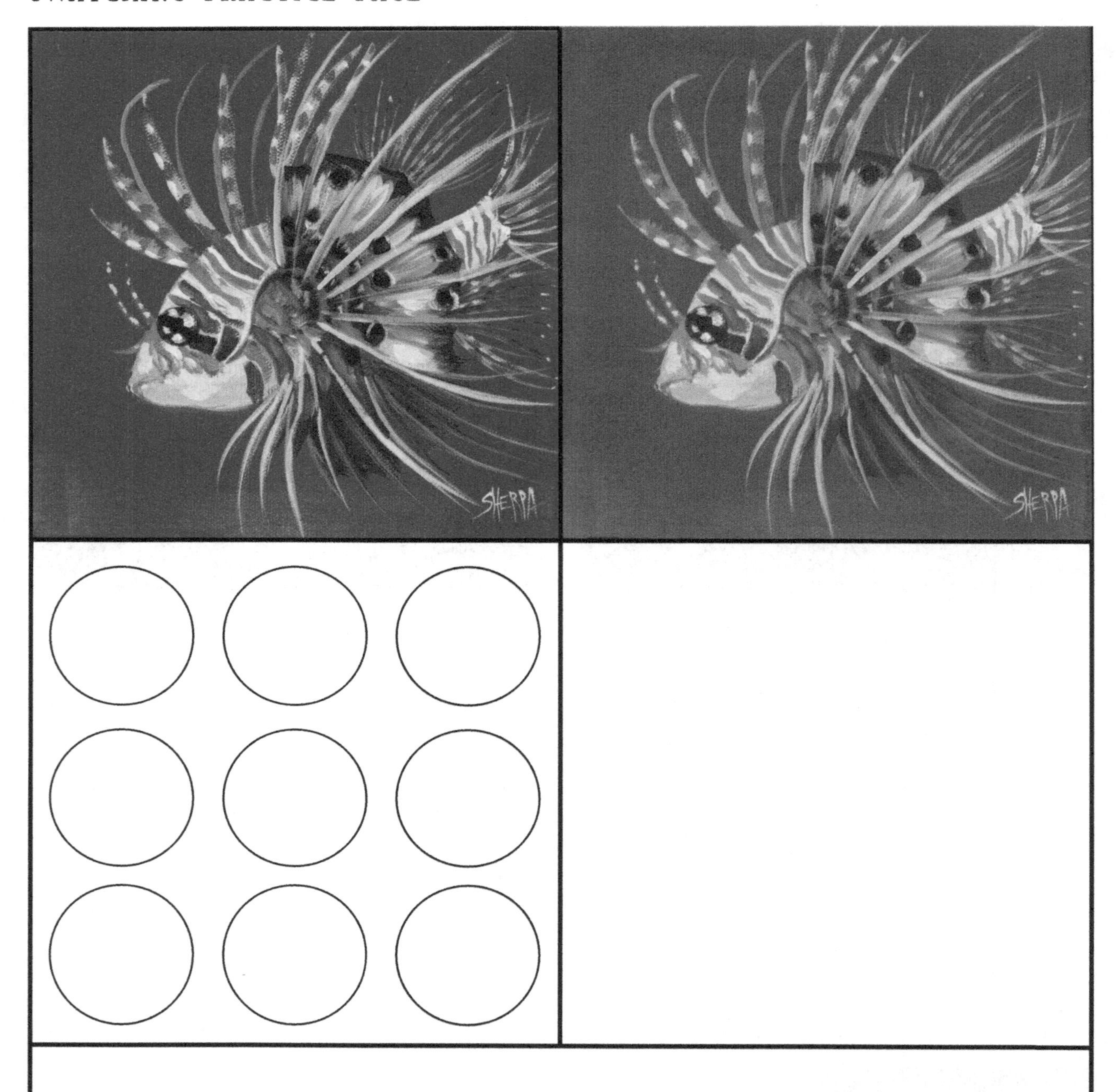

1. Practice mixing the colors from todays palette and paint in your circles with your colors.
2. Check your values and hue by swatching your paint mixes on the sample images.
3. Do a tiny fast grey scale sketch to help you express light and shadow - use paint or pencil, either is fine.

TRACEABLE

POPPIES

COLOR PALETTE:          

Today's color palette is Burnt Sienna, Phthalo Green, Ultramarine Blue, Phthalo Blue, Quinacridone Magenta, Cad Red Medium, Cad Yellow Medium, Naples Yellow Light, and Titanium White.

1. BACKGROUND AND GRID

A BIT DIFFERENT TODAY:

With your T-square ruler, make a mark at the 3" line and draw a line across to divide your sky from the poppy field. Use chalk or a watercolor pencil for your mark. With your big brush, load phthalo blue and naples yellow with a touch of white, to a bluish green and paint the sky this color. The bottom part is phthalo green and burnt sienna.

Take a deep breath and remember, if you have to change any lines, the chalk is removed easily with just a damp brush and clean water.

GRID:

With your t-square and chalk, create a 1" x 1" grid on your canvas. Number the squares across the top 1 - 8 and along the left side, top to bottom, 1 - 8. Duplicate the image exactly as shown in the reference, one square at a time. Only draw what's in that square before you move on.

2. SPECTACULAR SKY AND HORIZON LINE

To start the spectacular sky and create a horizon line glow that transitions into blue, get the smallest bit of cad red into cad yellow, just enough to warm the yellow up. You can add naples to it if you think it needs to be lighter, to an orange-yellow. The center part should be lighter. As you move up, it will be important to get some white and phthalo blue for a half tone. Blend that from the yellow up wet into wet, going right over the background.

Adding more blue, blend the darker tone from the top down to imply light far away clouds. A little darker at the top. Be careful not to blend this blue all the way into the yellow. Can you see the transition in the sky?

3. SUN AND GLOW THE SLY

Mix equal parts ultramarine blue and phthalo blue. On the corner of your #8 Cambridge, dry brush in those airy far away stratosphere clouds. Still on the corner of the brush put in some little cloud forms. You could cloud with a pallet knife or your finger or one of my cloud brushes if you prefer. The cloud is in you. For the lighter half of the cloud mix a peachy color with naples and a smidge of quin, smidge of cad and white, peach at the bottom and then bring in those highlights. You can always add a little cad yellow to warm up the peach to increase the value of the hue. Refer to your reference.

4. SUN AND GLOW THE SLY

You can always add paint to increase the value of the hue. To refine these little clouds and get the rest of the glow in the sky. Grab the #4 round and a bit of yellow and tiny bit of cad red just to warm it and add your sun and that glow. Pure yellow highlights are wonderful.

The halo outline around your clouds might be our peach with some white or pure white is so very powerful. Around the sun, yellow and white. Don't paint away the little dot but give it a bit of shimmer.

5. DISTANT LANDSCAPE

Mix green and burnt sienna with a bit of ultramarine, for an almost black-green. On the toe of your round brush, tap in little bits of greenery and leafery. Catch those little distant trees, be loose, little moments of magic. Let some sunlight peek through. Dot, dot, dot, keeping shapes irregular, no cloning.

Get your #8 bright, not too wet, and with that dark green foliage color, come along the bottom of your tree line and with little up and down strokes, dry brush that color, blending up a little and then back and forth strokes across creating little shrubberies. Rinse out and mix a lighter green and blend that brighter color back and forth down to your horizon line.

If you painted something out, just come back in and add it in when you can. No worries.

6. FARAWAY POPPIES

Mix your cad red and quin magenta, add a bit of ultramarine for those distant little poppies. Blend it a little up into the green, wiggling that brush lightly across your horizon line. As you come forward, rinse your brush and make a brighter red. Create random spaces. Rough little up and down marks. Mix quin magenta and cad red, brighter than before, but not the brightest mix. Tap in more defined shapes as you get closer. Step back and review from time to time with your reference.

Time to add some underlying greenery to your poppy field. Make little up and down strokes. Rinse out and get burnt sienna and green, maybe some cad yellow for the greenery. Add a bit of red to mute the green. Add more green to the mix for the darker values. Keep things loose and slightly spaced. Darker green on the outer edges, maybe some well lit peaks. Do you sense a sort of almost Monet impressionistic style here?

Use your reference photo as a guide. Evaluate.

7. MORE REFINED MID RANGE POPPIES

For the slightly more defined poppies, mix quin magenta and cad red, not too much water. With your #4 round create dot shapes that give illusion to the shape of a poppy. Some flowers will have a lot more magenta and some more cad red. Make little individual touches. Some will catch light and the centers should be darker. Start to pick up bits of cad yellow with your reds on the toe of your brush and play with light and dark values to create a corridor of lighter poppies in the center. Remember the sunlight will be brightest in the center so you want to make those flowers brighter. Poppies would be darker on the outside edge. You should start to sense definition. Tap in some cad yellow in some areas. Tap in naples yellow in some places.

With your filbert or your bright, mix your darkest green with ultramarine blue, phthalo green, and a bit of burnt umber. Paint the remaining bottom of your canvas this dark green base. Add some cad yellow to your green and add lighter bits in the center.

Refer to your reference and remember that you can always go back and view my video at any time for additional support.

8. CLOSEST POPPIES

This is very similar to the previous step. As you paint your field of poppies moving closer, they become slightly larger, brighter and a bit more defined.

Rinsing your brush and getting clean water can help keep your colors bright when transitioning to lighter hues.

Still on the #4 round, mix quin magenta and cad red and start to address the bigger poppies. Create little roundish shapes with the toe of your brush. Not the exact shape of poppies but implied poppy shapes. Define them as separated when you put in the little dark center. Add a little cad yellow to your brush for lighter hues. Then add a little naples yellow. Play with little bits of reds and yellows to create lighter poppies in the center of the canvas, creating that keyhole of light effect. They are all different sizes. Some have an almost rosey bud, some are open, some are thinking about opening. Definition will happen once we have the general placement established and we come back with highlights and depth and perspective. Red does not like to go over green, so don't hesitate to paint a little area white before you add the red if you need to.

We're almost done here. Step back and compare your painting to the reference. Is there anything you feel needs refining and are you ready for the next step?

9. HIGHLIGHTS ON POPPIES AND CORRIDOR

Mix cad red and cad yellow to an orange red. As you come forward, add more red to make a darker orange. They're still in the corridor, but not quite in the hot spot of light. Paint loosely and find those little bits of highlights from the sun. Get into just cad red for some individual petals. Get a little ultramarine and burnt sienna to pop in the dark centers.

Do your dots portray that the poppies are facing different directions? Do your highlights portray the source of light? Do your shadows show that the sun is being blocked?

Use your reference to help you determine your progress.

10. BRIGHT PETALS AND SIGNATURE

To add highlights to the closest poppies, your brightest colors would be cad yellow and little cad red, maybe even some white to lighten up the poppies. Lastly, come in with cad red and add petals. Leave some of them open, some of them more round, defined shapes, some of them closed, just irregular lovely little poppies. Use thick paint as if it were impasto. This will bring the poppies into focus.

Sign your name to your incredible painting and please share it with the community.

SWATCHING PRACTICE PAGE

1. Practice mixing the colors from todays palette and paint in your circles with your colors.
2. Check your values and hue by swatching your paint mixes on the sample images.
3. Do a tiny fast grey scale sketch to help you express light and shadow - use paint or pencil, either is fine.

TRACEABLE

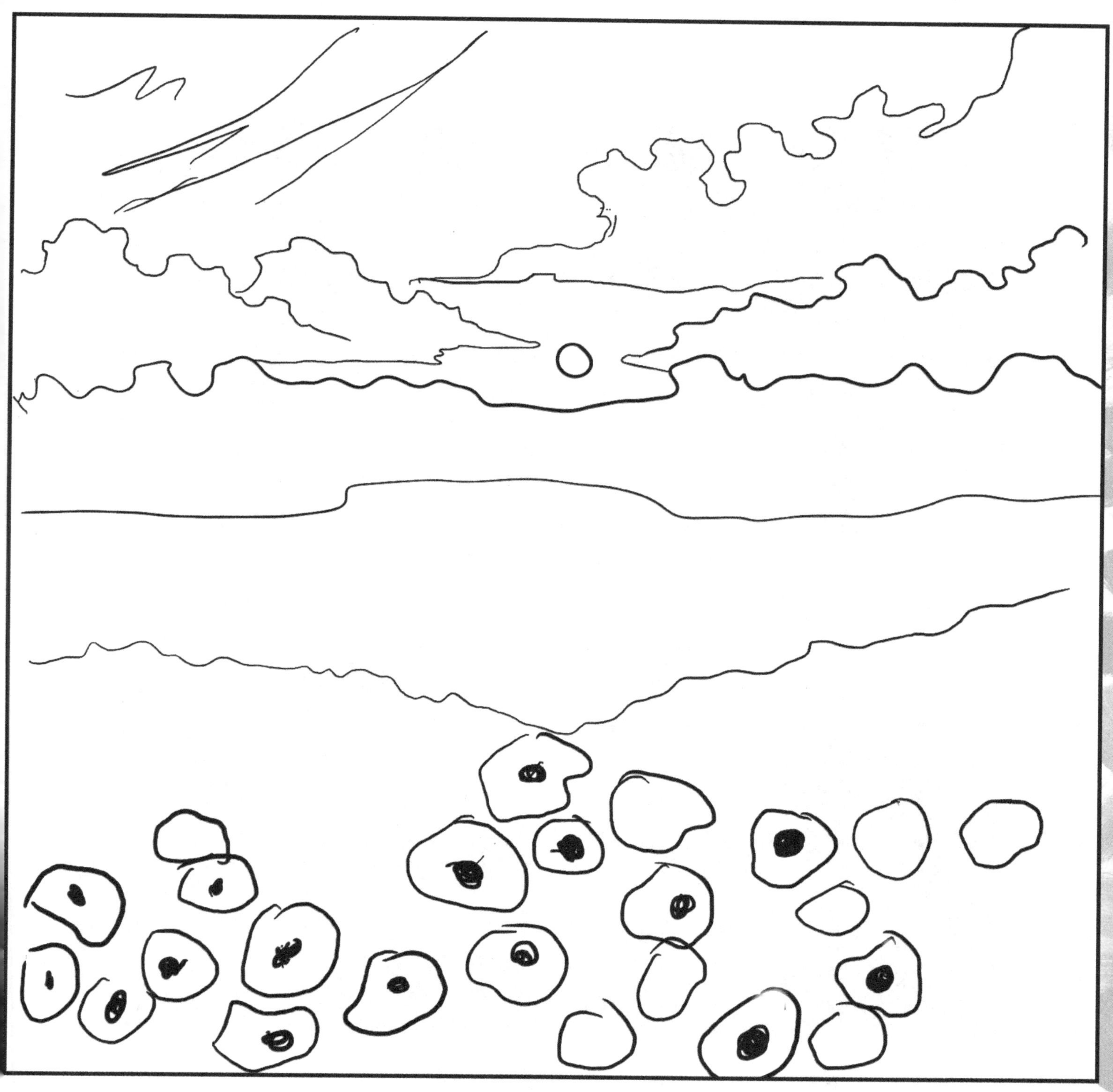

THE ART SHERPA

BLUE ROSE

COLOR PALETTE:        

Today's color palette is: Dioxazine Purple, Phthalo Blue, Ultramarine Blue, Phthalo Green, Quinacridone Magenta, Mars Black, and Titanium White.

1. BACKGROUND AND GRID

COLOR MIX: Dioxazine purple. Get some water on your background brush, just enough to help your paint flow. Paint your entire surface. Dry completely.

GRID: With your t-square and chalk, create a 1" x 1" grid on your canvas. Number the squares across the top 1 - 8 and along the left side, top to bottom, 1 - 8. Duplicate the image exactly as shown in the reference, one square at a time. Only draw what's in that square before you move on.

2. STEM AND LEAVES

Start by cleaning up the chalk grid lines only keeping those grid lines that are necessary because roses are visually complicated. Use a clean brush with clean water or, if you need, you can paint over the lines you don't want with diox purple.

With your filbert get phthalo green with a bit of white and paint in the stem and leaves at the bottom. Go ahead and imply some distant leaves around the outside of the rose. Then come back and get white and a titch of diox purple and make the more implied leaves in and around the green. If you need to add a smidge of purple to the white to cover, please do so. Purple and green blend incredibly well together. They add a mystical feeling.

Dry your painting and grab some sippy sippy or water, anything to keep you chill.

3. THE ROSE

Starting at the top of center section of the rose, with the #4 round, mix some phthalo blue and white. Not the darkest phthalo blue, and begin the inside petal space. Roses are a contrast of light and shadow, so you must retain a good amount of shadow. The shadow is dark in the center. Lighter on the edge. Phthalo blue and phthalo green and white for turquoise. One side is definitely more in highlight, use feather blending technique.

Rinse out your brush and get clean water when you need to. Don't forget to highlight the lip of the petal.

Pure phthalo blue where the shadow is deeper, purple and blue for another shadow color.

4. CONTINUING THE PROCESS

Changing to the #8 filbert if you like, continue the same process from the last step, staying on the toe of the brush. Put some highlights in and then the dark shadows in the petals and highlighting the edges of the petals. As you come down, add more and more dark blue. Make sure the petal stands out from the one in front of it. Turquoise for your light color.

You will want an alternative aqua for more color play. Mix ultramarine blue and green with a bit of white and come along the outside edge of your petal into the corner. Blending wet into wet, exaggerating the elements of the flower. Phthalo green and purple for deepest shadows. Not too much water.

Come back with any colors you need to reinforce your progress before stepping back to compare it to your reference. If you painted something out, just come back in and add it back in. No worries.

5. BRINGING LIFE

To bring your rose to life you will want to play shadow against light to form separate delicate petals. The petals curve and roll so don't forget to catch those shadows. For the large outer petals, use diox and a bit of green for the shadow and then get magenta and blend that in. Very unexpected. Wipe off any excess on your brush and soften hard lines.

If you're not already on the #8 cat's tongue, you can switch and work the toe with a mix of magenta and white on the outer edge with very little water and blend wet into wet. Pink and white for some soft drama, light pressure.

6. OOOOMPH

As we continue to resolve, we need to work this nice folded out petal so get some purple, and catch the deep shadow along the inside. Come back with phthalo blue and phthalo green and blend.

Contemplate your progress. Do you feel like you have enough magenta on your petals? Does the underside of your curved petals show shadow and does the uppermost edge show highlight? Get back into the pure magenta and blend in to any of the petals that need more oooomph. Add white when necessary, wet into wet. Wiping out your brush and changing water when necessary. Find a zone and play with it in the zone, small steps. It's your rose, be happy with it.

Refer to your reference and remember that you can always go back to video my video at any time for additional support.

7. EXTREME FINISH AND SIGNATURE

Extreme highlights and shadows will really refine our beauty, so go into the black and get a little purple, almost a periwinkle lavender. With the #4 round, just put that on the lip edge of the rose. A little fine line. Thin your paint with water if you need to. Light pressure, curved strokes, paying attention to the shape of the rose. A little bit of dry brush highlight in places. Bright highlights with diox and magenta, some white. Dry brush with the lightest of touches. Catch those shadows with your turquoise and deep aqua. Edge those little pink areas with aqua - outstanding.

Step back and compare your painting to the reference. Is there anything you feel needs refining? Use your reference for that final check.

8. SIGNATURE

Sign your name to your incredible painting and please share it with the community.

SWATCHING PRACTICE PAGE

1. Practice mixing the colors from todays palette and paint in your circles with your colors.
2. Check your values and hue by swatching your paint mixes on the sample images.
3. Do a tiny fast grey scale sketch to help you express light and shadow - use paint or pencil, either is fine.

TRACEABLE

THE ART SHERPA

BALLET SHOES

COLOR PALETTE:  

Today's color palette is Mars Black, Burnt Sienna, Ultramarine Blue, Phthalo Green, Cad Yellow Medium, Naples Yellow Light, Cad Red Medium, Quinacridone Magenta, and Titanium White.

1. BACKGROUND AND GRID

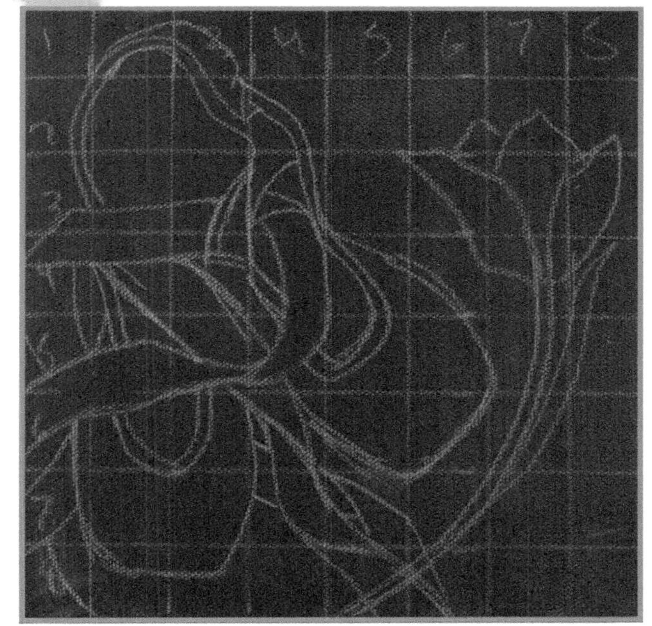

COLOR MIX: Ultramarine blue and burnt sienna. Get some water on your background brush, just enough to help your paint flow. Paint your entire surface. Dry completely.

GRID: With your t-square and chalk, create a 1" x 1" grid on your canvas. Number the squares across the top 1 - 8 and along the left side, top to bottom, 1 - 8. Duplicate the image exactly as shown in the reference, one square at a time. Only draw what's in that square before you move on.

2. THE BACKGROUND AND FURTHEST

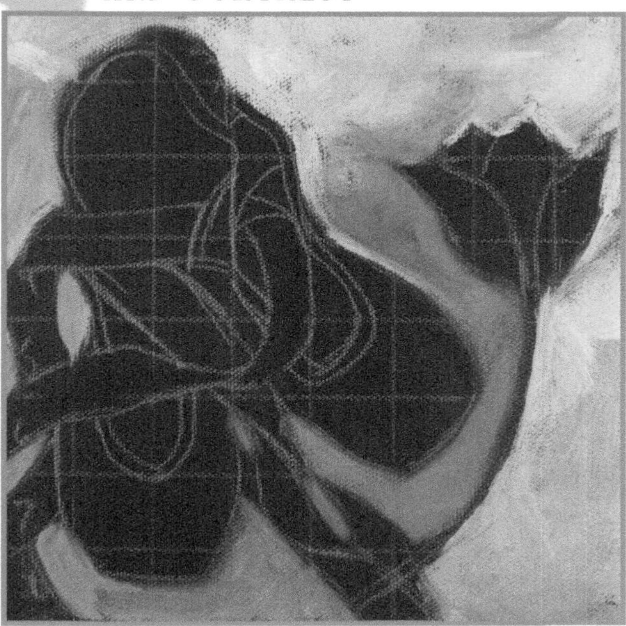

With the # 8 bright, and no excess water, get white and some ultramarine blue and make a light value blue hue. With relaxed, loose stokes, paint in your background. Try not to paint out the chalk lines you need for your ribbons and shoes, but if you do, you can always draw it back in. Adding more blue to your mix and going around the side of objects will add dimension as defined by shape and contour. Put this darker value in around the tulip and where the leaves will go. Add even more blue for darker values where you see them on your reference.

Check your reference. Have you gone around the ribbons? Does the background poke through the little areas in between the ribbons? Are there Shadows? because objects are blocking a small amount of light?

3. ADDING AN ELEMENT, INSOLES, HIGHLIGHTS, AND SHADOWS

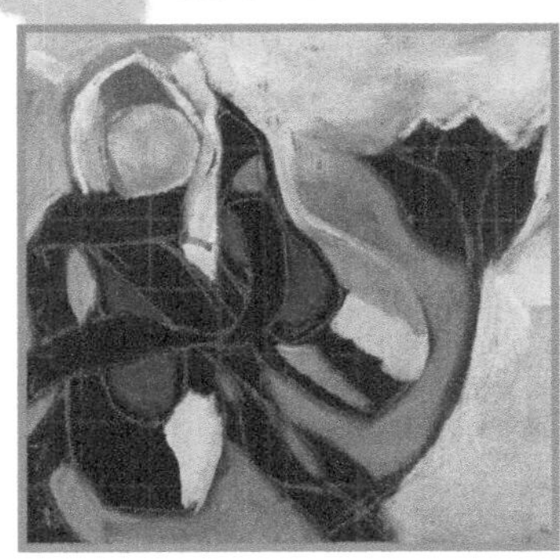

This is a big step, and you will want to have your reference handy. With your #6 bright, get white and very little quin magenta. Come into the inside of the shoe and work that out. As the insoles come forward, they get darker, use sharp, clean lines. With ultramarine and quin, perhaps some brown, take that to the inside to devalue our crumbled up ballet slippers. A little bit of white to the hue in places. The base seems to have a rose/mauve kind of reflection, so we need deeper values. A little lighter on the heel, darker at the toe. Rinse out often and clean your water.

Mix your pinks, take quin and cad red for one of your pink base mixes. Add naples yellow to some of that pink for another pink base. Adding white to each of these mixes will make them brighter. Add that lighter value as reflections on the shoes where you see them on your reference. You might want to take your value almost to white in places. More magenta into the pink mixes for darker values. Check your reference for where they go. You can add some cad yellow for another interesting value. Play with these values against each other. Refer to your reference to help you with color placement. Your shoes are glossy and satin, and your highlights are how you portray that. Stand back every so often and check your progress. Don't forget the top of the ballet slipper has a roll, with a little gathered edge.

4. BLOCKING IN DARK & LIGHT VALUES AND RIBBON

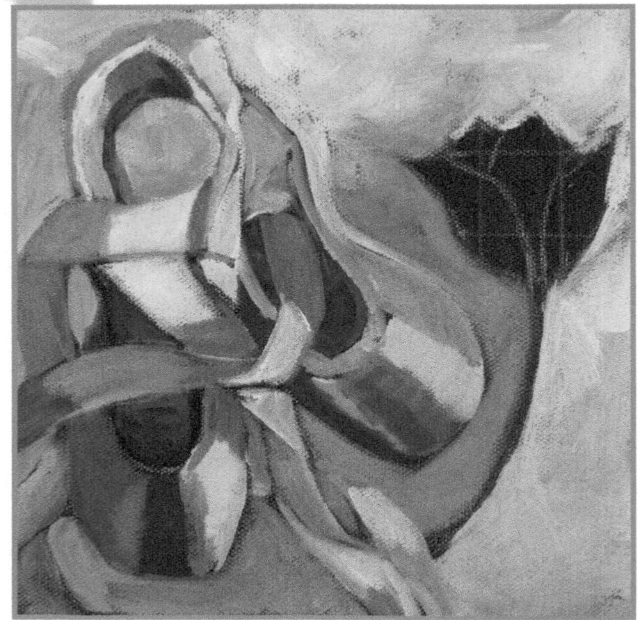

Remember not to overwork yourself or stress yourself out. Just work through the zones of each step and trust that the end will reveal a wonderful piece. Mix a little more magenta into the shoe mix with some naples, and a smidge of brown for a pretty dark satin value. Add that in and don't hesitate to add more white or brown if you need to. Still on the #6 Bright, does your ribbon have light and dark values where it should or do you need to add purple into the ultramarine or magenta for a value different from diox purple. Make any adjustment that you feel you need. Adding dark shadows and lighter highlights. White into naples for highlights. This is a very visual step. Step away often and assess. Let your reference be your friend. Do your brush strokes help define the flow of the object? Where there is a highlight, is there also shadow? Taking it slow. Using all our colors and values to refine our ballet slippers. Try making half tones, tones, and mid-tones.

5. BALLET SLIPPERS

With the #4 round, continue to refine the shoe with a mix of naples and cad yellow and address the brighter aspects of the binding and highlights. Put in some lighter pink highlights. Not quite yellow white highlights. Painting the edges of the highlights with brighter hues. Stepping back and assessing. Pink to capture the structural elements of the slippers. Magenta and the base mix for shadows.

Relax and enjoy this step but constantly looking for what you can take, what do you need to take away. Play with it.

Use your reference photo as a guide. Evaluate.

6. REFINING SHADOWS AND LINES

Let's put in more shadows, refine lines, and get some control. Get quin magenta into ultramarine with a titch of sienna and put back any strong bits of shadows, recapturing any bits you may have painted out. Maybe you need more magenta. Do your stitches have shadows? Mixing cad into quin for a shadow mix. You have shadow value and hue choices to make. Let dry and assess again. Come in with a little ultramarine and white and make any additional highlights you need. Some pure white highlights. You have finished the slippers, time to assess and see if you are where you think you need to be before moving to the tulip.

Refer to your reference and remember that you can always go back to video my video at any time for additional support.

7. TULIP

Mix phthalo green and burnt sienna for a deep green and paint in the stem, coming over the ribbons. Paint in some long, thin leaves and use shadows and highlights. Press and twirl as leaves tend to open much like a petal. Get some cad yellow in that green and add that to the stem. Work out highlights and lowlights in the green bits. Stems and leaves have shadows.

For the flower, rinse your brush and mix some quin and a smidge of cad yellow into the center petal and the side petals. Don't hesitate to use ultramarine blue for the shadow along the stem, and yellow and white for bright highlights. A very easy, soothing step.

We're almost done here. Step back and compare your painting to the reference. Is there anything you feel needs refining and are you ready for the next step? Use your reference.

8. TULIP AND SIGNATURE

Finish your tulip with white with a titch of pink, maybe some naples yellow to make it less bright. Come underneath the flower and brush forward. Maybe add a bit of that yellow green from the leaves. Control the values. Blending back, feathered blending. Come back with white for focus. A little naples yellow, bits of green. Pinker hues in some places and whiter hues in other places. Deeper pink on the inside petal. The ridge should have highlights. Ultramarine and quin magenta for that wonderful purple for shadows.

Is there anything you feel needs refining? Use your reference for that final check.

9. SIGNATURE

Sign your name to your incredible painting and please share it with the community. You should be very proud of yourself.

SWATCHING PRACTICE PAGE

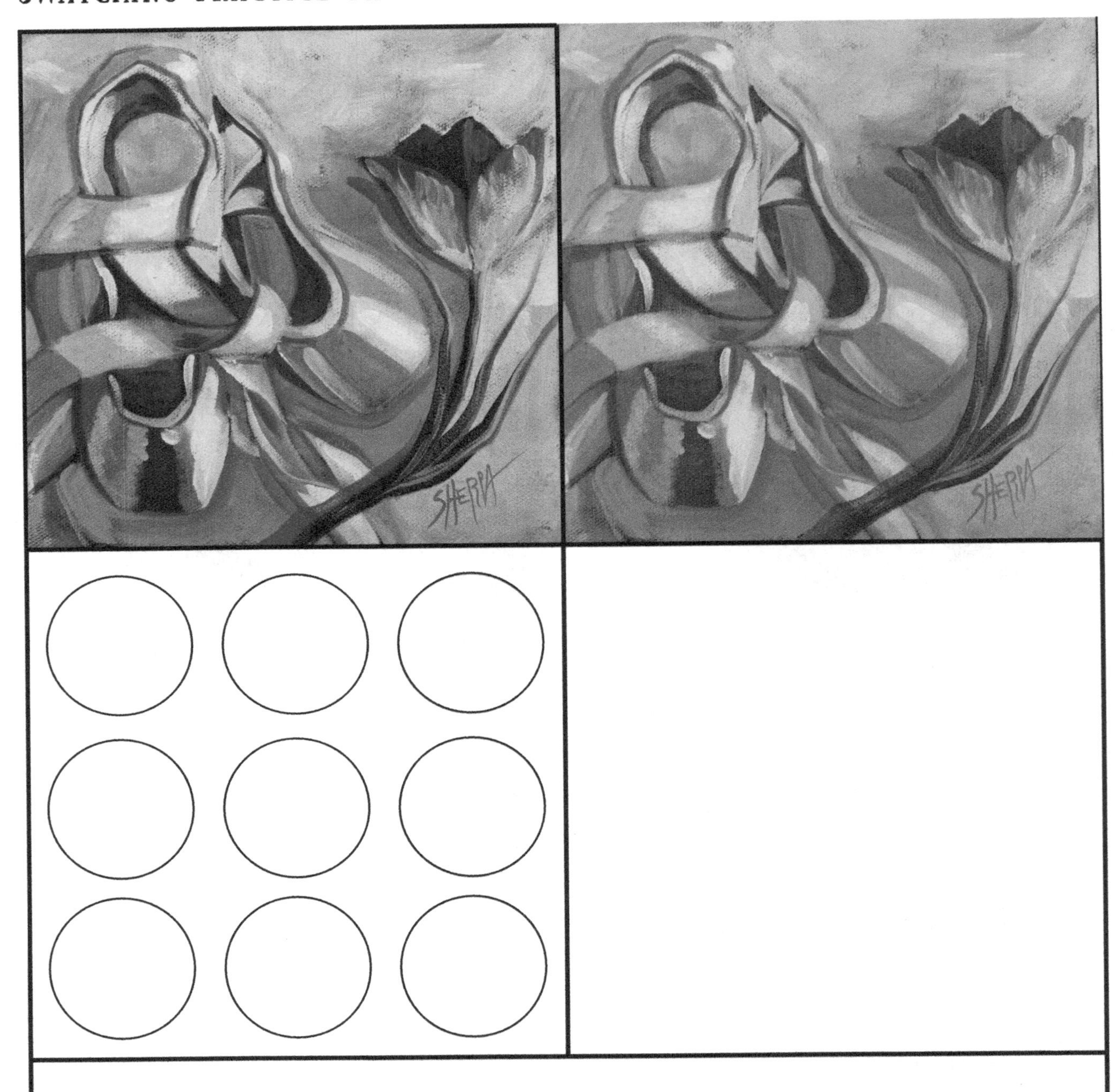

1. Practice mixing the colors from todays palette and paint in your circles with your colors.
2. Check your values and hue by swatching your paint mixes on the sample images.
3. Do a tiny fast grey scale sketch to help you express light and shadow - use paint or pencil, either is fine.

TRACEABLE

THE ART SHERPA

RED FOX

COLOR PALETTE:     

Today's color palette is Phthalo Blue, Mars Black, Burnt Sienna, Cad Yellow Medium, Cad Red Medium, Naples Yellow Light, and Titanium White.

1. BACKGROUND AND GRID

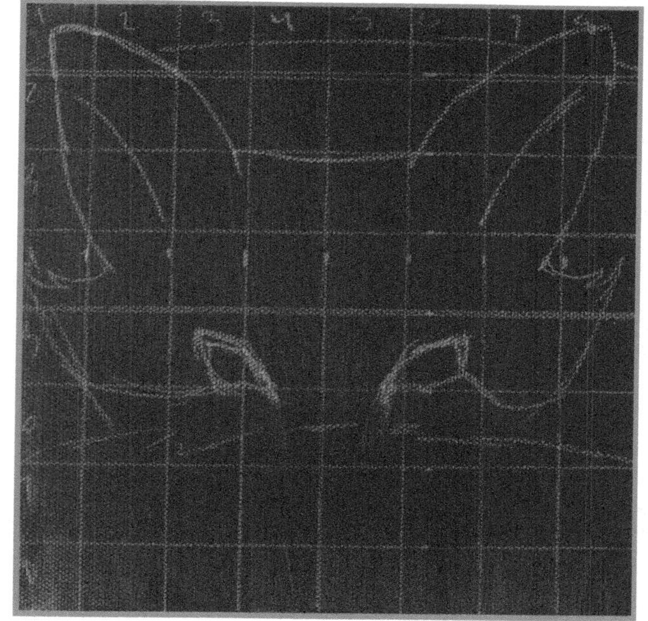

With your biggest damp brush, mix burnt sienna and black to a deep chocolate brown and paint the entire canvas.

Let dry and when you dry, even on low heat with a hairdryer, remember to allow the canvas to cool completely before moving on. With your t-square and chalk, create a 1" x 1" grid on your canvas, number the top squares 1 - 8 and the side squares 1 - 8. Using the reference, duplicate the image exactly as shown in the reference, one square at a time. Only draw what's in that square before you move on.

2. DISTANT AND OUT OF FOCUS

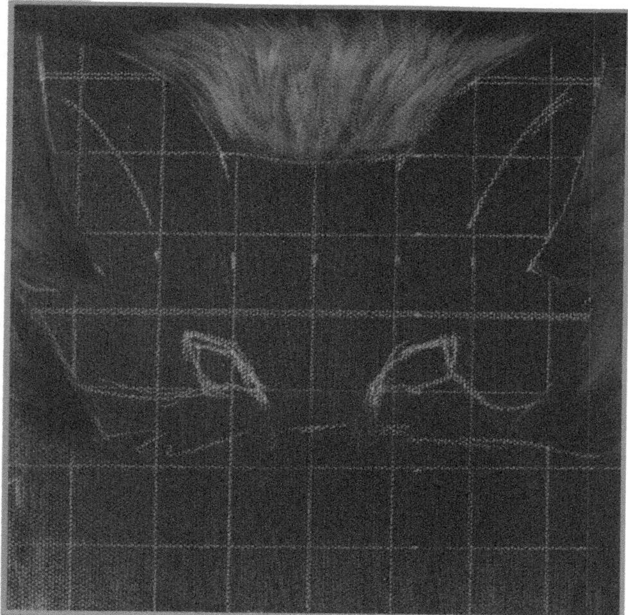

Dampen the #8 Cambridge, and mix cad yellow and cad red with a bit of sienna to a distance orange, maybe more to the red. Across the top of the background, out of focus, short upward strokes that lend themselves to fur, feathering.

As you come forward, add more brown to the mix to bring the fur forward. Perhaps black and brown again coming from the back, really defining those edges where his fur is. Flicking in shadows and subtle changes. Get brown, yellow, and red and bring the fur around the sides. Add some naples yellow for another fur mix. Still staying distant, blurry, and out of focus.

Refer to your reference.

4. EARS AND FUR

In this order, get some black with a touch of brown for a dark gray, a dark value for the ears. With flicking strokes, paint the inside ear line, and along the outer edges to the tip. Add a bit of white and flick in some gray. Red and naples for the lighter edge. Now rinse all the pigment out of the brush.

Get back into the gray, maybe with a bit of blue, brush should be dry, and go back in the opposite direction with your strokes. Redefine that dark part if you need to. Curve the brush strokes to imply fur. Maybe yellow and red and temper with brown. Layering and bringing hair up into the ear.

Wipe your brush out again and grab red and yellow toned with brown for the richer inside of the ear. Clean out your brush water through this step as necessary. Refer to your reference if you need help with this step.

5. FURRY FURRY FUR

Now we move to the hairs under the eye. Brown with cad red and a little yellow for a brighter orange. Dry brush this color fur under his eyes and maybe brush a little into his head using arabesques and s-curves. Do the hairs reflect movement above and around his eyes?

Rinse your brush and mix cad yellow, naples and a bit of red brush this over his eyes, more arabesques and s-curves over and between his eyes. Add some red for another fur color and flick in some more fur. Losely mixed color mixtures, plenty of s-curved strokes. With an unwiped brush, grab some white and add tips to the guard hairs.

Rinse your brush really well. With brown and black, add some darker bits of hair. With your round brush, outline the contour of his eyes and all the way to the edges with black and a bit of brown.

Come back with any colors you need to reinforce your progress before stepping back to compare it to your reference. If you painted something out, just come back in and add it in when you can. No worries.

5. MORE FUR - TAIL

Brown and cad yellow with a little white, at the tear duct, brushing up in the direction that fur grows. Mix brown and cad yellow for the first layer on that nose. Red and yellow fur again. That off color we used before for the lighter fur, in the center a bit.

For the fox tail, burnt sienna and cad yellow, deepend with the gray if you need, and bring that tail across. Add some lighter values for contrast. The tail hair goes in many directions.

Rinse out and get some black and brown on the guard hairs. It's lighter on the underside against his nose. Get all these deep dark values in Mr. Fox. Don't be afraid of pure black. Lots of arabesque stroves, s-curves and calligraphy marks. A bit of drama with white. Our neutral white from earlier. Mostly a dry brush effect. Don't paint out the black guard hairs.

Use your reference photo as a guide. Evaluate.

6. MR. FOX'S FINALE

The eyes tell the story of the soul, so grab your #4 and make sure it has a nice point. Come into the tear duct with black and flip out some lashes. Below the eye is darker. You're not giving him eyelashes, you are just exaggerating. Mix a bright orange for the center orbs of his eyes. This is going to make them glow, add a touch of sienna. Shade the eye with some brown and black. The lids tend to cast a lot more shadow that you think. With just black and on the tip of your round brush but in his pointed pupils. Come in with blue and black and quite a bit of white to a light blue gray and put in the little highlights, some bright bright white highlights.

Refer to your reference and remember that you can always go back and watch video at any time for additional support. Step back and compare your painting to the reference. Is there anything you feel needs refining?

9. SIGNATURE

Sign your name to your incredible painting and please share it with the community. You should be very proud of yourself and Mr. Fox.

SWATCHING PRACTICE PAGE

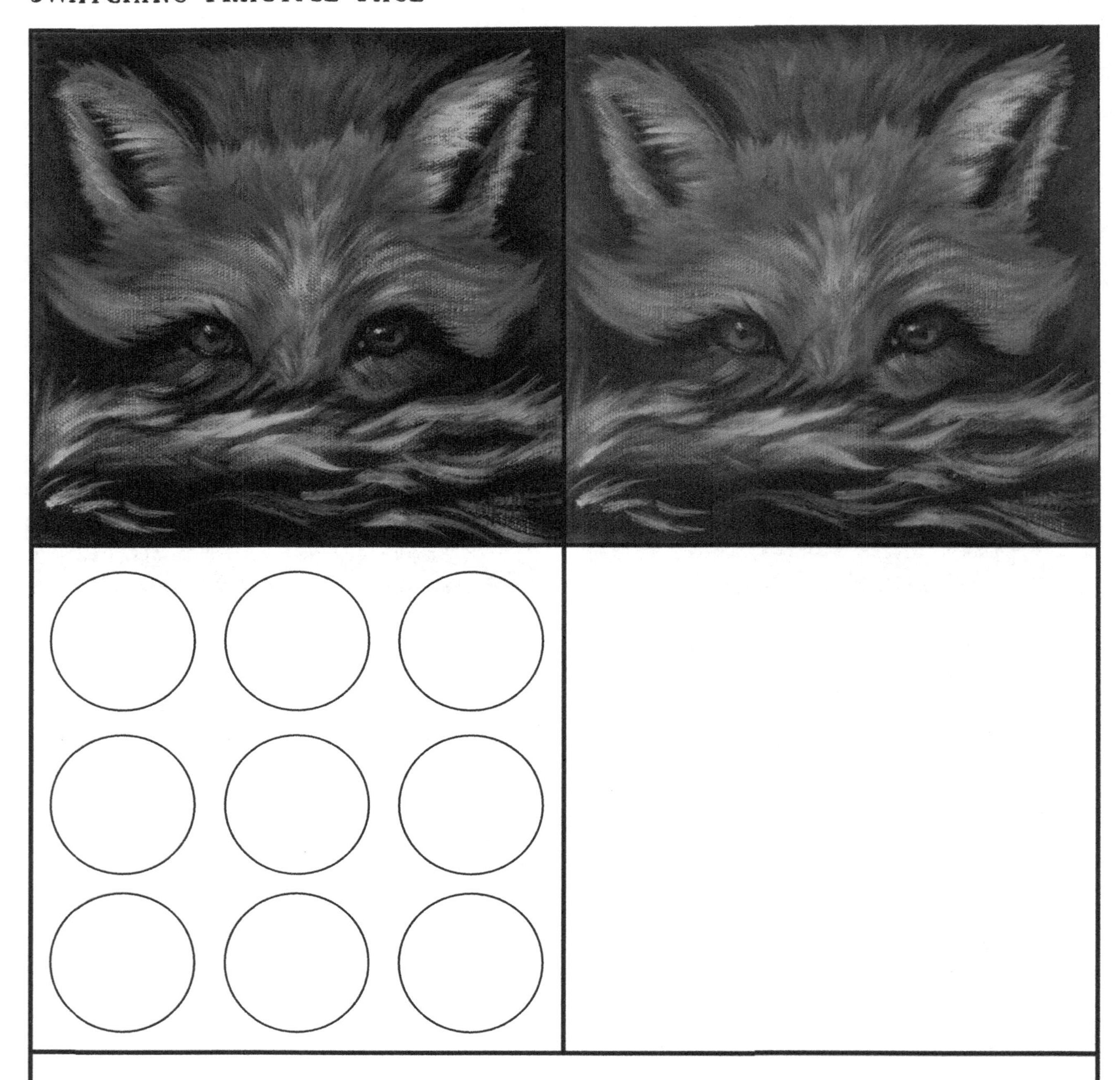

1. Practice mixing the colors from todays palette and paint in your circles with your colors.
2. Check your values and hue by swatching your paint mixes on the sample images.
3. Do a tiny fast grey scale sketch to help you express light and shadow - use paint or pencil, either is fine.

TRACEABLE

THE ART SHERPA

GIRL IN HAT

COLOR PALETTE:           

Today's color palette is Mars Black, Burnt Sienna, Cad Yellow medium, Quinacridone magenta, Cad Red Medium, Naples Yellow Light, Phthalo Blue, Phthalo Green, Dioxazine Purple, and Titanium White.

1. BACKGROUND AND GRID

With your damp big brush, paint the entire surface of the canvas block. Put out more black on your pallet if you need it.

Let dry and when you dry, even on low heat, with a hairdryer, remember to allow the canvas to cool completely before moving on. With your t-square and chalk, create a 1" x 1" grid on your canvas, number the top squares 1 - 8 and the side squares 1 - 8. Using the reference, duplicate the image exactly as shown in the reference, one square at a time. Only draw what's in that square before you move on.

2. SKIN VALUES

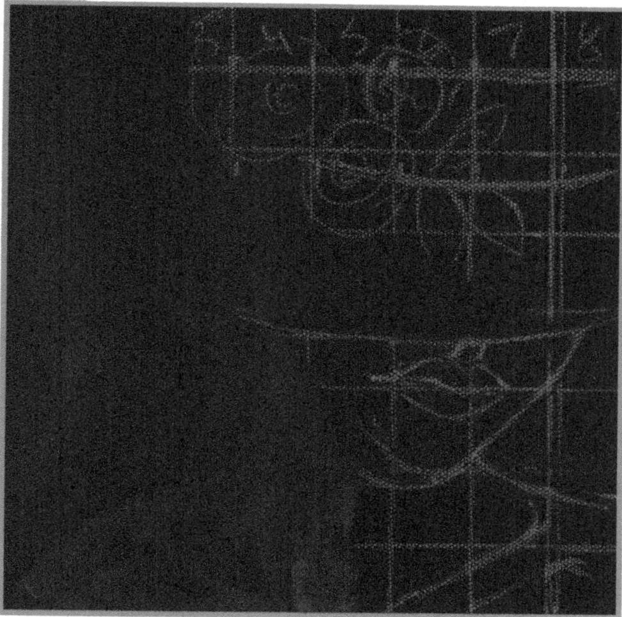

Most of this picture is in shadow, but let's talk skin tones, which are a combination of reds, yellows, browns and white and always best if you have a master mix. Mix your master skin tone with quin and naples yellow, maybe a smidge of cad yellow to warm it up, and you have a nice lip color. Add a little bit of brown for warmer tones. Add more yellow if you need it, or more brown or white to get these tones to the hue you want.

Take your base skin tone and add either blue or black to darken it to be just lighter than where you will begin to paint her in, making subtle changes and blend into the background. I actually started with black, a very dark value, on the #8 Cambridge, and catch her body fading into the background. Hint at a bit of delicate collar bone. Some elements will be delicate and subtle, not big changes and not in huge amounts. Catch those shadows, and imply a tendon in the neck. White is a great highlight, just a hint, not big somethings. Make sure you've got some good shading and blending happening right up to the chin. Where you need to come in with a darker value, you just add more black and blend into the background.

3. SHADOWS AND HIGHLIGHTS

For shadows and highlights around the face and neck, go back into the black and skin tone and start adding those warmer highlights coming forward. Don't be afraid to add more black if you need to, but do paint the brush in a curve down manner, the direction of your brush strokes does impact things. A warm shadow under the lip and under the brim, around the chin, on the collar bone. Darker on her shoulder, and working lighter and lighter on the skin tone as you move out of the shadows. You'll want dark and light values in the divot above the nose, and on the shoulder.

Switch to a flat brush for control in needed. As you come forward into the full skin tones, add more white, maybe even yellow. Come back with the Cambridge if you need to soften. Don't be afraid to get scruffy with your brush. The chin seems to be directly in light, but the tone is dark under the chin. This is a big step, so try to stay loose. Be easy on yourself and play with your tones and hues.

It's the moment to kind of introduce yourself to the idea of skin tones and values in relationship to human faces. Refer to your reference.

4. REFINING THE FACE

As we continue to refine, switch brushes if you need to between your #6 Bright and the #4 round. Start with the divot shadows that pull into the hat. One side is slightly lighter. Lighter skin values come in as we move into the light. The divot needs to taper a bit, otherwise it's just overwhelming in it's divotness. Back to the base skin tone, maybe more magenta and white for our light value. Capture those senses of light on the face. A lot more naples and white for a high reflection. The chin has a reflection. Just trying to find that balance between shadow and light. Clean up your black line along her face if you need to. Clean out your water when it needs it.

Come back with any colors you need to reinforce your progress before stepping back to compare it to your reference. If you painted something out, just come back in and add it in when you can. No worries.

5. Lips, Shiny Reflective Lips

First the lips will start with a master mix of cad red and magenta, to the magenta side, deepened with black. Get enough water for flow. Arc that little bow up. The lower lip curves down a bit. Where the lips join is quite in shadow. Get the shadows in for now. Lighten that color up a little, rinse out, and get more cad in your base for the center. Just a bit brighter. Catch the little curved strokes, leaving some of the darkest value showing. A titch in the center of the lips. For a light color, you could add some naples and make small little marks. If you add too much, get some more magenta. Add more cad for the brightest lip color. Make them glowing, full lips. The last bit is highlights with a bit of magenta and a lot of white. Get those shiny reflections. With naples and a lot of white, get the top of the lip, on the skin, highlight it just a bit.

Use your reference photo as a guide. Evaluate.

6. Hat and Flowers

With the #6 bright and blue and black, paint the hat band. You will paint your flowers back in after the layer dries. Highlight mix can start with blue, a little black, and white. Keep your hat in the blue ranges, even the highlights, where the most light hits the hat. Be light and subtle on the brim, just a little of it is showing. Back into the black to help the hat have a clean line. Try not to be overly harsh or judgmental of your art.

For the leaves and flowers, mix your darkest green value with green and sienna. Little pulled in leaves. Naples and yellow for reflections as they come forward. The center of the rose begins with quin, and a smidge of naples. Our flowers have very tight petals and we may only catch some of them on the tip. Use small round brush strokes. More naples yellow to lighten, more on the outside. Warmer in front, so more naples and white in the front. Add some smaller, lighter highlights to show just the tips of the petals. Don't forget to add some thoughtful little buds. Does the shadow of her face and the shadow of the rose match?

7. Final Touches and Signature

Dry your canvas. Take some blue and purple, tiny bit of white loosely mixed, and put in some little flower leaves. This will make an interesting texture in the hat. Phthalo blue and phthalo green and a lot of white, for highlights. These just pop when they have a highlight on them with white and yellow. She is a moody girl with a very happy hat. With black, make sure that she has a nice, perfect silhouette. Exaggerating the contrast of some of the flowers.

We're almost done here. Step back and compare your painting to the reference. Is there anything you feel needs refining and are you ready to sign? Use your reference for that final check.

Sign your name to your incredible painting and please share it with the community. You should be very proud of yourself.

SWATCHING PRACTICE PAGE

1. Practice mixing the colors from todays palette and paint in your circles with your colors.
2. Check your values and hue by swatching your paint mixes on the sample images.
3. Do a tiny fast grey scale sketch to help you express light and shadow - use paint or pencil, either is fine.

TRACEABLE

THE ART SHERPA

DESERT SUNSET

COLOR PALETTE:     

Today's color palette is Dioxazine Purple, Quinacridone Magenta, Cad Red Medium, Cad Yellow Medium, Phthalo Blue, Mars Black, and Titanium White.

1. BACKGROUND AND GRID

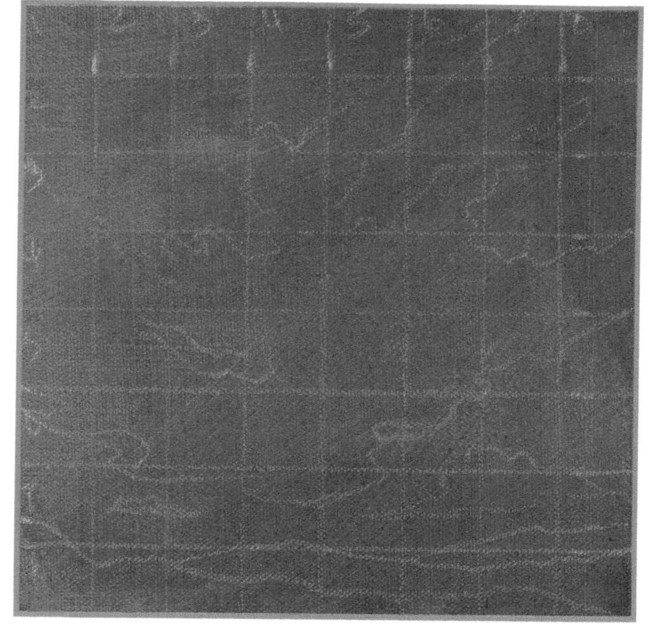

Get your biggest brush and paint the entire surface with quinacridone magenta. All pure pink. Add water to improve the flow.

Let dry and, when you dry the canvas, even on low heat with a hairdryer, remember to allow the canvas to cool completely before moving on. With your t-square and chalk, create a 1" x 1" grid on your canvas, number the top squares 1 - 8 and the side squares 1 - 8. Using the reference, duplicate the image exactly as shown in the reference, one square at a time. Only draw what's in that square before you move on.

2. LAYING IN THE BACKGROUND AND SKY

With the #8 cat's tongue, begin the top left corner of the sky, with some phthalo blue and a smidge of white. Because the quinacridone is underneath, It's going to give us that slightly purple cast. Adding a lot more white, continue to paint in your sky. If you need, make a half mix to blend the center to help make a smooth transition of value. Add some brighter highlights. Softly, with the side of your brush, soften any hard lines. Use your grid and references to help with cloud placement.

3. BRIGHT SKYE

Great tip to keep your colors bright is to have a couple cups of clean water, one for blues and purples, one for reds and yellows. Use some pure cad yellow, and paint in this first layer from the side down along the bottom of the next cloud. The yellow is very transparent, this lets the quinacridone show through. For the next layer, add a lot of white to your cad yellow and start painting in this bright yellow cloud layer. Soften the edges of the two yellow layers together using the edge of your brush. Mix orange with cad red and cad yellow, blend wet into wet for the bright orange layer. Your darkest value is along the mountainscape.

Refer to your reference and go back to the video if you need to. Let dry before you move on.

4. DEEP DARK SKY

In a sunset, the light source is low and clouds actually do block light. They have shadows and highlights. Because the light source is from below, it means that the upside of the clouds, the top of the clouds is quite dark and you'll see some of that. Switch to a #8 Cambridge, which is a mix of hog bristles and synthetics, with short filaments and it's very stiff and scratchy. Get the brush mildly damp. Start with just a little mix of dioxazine purple, quinacridone magenta on the corner of the brush. Scumbling here as you do and some of the pink is going to show through. Work with the purple and the blue water. The brush makes little bits of distant and airy clouds that are maybe not solid. Rinse out very thoroughly. Down low, there are some clouds that are a mix of dioxazine and quinacridone. Wiggling the brush back and forth, making those little wispy clouds.

5. SUNSET CLOUDS

Using the quinacridone, cad red, cad yellow and a small amount of white. More to the quinacridone side in tone. Continue with the #8 Cambridge, hog bristle or scratchy brush you have. Use a wiggling stroke to dry brush this color into your clouds utilizing the reference picture or video as needed.

Come back with any colors you need to reinforce your progress before stepping back to compare it to your reference. If you painted something out, just come back in and add it in when you can. No worries.

6. LANDSCAPE

On this landscape, we want to put some further back mountains, some stuff coming forward, and then little bits of low light trees. Start with a #4 round. Using the purple with a bit of cad red, and even a little cad yellow, grey the mountains a bit.

Now, coming forward, get a little purple and a bit of blue. Don't lighten it too much, but a small amount of white. Just paint that all in. Terrain is the look you want. The last part is the black. Thin the black with water to improve the flow. Do two coats because the first one gives the basic landscape and then the next coat is going to give the depth of the black and show the little plants.

Refer to your reference and remember that you can always go back to video my video at any time for additional support.

7. PAINTING IN THE BODY

Use the #8 cat's tongue and darken up with the black. Paint in the bushes and grasses in the distance. Use your reference photo. Rough up thin branches with the black, just on the very tip of the brush. Then paint in the desert cactus.

8. SIGNATURE

Only thing left to do is sign your incredible painting and please share it with the community. You can be very proud of yourself. So to make the signature line pop and blend well use the blue with a bit of the white.

SWATCHING PRACTICE PAGE

1. Practice mixing the colors from todays palette and paint in your circles with your colors.
2. Check your values and hue by swatching your paint mixes on the sample images.
3. Do a tiny fast grey scale sketch to help you express light and shadow - use paint or pencil, either is fine.

TRACEABLE

THE ART SHERPA

RACCOON IN FLOWERS

COLOR PALETTE:        

Today's color palette is Mars Black, Naples Yellow Light, Cad Yellow Medium, Burnt Sienna, Cad Red Medium, Phthalo Green, Phthalo Blue, and Titanium White.

1. BACKGROUND AND GRID

With your biggest brush dampened, paint the entire canvas with black.

Let dry and, when you dry even on low heat with a hairdryer, remember to allow the canvas to cool completely before moving on. With your t-square and chalk, create a 1" x 1" grid on your canvas, number the top squares 1 - 8 and the side squares 1 - 8. Using the reference, duplicate the image exactly as shown in the reference, one square at a time. Only draw what's in that square before you move on.

2. SETTING THE STAGE

We need to make sure Mr. Raccoon is in a greenery environment, so grab your #8 cat's tongue and mix a bit of your phthalo green and burnt sienna to start putting in the distant greenery. Paint the sides if you'd like but make sure to go down into the corner. Catch those deep green values. Use your reference to help you with placement if you need.

Add some yellow for some of our distant plants, delicate loose lines. More yellow where you need to elude that something is catching the light. Tone yellow with a bit of brown and add this dimmed yellow, even peaking it in places. We don't want him to appear to be "floating", he's in his natural environment.

Allow to dry, change your water if you need to, rinse your brush, and heat up your sippy sippy. Ready for the next step?

3. EVERY STAR NEEDS BLOCKING

Mr. Racoon needs to be blocked in. Start with black and sienna to address his most distant value, working that in. Get his ears, his little nose, that kind of a "panda" patch. Add some yellow to our mix for a neutral fur color and don't forget down the middle of the nose is a little "V" thing. Just blocking in, blending. Even though there will be plants in front, you want continuity. Add some white and work those ears, roughing them in, not too particular yet. Loose little hairs, furry, by no means our lightest value and letting the dark values show. On the nose, we already have black on the canvas, we don't need to repaint the black, just allow for it. More brown where you need it, building those layered fur textures. Work the ears. Very dark on the inside. Create little fur areas. A shadow into his inner ears. Switch to the #4 round for control and thin lines. Feather stroking in places to exaggerate little hair motions. Brown values where we have some shadow. Black with a little blue for a blue-gray color that might be in his fur. Still working the ears, don't forget the black-brown guard hairs.

Rinse out and change your water if you need to. Grab some blue and black with a little white to a cool gray, lightly flicking this around. More little guard hairs that are backlit and shining. Back into black to blend, layering. Not painting every single hair but painting with overall directionality. Yellow and cad red to orange and work that into your brown. Thin your paint if you need. If you paint something out, you can always let the canvas dry and paint it back in. Take your dirty brush and add some white and put a few of that nondescript color in. Play with it.

Refer to your reference as needed. This was a big step. Relax, step back and access your progress.

4. EARS ARE IMPORTANT

Let's continue with the ears and layering in the fur. Be sure to replenish any colors that are low on your pallet. Pay some attention to the nose with your blue-gray. Catch that curve. A little phthalo blue and burnt sienna, maybe more brown. Another gray neutral tone. A great mix for lighting is yellow and brown to a cream color. Dry brush that light color in, up his head, and all those places where you see the lightest values in your reference.

Deep brown and black in those dark shadowy areas. His face has some of that lighter brown fur around the side. Do some individual hairs, play, maybe add some green. Be daring. Try to stay on the toe of the brush. Little fly away hairs happen, are you catching all the little reflections? Blue and black and a touch of white. Pure black where you need the deepest value. Everything around his eyes will be minimal. Find the reflections. A little blue in there. A little gray-blue reflection there. Be subtle. We see his eyes because of the lighting.

5. BUILDING UP A RACOON FACE AND EYES

Let's continue to build up the hair around his cute little face. We are going to do several cool gray mixes to build the layers of fur. With mars black and burnt sienna, using the Cambridge brush. Begin to dry brush this color on his nose in an upward stroke, up in between his eyes, nice fluffy fur up over his eyes. Add some cool gray with phthalo blue, burnt sienna and white. brush some of this lighter fur color up the center of his nose and around the top of the eyes. Next a layer of very dark gray. Repeat these same layers around the sides of his face to fluff him up. Black with just a little brown and take this dark fur color around his eyes flicking, feathering, and layering this last layer over the previous layers. This is a tricky step. Feel free to watch the video for help if you need help.

To begin his eyes, Switch to the #4 round and add little blue hairs under and around the outside of his eyes with a mis of blue and white. Paint the eyes black.

Rinse out. Add some blue gray highlights around the rim of his eyes and then some little white highlights. For the center of his eyes, add a gray, just a little lighter than black, in the center, and then tap in a couple white dots.

Come back with any colors you need to reinforce your progress before stepping back to compare it to your reference. If you painted something out, just come back in and add it in when you can. No worries.

6. THE NOSE AND FINISHING THE FACE

The nose is just a lot of reflection, much like the eye. With the #8 Cambridge, mix some white, naples, and brown, paint more little gray furs. Adding brown and black for value, red, yellow, no rinsing. Be playful, make the fur interesting. Go for shaggy. Blue and white where it pleases you. Trim up the little chin with some dark hairs. Blue, black and white to imply some dark fur in shadow. Naples added as a feather stroke to accentuate that underbite. Pulling darker and darker values so that we see shapes, finding balance. Make the guard hairs fun with maybe a little naples using curvy little s-curve strokes. Defining individual hairs, whimsical and interesting.

If anything gets out of hand just blend it in. Does he feel playful? Does he feel arty? Do you like him?

Refer to your reference and remember that you can always go back to video my video at any time for additional support.

7. RESOLVE BODY FUR AND DEFINE MOUTH

I added a couple little white highlights to his eyes at the beginning of this step before moving on to his body. On the Cambridge brush, mix a very dark color with black and a little blue, dry brush this dark layer of fur below his chin and down the front center of his body.

For the next layer, add white to your brush, you want a light gray fur color. Add that little bit of light gray under his mouth to define. Dry brush some of this light fur color from his shoulder area all the way down the sides of his body. Long flicking strokes creating hair and fur. Play with fur colors and values as you go and make lots of weird little color mixes. Don't worry if your colors don't match mine exactly. The important thing to get is the light and dark values. For his chin, get some little fur layers trimmed and raggedy. Put in that little mouth with a very dark gray and a highlight.

8. GREEN ENVIRONMENT

Time to work on his environment, so grab the #8 cat's tongue, mix green with a bit of burnt sienna, and cad yellow. On the toe of the brush, start encroaching on his space. Building up layers from dark to light. Little leaves touching him and each other. Stems happen. Lighter bits with just cad yellow. Don't paint each individual stem, just the feeling of a stem. Add some white for those highlights where the foliage is just bathed in sunlight. More yellow in places, more white in others. Rinse out. Sienna and cad yellow in front of him.

9. FLOWERS

Now, for the pretty little flowers, you will actually start with a bit of red in the yellow, mixed to orange and create some basic petal shapes. Capture those gestures, pulling the brush around into shapes. Wildflowers do not hide their petals, but sometimes petals get bent in weird ways. Don't make your flowers uniform or regular in any way. Highlight using cad yellow and naples, not on every petal, just where the sun has caught them. Loose. Now the brightest highlights with white and a touch of yellow.

You want the whiskers to really stand out.With the #1 monogrammed liner and yellow and red to orange. little touches. Yellow and white for highlights and reflections. Don't paint every whisker.

10. SIGNATURE

Sign your name to your incredible painting and please share it with the community.

SWATCHING PRACTICE PAGE

1. Practice mixing the colors from todays palette and paint in your circles with your colors.
2. Check your values and hue by swatching your paint mixes on the sample images.
3. Do a tiny fast grey scale sketch to help you express light and shadow - use paint or pencil, either is fine.

TRACEABLE

KOI FISH POND

COLOR PALETTE: 

Today's color palette is: Phthalo Green, Mars Black, Burnt Sienna, Cad Yellow Medium, Naples Yellow Light, Cad Red Medium, Quinacridone Magenta, Phthalo Blue, Ultramarine Blue, and Titanium White.

1. BACKGROUND AND GRID

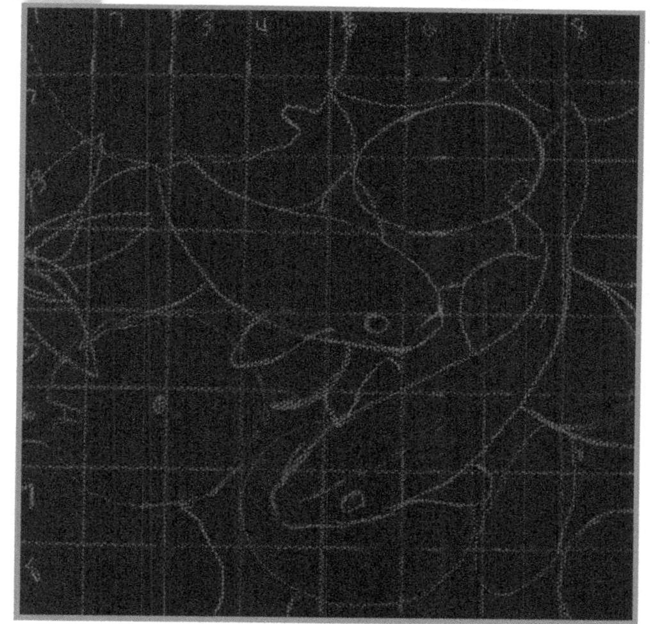

Paint the entire surface of your 8 by 8 canvas, black. So get your big brush, load up your black paint, and paint everything black.

Let dry and when you dry, even on low heat with a hairdryer, remember to allow the canvas to cool completely before moving on. With your t-square and chalk, create a 1" x 1" grid on your canvas, number the top squares 1 - 8 and the side squares 1 - 8. Using the reference, duplicate the image exactly as shown in the reference, one square at a time. Only draw what's in that square before you move on.

2. STONES WITH A DRY BRUSH

To start on our Koi in Lily Pads, begin with a #8 Cambridge and a series of neutral and gray colors, combining black, blue and white. start pulling the color across the stones using a dry brush. Paint all the stones this way making some a little bluer and some with black stripes, flecks or stippling.

Use the reference picture and enjoy making the stones deeper in the water or highlighted with sunlight. Note that some of the stones are made using ultramarine blue, burnt sienna and a bit of cad red.

3. SHADING IN STONES WITH DEEP SHADOWS

Our water and landscape will begin with the #8 Cat's Tongue Brush. Mix phthalo blue, phthalo green and a bit of burnt sienna with a palette knife. The stones edges will be brushed to create a deep value where the shadows are to create depth. A few of the stones will be brushed with a tiny amount of white mixed in. On top of these shadows use a mix of phthalo blue and ultramarine blue with a smidge of burnt sienna and outline the stones creating and casting shadows. Crisping up those lines and paying attention to where shadows might be cast. This color mix will be a bit transparent and that is going to help create deep shadows on the floor and lighter ones that are closer to the surface. Mix the same colors again and add the smallests titch of white, place this around here and there indicating depth levels in your water.

To glaze the stones closer to the water, mix ultramarine blue, phthalo blue and a smidge of brown and make a dark transparent glaze and put show shadows on some of the stones. A dry brush technique will help create this effect. Refer to your reference

4. RIPPLING LIGHT

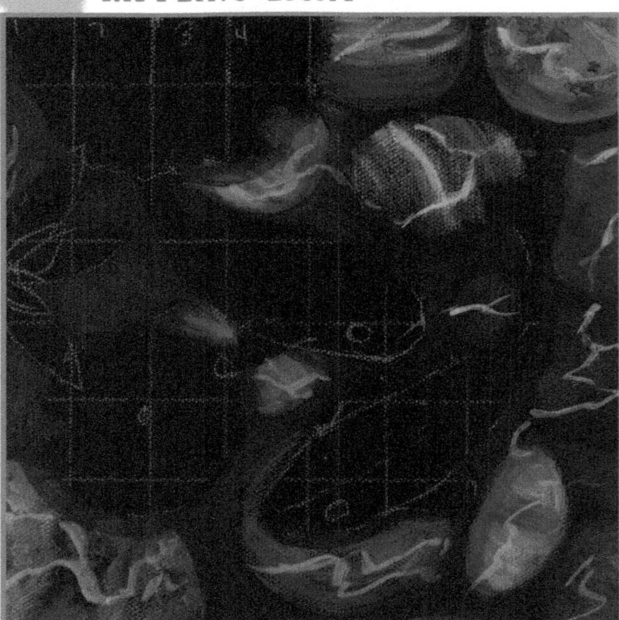

Rippling light and drop shadows from the fish are super dramatic touches. Mix a very light yellow with cad yellow and white. On the toe of the #8 cat's tongue begin to place ribbons of light onto the rocks and water. Lighten with naples if you want too. Water is a lens and it ripples. It breaks and casts a light onto the rocks. More white where you need it. Maybe a bit of yellow. Reflecting light. Relaxed. You can come back with a little phthalo blue and phthalo green to glaze some area where maybe the shadow is. Just a smidge of black for the deepest deepest deep water.

5. FISH

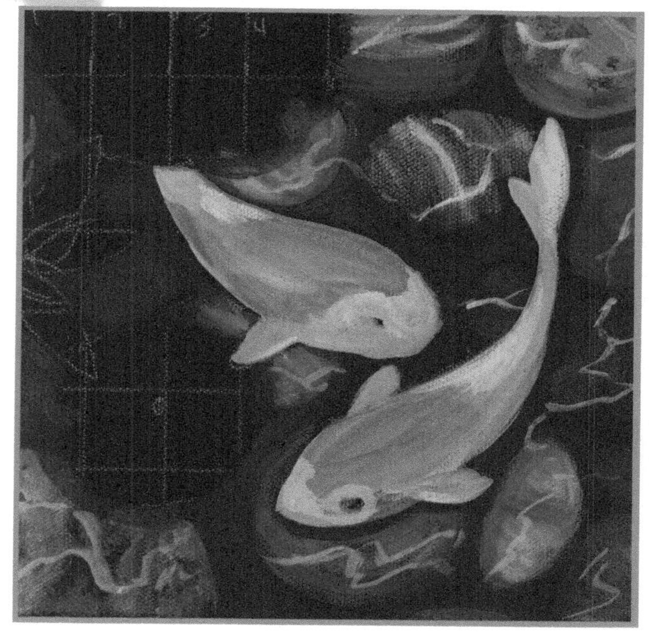

The fish tones are made with quinacridone magenta and cad red with more quin than cad. Adding naples and white to make it a peachy color. Paint the fish this base color. Leave the eye black and unpainted. I went ahead and drew in my large scale pattern and then on the #4 round paint in the large white ccales as shown or as you designed. Add a touch of ultramarine into your mix for a shadow color. Pay attention to the depth of the water. Some of the fish near the top will be lighter with deeper tones underneath. Use the reference photo and evaluate.

6. PATTERNING THE FISH

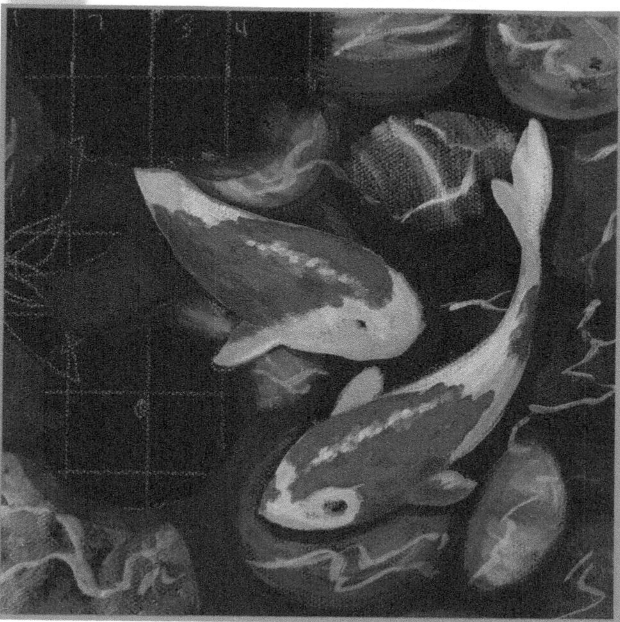

Fish scales are cad red and cad yellow, and sometimes a touch of magenta, this will be our scale patterning color. Tap out some short little brush strokes that imply scales. More magenta where you need it, use bright oranges. The top will be brighter, but the brightest highlight color will come later. Get the pattern in. Maybe some implied red on sides in shadow. The more orange scales are cad red and cad yellow. Make little interesting in and out patterns. More yellow here. Tap, tap, tap. A little strippling. More red in places, more magenta in others. Yellow and white for the bright and shiny scales and reflections, mix the two for the nearly white highlights along the spine. Where does the light hit the scales?

Rinse out and check your water. Breathe. Don't forget to use your reference.

7. LIGHTEST HIGHLIGHTS

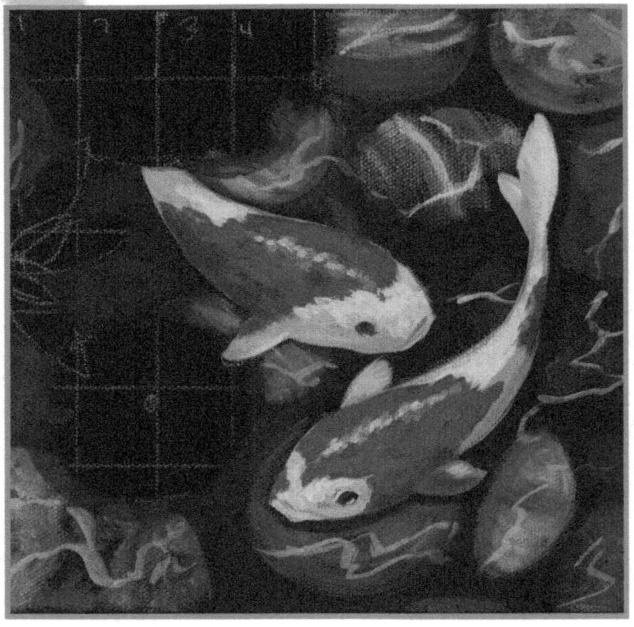

Come back with a bright white (not pure white just yet) and catch the center of our nearest Koi's back and shape out his face. Maybe a highlight on the tail or the edge of a fin. Brighter pink where necessary. Over the eye, feathering that a bit. A little more yellow white for a little warmer glow of reflection. Blue and black, thined, for the eyes. The eyes are just little squished circles. Bright white where it needs to be. Use the reference for placement. Add the little lips and little blue highlights to the eyes.

8. REFLECTIONS, LILY PADS AND LILY PAD REFLECTIONS

For rippling water reflections over the fish, repeat step 4 and add some rippling reflections on your fish. Make your shadow glaze color and add a few more shadows.

Switch to the #8 Cambridge for texture and dry brush in lily pad Shadows with a dark mix of green and brown. The lily also casts a shadow across the fish and covers one of the fins. Pulling the brush strokes in towards the center. Grab some cad yellow to the green for the brighter green part of the center of the lily. Catch the fin's reflection on that leaf. A leaf comes over a part of the fin in another place. Look for those little shadows in the reference if you need help. The fish cast shadows onto the stones that are underneath them. Be sure your brushstrokes are radiating out in a fan-ish way.

9. LILY PADS

With the #8 cat's tongue, yellow and green, for the brightest of bright greenery highlights, you'll add some radial patterns. Add bits of wrinkles and play with these highlights on the edge of the brush, leaving dark shadows in between. Naples and white for a bright color on the center of the lily. Where is the lily in sunlight? Very light pressure. Play with the lily until you are happy. Be random in color placement. Paint all the highlights.

We're almost done with the tutorial. Step back and compare your painting to the reference. Is there anything you feel needs refining and are you ready for the next step? Use your reference for that final check.

10. FLOWER

We are going to stack the layers of petals, bottom to top. Mix ultramarine and quin, to dark purple,a bit of white, add water for flow if needed. Paint the first layer of petal. Next layer of smaller petals is magenta and naples and comes between the purple petals. Add a lot of white to that same color mix and paint those petals. You are stacking. Naples and white to highlight some of the edges. Blend if necessary, crisp up where you want definition. Mix an orangey yellow and bring that into the center. Your naples and white for a highlight.

11. SIGNATURE

Sign your name to your incredible painting and please share it with the community.

SWATCHING PRACTICE PAGE

1. Practice mixing the colors from todays palette and paint in your circles with your colors.
2. Check your values and hue by swatching your paint mixes on the sample images.
3. Do a tiny fast grey scale sketch to help you express light and shadow - use paint or pencil, either is fine.

TRACEABLE

COLORFUL DOG

COLOR PALETTE:          

Todays Color Palette is: Phthalo Blue, Mars Black, Titanium White' Phthalo Green, Burnt Sienna, Naples Yellow Light, Cad Medium Yellow, Cad Medium Red, Quinacrodone Magenta, and Dioxazine Purple

1. BACKGROUND AND GRID

COLOR MIX: Mix a cool blue gray with phthalo blue, black and some white. Get some water on your background brush, just enough to help your paint flow. Paint your entire surface. Dry Completely.

GRID: With your t-square and chalk, create a 1" x 1" grid on your canvas. Number the squares across the top 1 - 8, and along the left side, top to bottom, 1 - 8. Duplicate the image exactly as shown in the reference, one square at a time. Only draw what's in that square before you move on. Take a deep breath and remember, if you have to change any lines, the chalk is removed easily with just a damp brush and clean water.

2. BLOCKING IN BASE FUR LAYER

For this step we will be mixing many warm and cool fur colors. We will use the value of these light and dark colors to build the base layer of his fur with lots of energetic, directional, c-curves, s-curves, arabesque stokes and long flicking strokes. First, base fur mix is red, cad yellow and brown. With the #8 cat's tongue brush, begin at the top of his upper ear and flick in some directional fur. This fur mix can be lightened and darkened to create variation with more brown or more red. Play and get those darker base values in. Use the reference photo to help with placement.

For the lighter fur mix, add more yellow and some white into the mix and come under the ear and over the top of his shoulder. Use curving directional strokes to show how the fur is almost curling around his face.

3. COLORFUL VALUE

Mix cad yellow, red, naples yellow and some white to a very light color. I used this on the tip of his shoulder and under his upper ear. More of this light fur on the top of his head, flicking those energetic flying fur strokes that imply direction and movement. For the colorful shoulder, add a lot of cad yellow to the light fur color, warming it to bright yellow and add a layer just on top of the light fur and then add red for a bright orange layer. Under his chin is very dark. Mix blue into purple with a bit of white so it shows,and begin making long curved directional strokes from under his chin all the way down, curving lines. Get lots more blue on your brush with a touch of white and add some of those long splashy dark blue strokes. For that bright green layer, mix green-brown and even just a bit of cad yellow, making a very dark mix. Put in some nice long dark green fur then come back add some more yellow and some white to lighten it.

Remember to check your reference and even go back and watch the video again to help you with placement for all these splashy colors.

4. MORE SPLASHY COLORS

For the bright pink in his upper ear, mix cad red into quin magenta for a dark value and then add naples yellow and a bit of white for that lovely light pink value. With a little more naples, make a peachy pink for the top of his head, wispy splashy fur. More bits of yellows on his ear. Keep your water clean to keep colors vibrant.

Rinse and wipe your brush when you need. Under his jaw, mix turquoise with phthalo blue and phthalo green for a dark value. Add naples yellow and white for a very light turquoise for his face and around his eye.Be playful and look for places these colors will be fun. Check the reference to see if there are any adjustments you want to make.

5. NOSE AND TEETH

Switch to the #4 round and mix blue and black, a very deep color, paint in his mouth and flick in those tiny little eyelashes. Use this dark color to put in that dark shadow where his other eye is, and his nose. Dark shadows on his nose and mouth with purple and then a highlight that lower lip.

Look for those bright yellow orange reflections that pop, just little highlights. Light gray for those fun crazy teeth. Check your reference and make any changes you need.

6. FINISHING SPLASHES OF COLOR

Go back and get that lovely pink, mixing some cad red into quinn, and some bright oranges for his other ear. Layer some beautiful bright yellow highlights on top of that with cad yellow, naples yellow and white. Use warm and cool colors next to each other. Cad red, quinn for the dark reddish pink under the lower eye, blend a little blue into the corner of that eye for a shadow. Flick in some deep orangey reds and then some lighter value layers. Be playful and enjoy him. Check the reference photo for help and remember you can watch the video.

7. THE WATER SPLASHES

Make a very light blue and on the tip of either brush, begin to dot in the water splashing off Mr. Cuteness. The trick is to have big and small, misshapen water marks. Some that are lighter and others are darker to say that some of the water is more in shadow, like under his chin. Some water droplets are heavier and some are just teeny tiny dots. Step back and take a look. Is your fur and your water sort of circling around his face?

9. SIGNATURE

Sign your name to your incredible painting and please share it with the community. I hope you are pleased.

SWATCHING PRACTICE PAGE

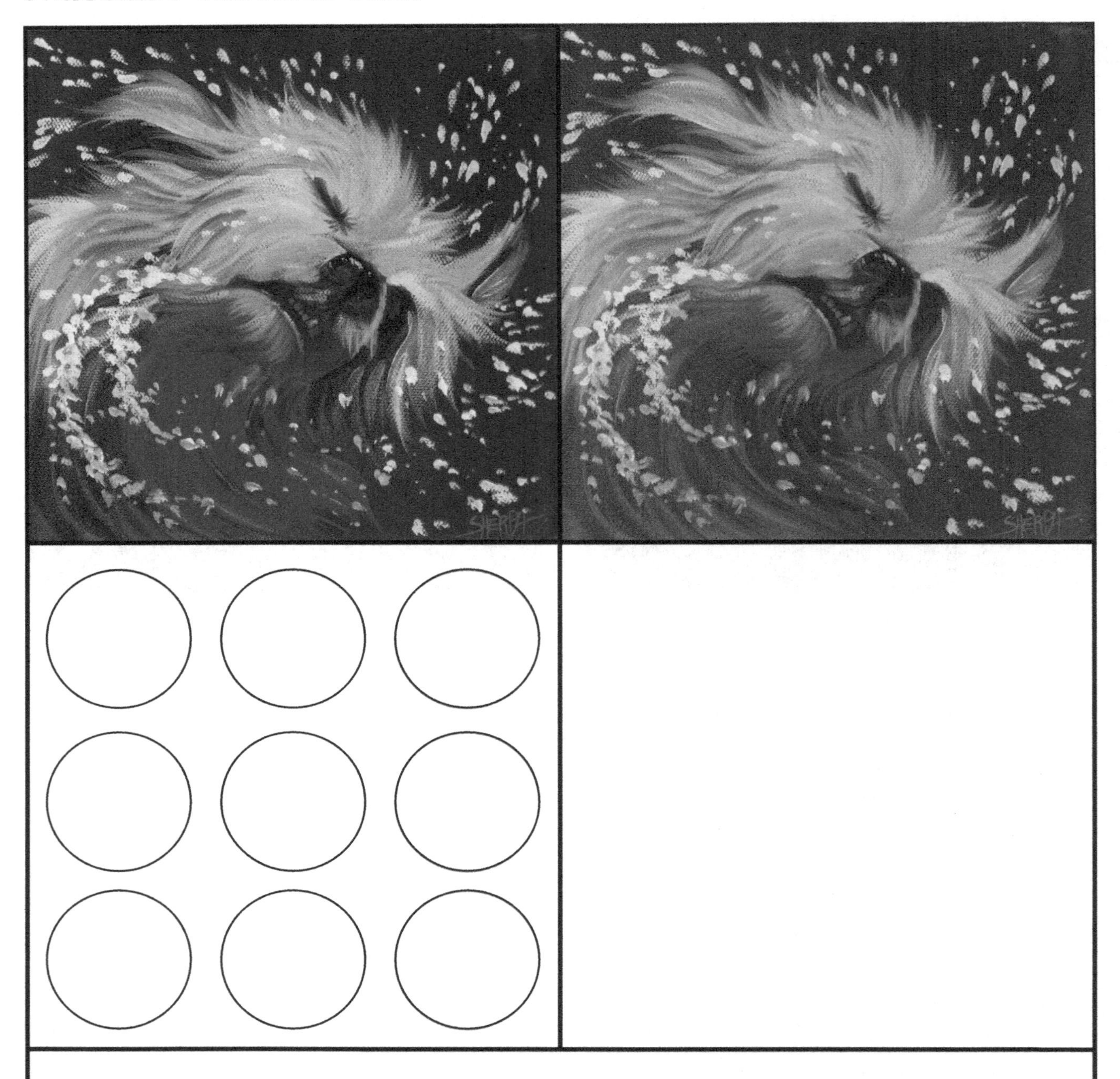

1. Practice mixing the colors from todays palette and paint in your circles with your colors.
2. Check your values and hue by swatching your paint mixes on the sample images.
3. Do a tiny fast grey scale sketch to help you express light and shadow - use paint or pencil, either is fine.

STORM HOUSE

COLOR PALETTE:         

Today's color palette is Naples Yellow Light, Cad Yellow Medium, Cad Red Medium, Phthalo Green, Phthalo Blue, Ultramarine Blue, Burnt Sienna, Mars Black, and Titanium White.

1. BACKGROUND AND GRID

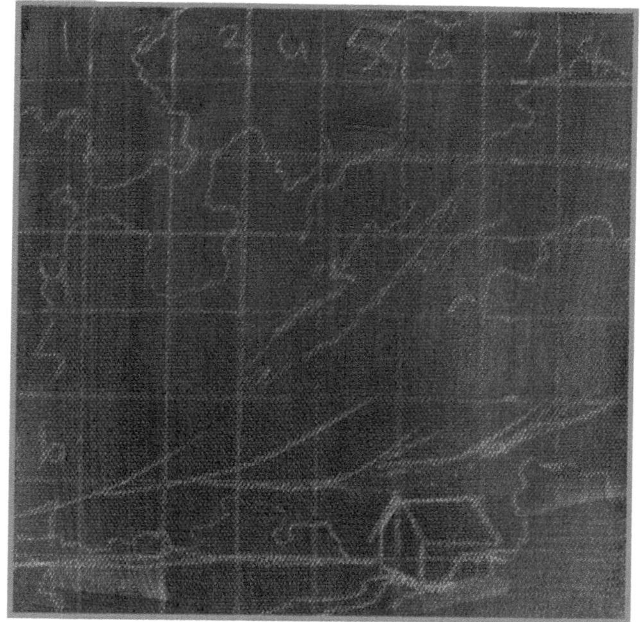

Blend ultramarine and sienna with an artist knife and with a damp, big brush, paint the entire canvas this color.

Let dry and, when you dry even on low heat with a hairdryer, remember to allow the canvas to cool completely before moving on. With your t-square and chalk, create a 1" x 1" grid on your canvas, number the top squares 1 - 8 and the side squares 1 - 8. Using the reference, duplicate the image exactly as shown in the reference, one square at a time. Only draw what's in that square before you move on.

2. LIGHT GRAY STORMY SKY

Our sky has several combos of grays and aquas, as well as a keyhole of optimistic light. Start with the #8 Cambridge and a bit of ultramarine, toned with a smidge of brown, and white to a very light color into it and brush this in over the house and trees. It's ok to brush right into the trees a bit so that later we can add some nice details. You can put the roofline back in if we need to. You are exaggerating the light, it's the foundation for the bright glow effect in the end. For the keyhole of light, ultramarine with a smidge of brown, white, add a little naples to green it up a bit for that stormy sky look. Next, mix a darker value of blue and along the outside edge of the sky, brushing it in on the edge of your brush, pushing little clouds in. Darkening the outside and creating this sort of light trajectory. Paint in the top left corner. An atmospheric stormy day. Refer to your reference.

3. STORMY DAY CLOUDS

For the first layer of dark clouds, blue and black to a blue-gray, a little white and a bit of water for flow if needed. Very dark. Take this to the area between the layer over the trees and the corridor of light. Lay it in with sweeping strokes and then fill in the little cloud shapes on the right. I hope you can already see that it builds a bank. More white to a more neutral gray, maybe a slight blue cast, and come up to the cloud in the top corner and push some of these light cloud shapes in using the side of your brush. Get back into your dark blue grey and push the darker color into the cloud space.

Refer to your reference to help you if you need to. If you have trouble seeing the shapes of clouds, you might want to resketch them with chalk. Light pressure. Another layer of much lighter clouds. Play with your cloud spaces light and dark until you are happy. With the # 4 round, get the gray and a lot of white for the light color, even lighter than the initial cloud, and make a little haloed edge. You want the lighter value defined on the edge.

4. SHADOW VS LIGHT VS SHADOW VS LIGHT

The sky areas are quite dark, darker than the cloud that it's against. Remember, your clouds should look like your clouds. Don't try to copy my clouds as much as try to capture the values. Work these areas by wiggling on the corner of my brush to put in the lighter clouds in front, making a stormy day by exaggerating the pockets in the sky with dark shadows. Add a little burnt sienna and a lot of ultramarine for a different, but still gray, color. Some get closer to the light but they are still stormy day clouds. Stormy days are really about having shadows vs highlights vs shadows vs highlights. Use blue and black, pulling this to add drama, little banks of clouds taking shape. Add white where you feel sunlight might be hitting. Scumbling. Random shapes, shaded and softened.

Come back with any colors you need to reinforce your progress. If you painted something out, just come back in and add it in when you can. No worries.

6. EVEN A STORMY CLOUD SKY NEEDS DRAMA

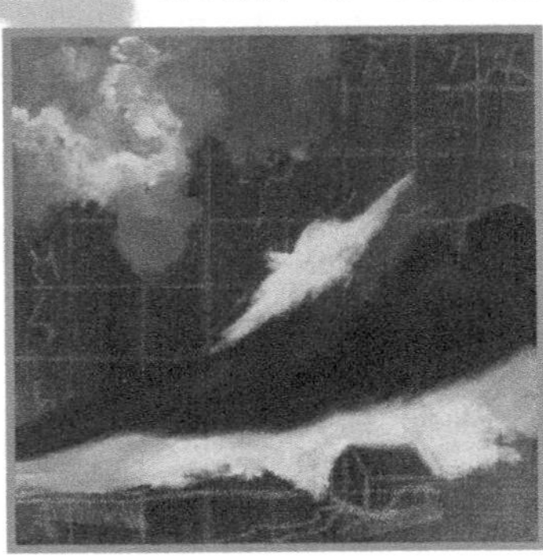

Drama in our sky. Light stormy green with ultramarine, phthalo green and a bit of cad yellow to a green-gold, Add white to a lighter value than before and on the #8 cambridge, tap in another layer of clouds on top of that stormy dark green layer. Using the #4 round get more white to a very light value and add the silver lining to these clouds as you did in the clouds above. Tap in little silver linings where there could be a cloud bank and soften by blending it into the cloud.

For more dynamic clouds and reflections in and around the keyhole of light, start with a mix of cad yellow, naples yellow and a smidge of red. Wiggle little yellow cloud shapes inside the keyhole that is allowing the sun to shine through, yellow, green, and white in the mix. Check your reference if you need help. Breathe, play with light and dark, shadows and highlights, softening that light before the paint dries. At the bottom fill in the landscape area with brown and black, very black, tap the shapes of bushes a bit. Make an orange and get some brown in and it makes a wonderful earthy color, brush this in to add dimension. Mix green and brown, a dark earthy color. For another layer of earthiness.

7. LANDSCAPE

Are you ready for more background, the line of bushes, and the house? Mix a very dark green with burnt sienna and phthalo green, with a bit of ultramarine. On the toe of the #4 round, start tapping in the tops of the trees. Little odd shapes that imply branches of leaves. Make sure there are some delicate edges that allow a bit of the sky to show through the greenery. The feel of something delicate. Get your scruffy brush, the #8 Cambridge, and the dark green mix and make a little run of bushes under the tree tops and blend it in. Make little bits of leaves that stick up. This bush line will tuck right in behind the house. Switch to a small bright brush and get cad red and ultramarine to gray it up a little and put in the hint of that roofline. Perhaps as the roof comes down, it gets redder gradually until it is bright red. Brown and black and yellow is the basis of the house and I think it looks like stucco. You need a darker gray for underneath the roof line and in front of the house, right under the eaves. Do the bushes go right up to the house? This brush will give you good clean lines.

We're almost done here. Step back and compare your painting to the reference. Is there anything you feel needs refining and are you ready for the next step? Use your reference for that final check.

8. A HUMBLE HOME & SIGNATURE

The bushes need highlights of phthalo green, burnt sienna and cad yellow to a brighter green, but not completely bright. The greens in front and farthest from the house will be the darkest greens. Feel free to switch to the #4 round as I did. Add some highlights in leaves. Delicate. Take your black, add water to make it fluid, and come under the roof and give yourself a door. You may as well add a walkway and a bit of window, because people live in this house. They are happy to be here. They think it's great. They love their humble home. Now cad red, toned with ultramarine and grab some yellow. A yellow orange inside the window because somebody has a light on. Naples and some cad for that highlight on the roof. A little yellow in bushes, a little white for where the sun might have gotten through.

For the rays of sun shining through,the #8 Cambridge and get some cad yellow and the tiniest twitch of blue or black to just barely tint it green. Dry brush the rays of sunlight with light pressure and long sweeping strokes. Wipe your brush and come back to diffuse them ifneeded. Less is more.

Sign your name to your incredible painting and please share it with the community. I hope you are happy with it.

SWATCHING PRACTICE PAGE

1. Practice mixing the colors from todays palette and paint in your circles with your colors.
2. Check your values and hue by swatching your paint mixes on the sample images.
3. Do a tiny fast grey scale sketch to help you express light and shadow - use paint or pencil, either is fine.

Acrylic April

STONE ANGEL

COLOR PALETTE:       

Today's color palette is Cadmium Red Medium, Cad Yellow Medium, Burnt Sienna, Ultramarine Blue, Phthalo Blue, Mars Black, and Phthalo Green.

1. BACKGROUND AND GRID

With a damp big brush, paint the entire canvas with a mix of burnt sienna and black.

Let dry and when you dry, even on low heat with a hairdryer, remember to allow the canvas to cool completely before moving on. With your t-square and chalk, create a 1" x 1" grid on your canvas, number the top squares 1 - 8 and the side squares 1 - 8. Using the reference, duplicate the image exactly as shown in the reference, one square at a time. Only draw what's in that square before you move on.

2. STONE FOUNDATION

With the #8 Cambridge, phthalo blue, black, and a smidge of white, paint in the background all around her, scumbling and being painterly, no particular brush direction, right over the white chalk. For the stone angel, black, pthalo blue and a bit more white this time, to a lovely gray which you will want to dry brush in to try to get that stone texture. Leave some dark underneath. We will be paying attention to how light and dark our objects are which will actually help you in dealing with skin tones in other paintings. Texture, smidges of additional blue, smidges of white. A little dark area on the forehead, at the cheek, adding this first layer of stone texture. Keep some of the chalk lines so you know where objects are. Catch a bit of the stripes and you can make out the carvings of the wings. Avoid water as much as possible. Imply little feathers on the wings, very loose. This is the stone underneath where the wings are and it will be overgrown. A bit more black, lightly working these dark values. Switch to the #4 round or clean your brush, and soften the edges. Just try to find all those darker values, like the shoulder.

3. BASIC FORM TO THE SCULPTURE

We will continue dry brushing, but we will add the lighter values and start to give some basic form to the sculpture. The base stone color of Phthalo blue, black and white with a bit of brown added for the areas that are a little more in highlight. Along the jawline, in the corner, the shade of the neck has a lot more light on it. Begin representing the light wherever you think your light source would be depositing light. The lip of the brow, some of the other brow. More blue and come down the bridge of the nose, keeping the lines very angular. More brown to warm it up, gray it up. A highlight where that stone is bent back, at the back of the head. Structured, chiseled. A little brighter over the top of the eyes, over the lip, chin and on the little structural bits of stone wings. A darker value in the eye corners. Green-brown into the stone because stones do patena, perhaps on the neck. Dry brushing, blending. Do you feel like a cool stone statue is emerging?

4. HIGHLIGHTS AND SHARP LINES

With the #4 round and black, get the spot that is the lips because the top lip is in shadow and must be captured first. Stone has distinctive shadows and crisp lines. Add that dimple that is carved in, a strong shadow under the lip, coming off the nose, and under the nose. The eyes have such deep cuts, define that hard edge. The hair has some sharp lines, a distinctive given shape. Catch the feathers on the stone wings. I clean up the chalk lines because I don't want them to confuse me if I need to make changes to her nose. Add more white to the top of the eye and any other stark white places be referring to the reference. The lid, the lip, the top of the chin, the temple. Instead of dry brushing I am now starting to wiggle in and soften the paint application. Not dry brushing, but softening. Are you starting to see a stone face?

Come back with any colors you need to reinforce your progress before stepping back to compare it to your reference. If you painted something out, just come back in and add it in when you can. No worries.

5. ADDING MOSS

Now, wet your brush to damp, and mix burnt sienna and phthalo green to a deep green for the plant life, the moss. Wiggling, kind of somewhere in between glazing and dry brushing. Some of the top of her will be in sunlight, be sure to go down the sides because it grows there, anywhere it can find purchase. That first sense of green. Look for shadows. As you come forward, add cad yellow for a lighter value. The front of her nose and places where moss might be.

Per John, "You gotta put the moss where the sun don't shine", which was responded by Sherpa with "moss don't grow on a rolling stone".

Add a little brown to your moss color for variety. Use your reference to help you with placement. Yellow to lighten, white for the lightest highlights. Dry brushing for the texture stone effect, blending for softness. Add a bit of moss to the nostril. You can come back with black to any hard edges you think need redefining. Do you feel the patena? Is she beautiful in your eyes?

Use your reference photo as a guide. Evaluate.

6. LEAVES AND GREENERY

For the leaves switch to the #8 cat's tongue, creating leaf shapes on the edge of the brush with some green and ultramarine, with a smidge of white. Be careful, a smidge can get away from you. This is our first value and will show up over the background yet still feel like they're in shadow. Some of the leaves will come over the stone wings and along the top. Get some cad yellow to brighten your leaves up, tone it with burnt sienna if you want to. You want a bright green, get more yellow and make them pop. Ultramarine, green and brown for a dark color, maybe phthalo green, and add water to thin flow to make the curling vines. Don't repeat patterns, roll the brush. Add highlights to the vines where light might be kissing them. Yellow and white for the brightest of highlights.

Refer to your reference and remember that you can always go back to video my video at any time for additional support.

7. FLOWERS

The flowers are mostly white, make sure you start with clean water to keep things bright,and replenish your pallet if needed. Mix a little red, yellow and a lot of white and just a twitch of green to tone it. On the side of the #8 cat's tongue, put in some background petals. Start from the center of the flower, playful curves, little s-curves. Messy little petals and messy little flowers. Next, layer what's next and in the center, add a lot more yellow, even a little more green. Brighten them up in the center. These are mums. They are full and messy, they face different directions. They are the lightest part of our painting, sort of the focal part. You'll be using pure white in places. Yellow in others. Rinse out often. Phthalo green and cad yellow and lots of white for some delicate little petals nearest the center. Dry your canvas and switch to the #4 round, yellow and red, and highlight a few centers with this color; not all of them, just a few. A few thoughtful white petals, just making sure that the center has highlights and shadows.

Step back and compare your painting to the reference. Is there anything you feel needs refining and are you ready for the next step?

9. SIGNATURE

Sign your name to your incredible painting and please share it with the community. I hope you are pleased.

SWATCHING PRACTICE PAGE

1. Practice mixing the colors from todays palette and paint in your circles with your colors.
2. Check your values and hue by swatching your paint mixes on the sample images.
3. Do a tiny fast grey scale sketch to help you express light and shadow - use paint or pencil, either is fine.

TRACEABLE

THE ART SHERPA

JUNGLE BIRD

COLOR PALETTE:          

Today's color palette is Mars Black, Phthalo Green, Phthalo Blue, Cad Red Medium, Quinacridone Magenta, Naples Yellow Light, Cadmium Medium Yellow, Burnt Sienna, and Titanium White.

1. BACKGROUND AND GRID

Get your big brush, water for flow, and paint that entire canvas black.

Let dry and when you dry, even on low heat with a hairdryer, remember to allow the canvas to cool completely before moving on. With your t-square and chalk, create a 1" x 1" grid on your canvas, number the top squares 1 - 8 and the side squares 1 - 8. Using the reference, duplicate the image exactly as shown in the reference, one square at a time. Only draw what's in that square before you move on.

2. BACKGROUND GREENERY

With the #8 cat's tongue, burnt sienna and phthalo green, start adding some of the implied little leaf structures in the background. You can add a little white if you have difficulty seeing this on the background. Imply different types of plant life. Remove the chalk if you need to. Like palm fronds. Mostly green back here. Paint around the bird but get the areas that would peek through. Catch around the branch, it's important. Adding texture. Add a little cad yellow for brighter greens, maybe a loosely highlighted stalk. Using the toe of the brush for our jungle structures. More yellow into the phthalo green for brighter highlights. He is surrounded by aspects of greenery that are out of focus because he does not want to share the spotlight.

Refer to your reference

3. BRANCH

Still on the #8 cat's tongue, with burnt sienna, let's catch that broken log. It's fine to pull a little of it into him. When the feathers go in, it will make the branch look like it is behind him. Paint his feet back over the log later because he needs a perch. Red and yellow to orange to highlight some parts of the log. On the toe of the brush, little, rough, short strokes. Beginning to speak of wood. Adding some yellow but have not rinsed out. Black and burnt sienna on the log branches. Yellow, maybe some white, some brown. Capturing light.

Check your water, breath, step back and refer to your reference. Make any modifications you feel you'd like to make.

4. DEEP CORAL BASE

Create a deep value coral color, mix cad red, and quin then add naples yellow. This is your base color. You will be adding naples and white for lighter values and more red and quin for darker values. Block in his body with the base color and lighten a bit for the wings. Don't go totally over the beak. Blocking him in, he's not fluffy yet, but he is pink. Check the reference for help if you need. With the #4 round, get black and blue and paint in the beak. At the front of the beak, a blue gray highlight to the front, wet into wet into wet, across that whole part of the beak. Wipe out your brush and get white and add another little highlight where the light might have caught a little more of his beak. I'm going to come under the beak a little bit with coral and carve back in so you can see just the tip of the beak. Curve that around into the wing. If you need to come back with black, you can always totally do that.

5. FIRST LAYER OF HEAD FEATHERS

With the the #4 round and a bit of light blue-gray, paint around his eye. Getting in this light area. Don't hesitate to mix up more base coral if you need to, you'll add cad yellow to some of it for a warm coral. Back to the #8 cats tongue, dampen brush and get your coral base with white and start to add directional feathers around the top of his head. Just a touch of yellow maybe at the top. Subtle, parts of the crown are shaded, some more in light. Pulling in feathers as you go. Maintain a dark coral and a lighter coral in parts. Use your blue-gray mix to tone the coral for feathers in shadow as shown in the reference. A strong shadow along the beak part not a full shadow. In front of the eye, blue to trim in the eye to shadow those feathers. Use your reference photo as a guide. Evaluate.

6. MORE FEATHERS. CREATING SHAPE WITH SHADOW AND LIGHT

Back into coral, maybe some white to lighten, not to the lightest, and pull downward little strokes, start to pull some of those feathers going towards his beak. Implying texture with the paint in this mid-tone. Layers. Lightening up as you go. He'll get lighter and lighter as we go through the painting process. Some of his feathers should go over the log. Deeper coral for the deeper value feathers, then add yellow to the coral for the bottom belly feathers. Maybe more cad yellow. Capture the tapered nature of the curls. Finding spaces. You can always add magenta and yellow to your base value. Catch values on the wing and the beautiful run of flight feathers. I've not rinsed out yet, but grab some white and add that muted highlight color where you'd like.

Refer to your reference and remember that you can always go back to video my video at any time for additional support.

7. LAYING IN SHADOWS AND VALUES

Let's start with a grayed coral, hues of blue, as we continue to highlight. Stay loose. With the #4 round and the base coral, but stronger to blue, comes under the beak in the shadow area, part of the chin, layering this deeper shadow color using your reference to help you with placement. More gray for a few feathers deeper in shadow. It's easy to come back and adjust if you need to. Shadow on the belly, lighter feathers on top, showing the coral underneath in sections. Naples to help with highlights.

Are you making good use of your reference? Remember, your reference is your friend.

8. MORE SHADOWS AND HIGH-LIGHTS

Shadows again, so grab our cool coral and add more quin, white if you need it; blue gray where you need it. Catching shadows but seeing our base coral peek through. Making him look very feathery. Do a serious rinse out. Now, add a lot of white to the mix for highlights. Part of his head is in sunlight, and add some outlines to a few feathers, especially on his wings. I have not mentioned this much, but you can always change up the positioning of the canvas when you need to. Work upside down if that helps you get some areas in, sideways if it makes sense. Highlight that little belly. He keeps getting pinker and pinker, but he is a fun bird. Grab some yellow on a few feathers, maybe a couple of little lines. Highlights and using your reference to help if you have difficulty locating where they should go.

Step back with your reference and compare. Does your bird show highlights and lowlights? Can you determine the source of light and do his feathers reflect that source?

9. FEET AND EYE DETAILS AND SIGNATURE

To create atmospheric perspective we use color and value to imply distance and shape by creating light, distant mountains which will darken as they come forward. Still using your #8 bright, take the master orange color, but make it one shade darker with a little more saturation of red. Starting at the mountains that appear furthest back. Bring this color about half way down this section of sky. Add yellow, and from the bottom of this section, scumble this lighter color up, softly blending wet into wet with the darker top color. This lighter color coming up from the bottom of the mountain will create a misty effect. Before you build in the next mountain, your edges should be dark and the base should have a gentle, warmer glow.

Sign your name to your incredible painting and please share it with the community. You should be very proud of you.

SWATCHING PRACTICE PAGE

1. Practice mixing the colors from todays palette and paint in your circles with your colors.
2. Check your values and hue by swatching your paint mixes on the sample images.
3. Do a tiny fast grey scale sketch to help you express light and shadow - use paint or pencil, either is fine.

TRACEABLE

BIG SHIP

COLOR PALETTE:           

Today's color palette is Dioxazine Purple, Ultramarine Blue, Mars Black, Phthalo Blue, Phthalo Green, Burnt Sienna, Cad Red Medium, Quinacridone Magenta, Naples Yellow Light, Cad Yellow Medium, and Titanium White.

1. BACKGROUND AND GRID

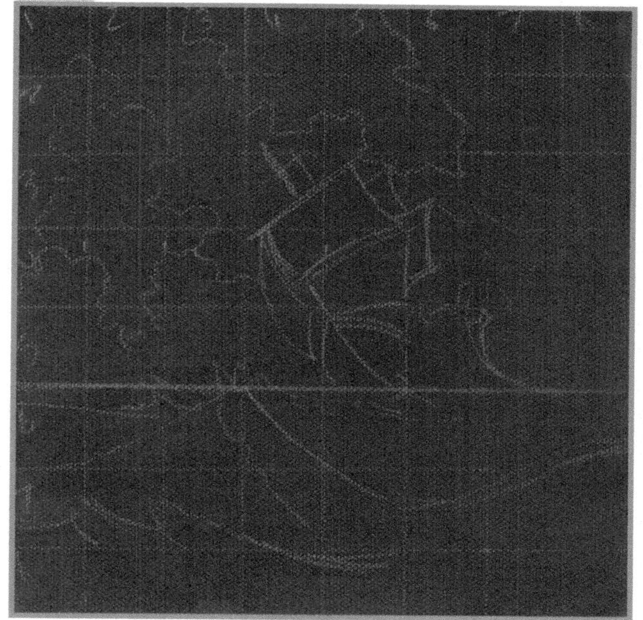

Paint the entire 8 x 8 canvas with a little bit of black and phthalo blue. Use the #30 brush. Let dry and when you dry, even on low heat with a hairdryer, remember to allow the canvas to cool completely before moving on. With your t-square and chalk, create a 1" x 1" grid on your canvas, number the top squares 1 - 8 and the side squares 1 - 8. Using the reference, duplicate the image exactly as shown in the reference, one square at a time. Only draw what's in that square before you move on.

2. BIG SKY BACKGROUND

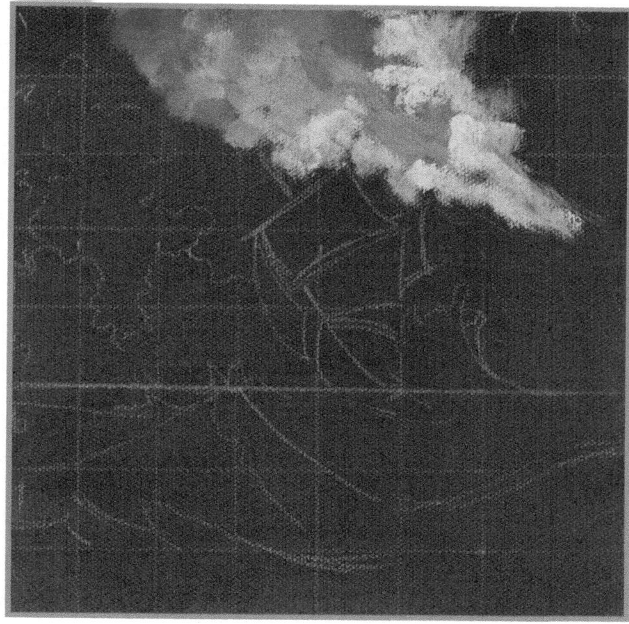

Mix with a palette knife ultramarine blue in the phthalo blue and a bit of white. Use water to improve the flow. #8 Cambridge and take this light sky color and be aware of the keyhole opening in the sky. Use the corner of the brush and scumble the sky in to get soft edges. Brush in some naples yellow light with titanium white. Add a few little clouds peeking through. The next layer lets light come around by using naples yellow with cad yellow and a lot of titanium white. Frame the clouds with this color forming a little halo. Refer to your reference.

3. STORMIER SKY

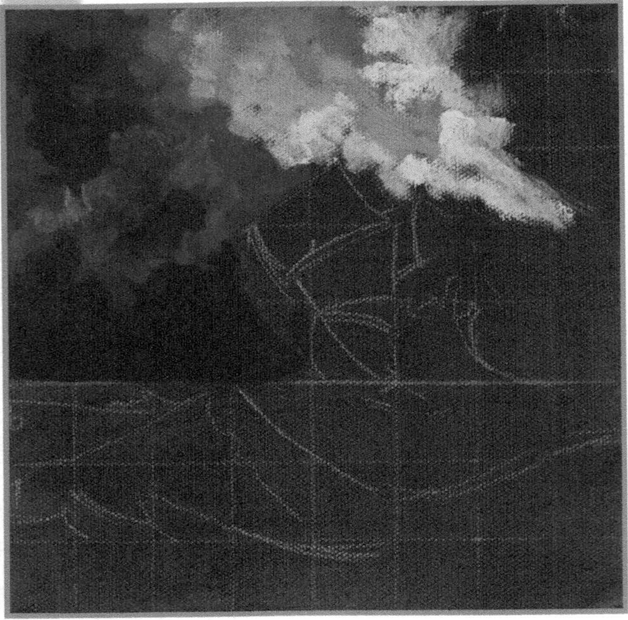

Use a palette knife to mix diox purple and burnt sienna to make a dark violet color. Paint this around the mast area and deepen the color with ultramarine applied in a circular fashion to make small clouds. Follow the references to place clouds throughout the sky. Use mars black in the deepest areas of color. The lighter highlights in the storm clouds are naples yellow and white. Refer to your reference.

4. BRIGHTER SKY

On the brighter side of the sky, the colors are cad red and cad yellow with the yellow predominating. Weave this color in and add in naples yellow. Take care not to lose the keyhole in the sky as you add in some highlights with white. Come back with any colors you need to reinforce your progress before stepping back to compare it to your reference. If you painted something out, just come back in and add it in when you can. No worries.

5. Refining the Sky

Using your lightest color and the corner of the brush pull in some sweeping cloud banks. Include some naples yellow and peach shaping around the purple. Carry some of these elements to the other side and use cad red, cad yellow and brown to create an orange cloud. Switch to the #4 round brush and outline with white silver lining, lightening up some of the darkest areas. Create a lavender color with cad yellow, purple and white to create some halos. Finish up the outlining of the clouds with naples yellow and white. Use your reference photo as a guide. Evaluate.

6. The Ship and First Layer of Sails

Use the #4 Round brush with blue/black dark color to define the space between the sails. The darker value in the sails is black, yellow and white. To light the sails up, use grey and white behind the mast.

Still using the #4 round begin the boat which is black brown in color. Refer to your reference and remember that you can always go back to video my video at any time for additional support.

7. SAILS AND RIGGING

Using the T-square will keep the rigging straight which is important. Use the darker black/brown color to imply rope and rigging. Add to the sails with grey and white. To highlight the sails use cad yellow/naples yellow half tone to give a glow to the sails. The sails also have a bit of the sunset in them with cad red and cad yellow. We're almost done here. Step back and compare your painting to the reference. Is there anything you feel needs refining and are you ready for the next step?

8. THE BOAT IN TWO PARTS

Make sure the canvas is dry. Use the #4 round brush on the toe to paint in the dark areas on the bow of the boat. Then start the highlights with the cad red, cad yellow with the burnt sienna. Add in naples yellow to lighten the brighter areas as shown in the reference.

9. THE OCEAN

Use a palette knife to mix phthalo blue, ultramarine blue and phthalo green for a deep aquatic color. The #8 Cambridge brush is used to brush in this dark color and then add in white to indicate far away crashing waves. Switch brushes to #6 Ruby bright or the cat's tongue to place the deep blue/black water crashing around the boat.Make a turquoise mix for the water churning around the boat. Use the #4 round and create a mix of sea foam color with black/ blue and the white. Tap in the foam with some highlights following the references. The final part of the waves are cad yellow and naples yellow with the lightest of the turquoise. Tap some fresh white as highlights. Use the references and evaluate.

10. FOREGROUND WAVE

#6 Bright brush. Mix phthalo blue, phthalo green and ultramarine blue lay the deep shadow under the wave. Use the deep turquoise color with naples yellow and some white to create the row of waves. Continue using the reference and video to create wave chop/churning. Detail the foam with white.

11. HOMESTRETCH

The final wave in the foreground uses the ultramarine, phthalo blue and phthalo green aquatic mix with a slightly lighter blue than the previous wave. Form this wave using the same techniques above and referencing the picture and video. Lighten up the highlights with the white and naples yellow.

Sign your name to your incredible painting and please share it with the community. You should be very proud of yourself.

JOHN AND I AND THE ART SHERPA TEAM WISH YOU AND YOURS THE VERY BEST. BE GOOD TO YOURSELF, BE GOOD TO EACH OTHER, AND I WANT TO SEE YOU AT AN EASEL REAL SOON.

SWATCHING PRACTICE PAGE

1. Practice mixing the colors from todays palette and paint in your circles with your colors.
2. Check your values and hue by swatching your paint mixes on the sample images.
3. Do a tiny fast grey scale sketch to help you express light and shadow - use paint or pencil, either is fine.

TRACEABLE

Thank you for being a part of
Art Sherpa Community

Made in the USA
Las Vegas, NV
28 December 2024

15489997R00125